THE
INTERNET
TRAP

THE INTERNET TRAP

TRAP

How the Digital Economy
Builds Monopolies and
Undermines Democracy

MATTHEW HINDMAN

PRIN
P

Copyright © 2018 by Princeton University Press
Published by Princeton University Press
41 William Street, Princeton, New Jersey 08540
6 Oxford Street, Woodstock, Oxfordshire OX20 1TR
press.princeton.edu

All Rights Reserved

LCCN: 2018934031

ISBN 978-0-691-15926-3

British Library Cataloging-in-Publication Data is available

Editorial: Eric Crahan and Pamela Weidman
Production Editorial: Nathan Carr
Text Design: Lorraine Doneker
Jacket/Cover Credit: Jacket art and design by Alex Robbins
Production: Erin Suydam
Publicity: Tayler Lord
Copyeditor: Linda Truilo

This book has been composed in Adobe Garamond Pro and Gothic

Printed on acid-free paper. ∞

Printed in the United States of America

1 3 5 7 9 10 8 6 4 2

for Elizabeth

CONTENTS

LIST OF FIGURES AND TABLES

FIGURES

TABLES

ACKNOWLEDGMENTS

This book is the product of many years of effort, and the list of intellectual debts that I have incurred in writing it is long.

First of all, I am deeply grateful to Bruce Rogers, my coauthor on chapters 4 and 5. Without Bruce this book would not exist in its current form. Most of what I have learned about stochastic dynamical systems I learned from Bruce, who brought to the project a mathematician's rigor and a deep curiosity about the workings of complex systems. If you find this book's models of dynamic audience and the attention economy useful, Bruce deserves much of the credit.

I am blessed to have an extraordinary set of colleagues at the School of Media and Public Affairs at the George Washington University, and their insights and criticisms of this project over many years have strengthened the final product immensely. Dave Karpf, Nikki Usher, Catie Baillard, Steve Livingston, Kerric Harvey, Janet Steele, Ethan Porter, Kim Gross, Jason Osder, Nathan Kalmoe, Emma Briant, Peter Loge, Silvio Waisbord, and Frank Sesno have all made contributions and suggestions that improved the book. Outside of GWU, Kenn Cukier, Daniel Kreiss, Chris Anderson, Russ Neuman, Talia Stroud, Jim Webster, Miguel Maduro, Aaron Shaw, Magdalena Wojcieszak, Homero Gil de Zuniga, Amit Shejter, Jay Hamilton, Phil Napoli, and Emily Bell have helped me to refine the arguments and evidence contained in this volume. I am grateful for the help even (or especially) of those on this list who will not endorse all of the book's conclusions.

Chapters 2 and 7 were drafted when I was a fellow at the Shorenstein Center on Media, Politics and Public Policy at the Harvard Kennedy School. Comments by Matthew Baum, Tom Patterson, Nicco Mele, Michael Ignatieff, Celestine Bohlen, Yavuz Baydar, John Geddes, and John Whibey were extremely helpful in those parts of the book. Both chapters benefited greatly from the help of Joanna Penn, who served as my research assistant during my time at the HKS.

An early version of chapter 3 was first published as "Personalization and the Future of News" in the edited volume *New Technologies and Civic Engagement* (Routledge, 2015). I'm grateful to Homero Gil de Zuniga for his thoughtful comments as volume editor, and for additional comments made by other authors in that volume that helped refine the chapter.

Chapter 5, in addition to the indispensable help of coauthor Bruce Rogers, also benefited from a series of conversations dating almost back to graduate school. Adrian Banner and Cynthia Rudin, in particular, helped shape the early thinking that went into chapter 5.

Chapter 6 began life as a report for the Federal Communications Commission. That report, similarly titled "Less of the Same: The Lack of Local News on the Internet," was published as part of the Commission's quadrennial review of media ownership rules. I would like to thank the FCC staff, particularly Jonathan Levy and Tracy Waldon, for their helpful comments and guidance in producing that report. Iris Chyi's peer review improved the report as well.

Lastly, I would like to thank my parents, my brother, and my wife, Elizabeth. Your love, support, and patience are a constant gift, and they made this book possible.

March 2018
Washington, D.C.

THE
INTERNET
TRAP

Rethinking the Attention Economy

The American Beauty rose can be produced in its splendor and fragrance
only by sacrificing the early buds which grow up around it.
—John D. Rockefeller, Jr. on trusts, quoted in Ida Tarbell's
The History of the Standard Oil Company

In early 2000, Google conducted one of its first online experiments. The
result was a disaster.

Google's mistake started with a simple question: How many results
should it return per search query? The young company had always given
users ten results, because that was what previous leader AltaVista had done.
Competing search engines like Yahoo! returned twenty, though, and focus
groups suggested that users preferred more.[1]

Google's researchers decided to try a real world test, splitting off groups
of users to receive twenty, twenty-five, or thirty results instead of ten. But
when they checked a month later, they found—to their shock—that more
results had produced huge *drops* in traffic. Searches in the thirty-result
group had fallen by more than 20 percent, and tens of thousands of users
had abandoned Google altogether.

The researchers rushed to figure out what had gone wrong. Were users
overwhelmed by more results? The data showed no evidence of this. Were
users just clicking the "next" button less? Few users clicked on the next
button to begin with, so this effect was tiny.

Google eventually traced the traffic drop to a surprising source: It took
a fraction of a second longer to return more results. The control group
waited 0.4 seconds on average, while those in the twenty-five-result group

waited 0.9 seconds. Over a day or two this added lag meant little. But as the weeks wore on, the effects of that extra half-second multiplied. People visited Google less often, and performed fewer searches when they did visit. Even when the experiment ended, slowed-down users did not come back immediately. Their usage started to increase again, but from the new, lower baseline.[2]

There are several morals to the story of Google's early experiments, which this book will unpack at length. But the most important lesson is about how to understand online advantage.

Digital survival depends on *stickiness*—firms' ability to attract users, to get them to stay longer, and to make them return again and again. Stickiness is like a constantly compounding internet interest rate, in which a small early edge in growth creates a huge long-term gap. Differences in stickiness do not add up, they *multiply together*.

Google's ascent from upstart to the world's most valuable company came from learning this lesson. Google spent billions to make its site faster—but it also did much, much more. It reinvented itself not as a search engine but as a bundle of the stickiest online activities: email, video, maps, mobile, even office software. And in its pursuit of an ever-larger slice of users' attention Google rebuilt the fundamental infrastructure of the internet: new data centers larger than any before, new fiber optic cables, new ways of running rich applications over the web and a speedy new browser to match, new forms of artificial intelligence running on new types of computer chips, even a new mobile operating system that now runs on two billion active smartphones.

How did online audiences and digital revenue get so concentrated? What does this concentration mean for business, politics, news, even national security? Is online oligopoly inevitable, or is there a way out of the internet trap? These are the questions this book seeks to answer. For us today, just as for Google two decades ago, the first lesson is this: small effects that compound quickly *are not small effects*.

A Scarcity of Attention

The World Wide Web is the most astonishingly successful technology of modern times, a technology that now underpins our social, economic, and political lives. You likely ordered this book online—or even had it wirelessly delivered to your phone or tablet or reader. The web is so popular, powerful, and omnipresent that we forget just how badly it has failed at its original goal.

The World Wide Web was built in an explicit attempt to eliminate hierarchy in communications. It tried to do this by combining other technologies developed with that same goal in mind. The first such technology was hypertext, originated in the 1960s by sociologist Ted Nelson. Hypertext documents were designed to be consumed nonsequentially. Links within the hypertext could point to other relevant passages, definitions, graphics, tables, or even other documents on the same computer. The second technology was the internet, which by the 1980s had become ubiquitous in universities and research labs. The internet had been created as a peer-to-peer network, in which there were no central hubs: each computer could send and receive data with any other computer.

Tim Berners-Lee, the creator of the web, saw that hypertext could piggyback on top of the internet. Instead of being sandboxed within a single computer, hypertext could link documents on computers continents apart. Berners-Lee called the project the World Wide Web to emphasize that "any node can be linked to any other," and to reflect "the distributed nature of the people and computers that the system could link."[3] In the opening sentence of the www's project overview, one of the very first pages online, Berners-Lee declared, "There is no top to the Web." All pages, and all sites, were supposed to be created equal.

If there were no "top" sites on the World Wide Web in 1991, there certainly are now. The fact that some sites and apps are far more popular than others is the most important fact of online life. We network on Facebook, while competing sites get less than 1 percent of Facebook's traffic. We search the web using Google or Bing, and competing search engines have minuscule market share. We read and write our email using Google or Yahoo! or Microsoft. We use eBay for auctions, and we buy our books (and increasingly everything else) from Amazon. Among hundreds of millions of sites on the web, the four largest internet firms—Google, Facebook, Microsoft, and Yahoo!—capture a third of all web visits.

Concentration in online revenue is even more dramatic. The ten largest digital firms have always dominated digital advertising, taking three-quarters of ad dollars since at least the mid-1990s. But the shift to mobile and video has intensified concentration at the very top. As of mid-2016, Google and Facebook together combined for more than 73 percent of digital advertising in the United States, a remarkable duopoly over a $60 billion-a-year industry.[4]

At its core, this is a book about the *attention economy*. It focuses on the interplay between money and attention, and how each is exchanged for the other. It shows how digital firms spend money—often mountains of money—to attract and keep audiences. The book shows why investments in things like server farms and fiber and backend software matter so much, and how sites with more content and better designs are able to tilt online competition in their favor.

The book also details how audiences are traded for revenue through ads and subscriptions. This exchange is highly unequal: for several reasons, larger outlets earn far more per audience member than smaller outlets. This reciprocal relationship between money and attention creates feedback loops, in which sites and apps that have early success can invest to become more successful still.

In itself, the idea of attention economics is not new. The notion is often traced back to Herbert Simon, political scientist and Nobel prize–winning economist. Writing about the problems of information overload in the 1960s, Simon wrote that

> in an information-rich world, the wealth of information means a dearth of something else: a scarcity of whatever it is that information consumes. What information consumes is rather obvious: it consumes the attention of its recipients. Hence a wealth of information creates a poverty of attention and a need to allocate that attention efficiently among the overabundance of information sources that might consume it.[5]

Simon's passage has been repeated so often that it verges on cliché, with Google claiming to find the quote on more than 4.5 million web pages.

Many scholars have claimed to pick up where Simon left off. In the past two decades many books and articles have been written about "attention scarcity," though this phrase has animated radically different ideas about digital media. Some discussions have been cloaked in business jargon or cyber-utopian rhetoric. One early treatment even declared that "attention transactions" would replace traditional money.[6] More recent works, such as James Webster's excellent *The Marketplace of Attention*, have relied not on an idealized vision of the web but on data on how digital media is actually consumed.

This book differs from previous work on attention economics in numerous ways. Too often attention economics has been invoked to argue that "old" economics does not apply, that the digital world is throwing off the shackles of the analog one. This book uses new data sources, together with models borrowed from economic domains such as international trade and mathematical finance, to show that the digital world is not so different after all. Large media firms still dominate for reasons economists will find both novel and familiar. Diverse preferences can serve to *concentrate* audiences rather than spread them out.

Even more fundamentally, this book challenges claims that "money cannot reliably buy attention."[7] This belief that digital attention cannot be bought is woven throughout internet scholarship and public debates—but it is flatly, undeniably wrong. Showing exactly how audiences are bought and sold is a central theme of this book.

There is one key point, though, in which this book is in agreement with previous work: understanding attention economics is crucial for understanding digital media's social impact. As James Webster writes, "Media need an audience before they can achieve a purpose."[8] Much is at stake beyond just commercial interests. Thinking about attention economics leads us to consider the *political economy* of attention—the ways in which attention economics impacts politics, and vice versa. On one hand, political choices and public policies help determine who wins and loses online. On the other, the digital attention economy increasingly shapes public life, including what content is produced, where audiences go, and ultimately which news and democratic information citizens see.

FORCES OF CONCENTRATION

Building a better version of attention economics starts with a key problem: *our understanding of the internet has been lopsided.* The forces that disperse digital attention are widely understood, while the forces of concentration are not.

This sort of asymmetric understanding in internet scholarship looks a lot like the historically uneven advance of knowledge in other fields. Consider the history of geology. When geology was organized as a scientific field in the late 1700s, it was mostly the study of erosion. While geologists quickly learned how wind and water wore mountains down, figuring out what built them up in the first place was harder. It was not until the surprise discovery of plate tectonics in the 1960s that geology had good models of geologic uplift.[9] In a sense, geology went for 150 years as only half of a discipline.

This sort of uneven understanding has occurred in the social sciences, too. Writing in 1997, Paul Krugman argued that economic geography—the study of where production and consumption happen in space—was like geology before the discovery of plate tectonics: "economists understood why economic activity spreads out, not why it becomes concentrated."[10] Economists had long understood how high rents push economic activity away from an urban center, a process modeled well by Econ 101 supply-and-demand models.[11] But such models had a critical problem: they could not explain why cities would ever form in the first place. Good models of city formation emerged only once economists understood how imperfect competition can create urban concentration—for example, how stockbrokers in lower Manhattan in New York City can outperform those in Manhattan, Kansas.

Those who write about digital media today face the same sort of problem that previously afflicted geology and spatial economics. The distribution of online audiences, like the distribution of people in the real world, is the result of a tug-of-war between forces of concentration and forces of dispersion. But while the forces of dispersion have been widely understood and celebrated, the forces that concentrate audiences have been systematically ignored.

Most writing to date has assumed that digital media will produce "centrifugal diffusion"[12] in audiences. Again and again, observers have said that the web is a "narrowcasting" or "pointcasting" medium, that it tilts the playing field toward small content producers, that it will, to paraphrase the U.S. Supreme Court in *Reno v. ACLU* (1997), make everyone a pamphleteer. We have been told that "the monolithic empires of mass media are dissolving into an array of cottage industries,"[13] that the internet has empowered an "army of Davids,"[14] that the internet will mean "the end of big."[15] Argument has focused not on whether audiences were diffusing, but rather how far and how fast they were spreading out.

Traffic data, though, show that audiences keep stubbornly refusing to decentralize. This book is, in part, an outgrowth of my previous book *The Myth of Digital Democracy*, which showed that online audiences follow concentrated power law patterns. Some commentators dismissed this evidence of concentration as premature, saying that it ignored the rapidly evolving nature of the internet. Micah Sifry argued, for example, that "it is dangerous to make conclusive statements about such a young and dynamic space."[16] The book's evidence of audience concentration online, Matt Bai suggested, "only reflects a particular moment in time."[17]

This wait-and-see argument is a natural consequence of our lopsided understanding of online audiences. If the only forces that shape internet traffic are dispersive, then, indeed, we should just wait, and all will be leveled. Like Vladimir and Estragon in *Waiting for Godot*, many still hold out hope that the internet they've been waiting for will arrive. Eventually.

All of these commentators are right that some old forces of concentration do not apply in digital media. There is no scarcity of spectrum on the web. There is no need for digital-only media firms to maintain printing presses or a fleet of delivery vans. Motivated citizens can share video without a broadcast license. Single journalists can start their own digital publications with only a laptop and a Starbucks latte.

But the unrelenting focus on new, small-scale sites ignores the elephants in the room—the large digital platforms where users spend the most time, and that soak up nearly all online profits. In celebrating the profusion of citizen blogs, we must also understand why the vast majority are abandoned and unread. The centripetal forces deserve just as much attention as the centrifugal ones do.

So the body of this book begins by documenting the other half of the story. Chapter 2 details how large internet firms can take advantage of a host of economies of scale, even beyond simple network effects. As a group, large sites load faster. They are prettier and more usable. They have more content updated more frequently. They rank higher in search results. They have established brands, and visitors are more practiced in navigating them. They are more efficient platforms for advertising. There is substantial evidence that each of these factors, individually, serves to concentrate traffic.

Chapter 3 goes further, showing that large firms and websites are far better at personalizing their content for users. Digital media defined by "The Daily Me" does not favor small-scale content producers, as most have assumed. Instead, it favors those with resources: money, staff, data, computing horsepower, intellectual property, an established audience.

BETTER MODELS

Detailing the forces that concentrate internet audiences is a start. But what has been especially needed are not new facts but *new models*, theories that explain the broad patterns of digital traffic and revenue from Facebook and Google all the way down to tiny personal blogs. What we need are simplified stories that can explain both the enormous concentration at the top of the web and the (very) long tail of smaller sites.

Chapters 4 and 5 take on the task of model building, using different but complementary approaches. Chapter 4 builds a formal economic model of online content production. This deductive model is based on three key assumptions. First, larger sites are assumed to have economies of scale, both in the production of content and in their ability to turn traffic into revenue. Second, users are assumed to have at least modest preferences for diversity. Third, users are assumed to face search costs or switching costs in seeking out new content.

Individually, these assumptions are uncontroversial—but combining them leads to some surprising results. Portal sites and aggregators are a market response to these stylized facts. Big sites can dominate *even if* smaller sites produce better content that perfectly matches users' preferences. The model suggests, too, that search engines or social networks can have countervailing effects: pushing readers further afield, but making audiences of the largest search engines and portals even more valuable. Facebook's push to host other sites' news articles, or the economic logic of content farms and so-called fake news, are captured well by this simple model.

Chapter 5 takes a different tack, using data on fluctuations in web traffic. The wait-and-see crowd is right about one thing: the web is a dynamic medium, and there have been big gaps in our understanding of how web traffic evolves over time. Sites gain and lose traffic every day. New sites constantly emerge, and old sites decline into irrelevance.

For perennial Internet optimists this churn is a cornerstone of their faith. Look at Facebook, the argument goes: barely a decade old, and now the most visited property on the Internet. Or look at the Huffington Post, founded in 2005, which became a top-ten online news outlet even before it merged with venerable AOL. Large web firms have been especially aggressive in pushing this line. Google has repeatedly told regulators that it does not need to be regulated, since "competition is only a click away."

But these views hide a basic error. The easiest way to see the mistake is to consider another venue defined by both ceaseless concentration and constant change: the stock market.

Though thousands of stocks trade on public exchanges, most of the market's value is concentrated in just a few dozen companies: big blue-chip firms like Apple, Microsoft, Google, Exxon, General Electric, and Bank of America. The smaller a company is, on average, the more volatile its stock price. Blue-chip companies are generally safer investments than smaller companies. Even when a blue-chip firm faces an unexpected negative shock—like, say, it spills hundreds of millions of gallons of oil into the Gulf of Mexico—its stock price drops only modestly. Moreover, the *structure* of the stock market is much more stable than the stocks themselves. We don't know which stock will be the fiftieth largest tomorrow, but we know how much it will be worth relative to the other stocks in the market.

Chapter 5 shows that web traffic follows remarkably similar patterns. Big sites have more stable audiences—day to day, month to month, year to year. Smaller sites are much more volatile. While individual sites constantly rise and fall, the overall structure of web traffic is largely constant. We cannot predict which site will be the one-hundredth most visited site tomorrow, but we know what share of traffic it will receive.

It is intuitive to think that the traffic of Facebook or Google varies less, in percentage terms, than the traffic of CNN.com or the *New York Times*. It make sense, too, that traffic to NYTimes.com is more stable than traffic to a small blog. The consequences of web traffic being structured this way are not obvious, but they are profound. As we will see, the "size equals stability" pattern—*by itself*—is enough to produce the power law patterns that dominate online life. This audience agglomeration is baked into the math. And while the notion of a dynamic, constantly changing web is often invoked to claim that the web empowers small sites, smaller outlets turn over *much* faster than big sites.

NEWS AND THE PUBLIC SPHERE

The models of the attention economy that this book proposes are quite general. Much of the evidence in the first few parts of the book comes from the commercial sphere of the web and digital media, where the dynamics of the attention economy are particularly stark, and where the online dynamics are not so different from familiar offline patterns.

But one of the biggest contributions of these models is illuminating areas of the web that go beyond purely commercial content. The most important implications of the attention economy concern the public sphere—the mix of news and information, citizen discussion and collective action, that is at the core of democratic politics. And so the last few chapters of this book focus on the online public sphere, and—especially—on online news.

This turn toward news comes for several reasons. Not only is the health of news of crucial democratic importance, but it is also the area where the digital attention economy has wrought the biggest changes. Local newspapers in the United States have always produced most of the nation's journalism, and employed most American reporters. But as online news consumption has reached a tipping point, we have witnessed a historic collapse in print readership and revenue.

Even beyond the civic importance of news, and the rapidity of change in the news business, there are theoretical reasons for looking at news content. News content provides some of the most challenging tests of our models of attention economics, and it is the area where the book's analysis most strongly challenges previous work.

So chapters 6 and 7 look at news through the lens of attention economics. Chapter 6 begins by looking at local news on the web. Many have hoped that new online news sources would take up the slack as newspapers and local broadcasters struggled. Using data from comScore, based on a panel of more than 250,000 web users in the one-hundred largest local media markets, this chapter provides the most comprehensive look at online local news to date.

Newspaper publishers have repeatedly claimed that local newspapers have a revenue problem, not a readership problem—that "lots of people came, but lots of advertising didn't."[18] In fact, local news sites get only about one-sixth of news traffic, or just one-half of 1 percent of traffic overall. Within local news markets, newspaper and television news sites soak up nearly all of the attention. Not a single web-native local news outlet—*not one* in any of the one hundred largest media markets—comes close to the traffic of a typical newspaper site or local TV site. Newspapers may be weakened, but these ailing monarchs are still larger than their upstart competitors.

Chapter 7 goes further, showing that our models provide actionable intelligence to strengthen local journalism. Publishers, technology leaders, academics, and policymakers have proposed a broad and contradictory set of "solutions" to the local news crisis. To date, nearly all of them are rooted in a misdiagnosis of the problem. Like it or not, preserving local journalism is mostly about helping newspapers make the transition to the digital age. Newspapers cannot monetize audience they do not have.

Any proposal to save local journalism must start from the dynamic nature of digital audiences. Local newspapers, and especially *smaller* local newspapers, have long broken all of the rules for building sticky sites. As a group they are slow to load, cluttered, and—let's be honest—often ugly. And while newspapers increasingly pay attention to digital traffic, they often do not understand what online metrics really mean.

Compounded audience is the most powerful force on the internet. The success of local news in the digital age depends on this compounding process, on measuring stickiness and optimizing for it. In contrast to repeated, contentless calls for "experimentation" and "innovation" in news delivery, this book provides real-world metrics by which to measure success.

There Is No Such Thing as a Free Audience

Building a more rigorous version of attention economics makes us rethink many "obvious" things about the web. It even challenges the single most important assumption about the digital age: the belief that the internet makes distributing content nearly free.

In the opening pages of *The Wealth of Networks*, Yochai Benkler argues that the internet has abolished the "industrial" economics that pertained to older communication technologies:

> The core distinguishing feature of communications, information, and cultural production since the mid-nineteenth century was that effective communication ... required ever-larger investments of physical capital. Large-circulation mechanical presses, the telegraph system, powerful radio and later television transmitters, cable and satellite, and the main-frame computer became necessary to make information and communicate it on scales that went beyond the very local. ... Information and cultural production took on, over the course of this period, a more industrial model than the economics of information itself would have required. The rise of the networked, computer-mediated communications environment has changed this basic fact.[19]

Many other scholars have followed suit. Clay Shirky writes in *Here Comes Everybody* that the challenges of "mass amateurization" center on two main questions: "What happens when the costs of reproduction and distribution go away? What happens when there is nothing unique about publishing anymore, because users can do it for themselves"?[20] Jay Rosen argues that the internet improves journalism by "driving towards zero the costs of getting it to people, and by vastly reducing the capital requirements for quality production"[21] Or as one book reported, "In one key area the Internet is reducing the cost structure of media firms and content producers: it lowers the cost of distribution."

Actually, that last quote was from me.[22] I was wrong, and this book aims to explain why.

It is true that the cost per byte of moving, storing, or processing information is now cheap, and getting cheaper all the time. But we now move, store, and process so much data that the total spent is massive. *Who pays* those costs has shifted, with important consequences. But the society-wide costs of web servers and site development are far larger, in constant dollars, than the cost of telegraph lines or mechanical presses or television transmitters. Google's data centers—or Amazon's or Facebook's—are exactly the sort of multi-*multi*-billion dollar capital expenditure that was supposed to be obsolete.

The more profound error made by those proclaiming free digital distribution, though, was an overly narrow definition of what counts as a distribution cost. Distribution costs, as Rosen's quote suggests, need to include all of the costs of getting content in front of citizens. But this involves not just data costs, or the costs of servers. Rather, the distribution cost of digital content is *the total cost of building up a digital audience over months and years*.

Distribution costs include the need to constantly post new content, since the volume of new content is a large factor in stickiness. Distribution costs include site design, and all the site features that increase reader engagement. Distribution costs include the staff and effort needed to personalize content, or even to just A/B test news headlines. Distribution costs include the expertise and infrastructure that go into search engine optimization. Distribution costs include the raw buying of traffic through ads and paid-for links. Distribution costs include the costs to build mobile apps and make websites mobile-friendly. Simply because the costs of online distribution are *different* than they are in other media does not mean that they are *small*.

Building an online audience is like pumping air into a balloon with a slow leak. One has to keep pumping, to keep up a constant level of investment, or previous efforts will quickly be lost. These indirect costs of distribution are not optional. For a news site or a blog, maintaining an above-average level of stickiness is a matter of life and death.

Chapter 8 thus concludes by offering an *evolutionary model* of digital audiences. Darwinian competition for attention does not produce the egalitarian internet many have assumed, because the traits needed for stickiness are not distributed equally. A tiny edge in stickiness allows winners to grow faster than the niches they occupy, monopolizing money and attention. Expensive distribution means that internet openness is neither intrinsic nor inevitable. And for all the cuddly talk of the internet as an "ecosystem," digital niches are just as brutal and fragile as those in the natural world.

Many had hoped that the web would make news and political debate less centralized, expand and diversify the number of journalists and news outlets, and make capital less important in gathering an audience. The number of outlets may have expanded, but the public sphere remains highly concentrated. The number of journalists has plummeted and "fake news" has multiplied, but digital media are just as dependent on a few corporate gatekeepers as ever. Building a consistent news audience remains hugely expensive. The attention economy has doomed most of our civic hopes for the web. This book is both eulogy and postmortem—an explanation of why things have ended up this way, and why this is not a passing phase.

The unwillingness of many to abandon those failed hopes now threatens to make the situation even worse. For all of the internet's faults, there are concrete steps that we can take to strengthen the online public sphere. But first we need to understand the gulf between our imagined, fictionalized internet and the less-inspiring reality.

A Tilted Playing Field

The best minds of my generation are thinking about how to make people click ads. That sucks.

—Jeff Hammerbacher

Outside of The Dalles, Oregon, in a nondescript industrial park along a barren stretch of the Columbia river, sits a $1.2 billion complex of hangar-like buildings. It was here, in 2006, that Google built its first mega data center. Google's mammoth computer warehouses squat alongside other industrial facilities: grain elevators, a derelict aluminum smelter, a plant that turns potatoes into French fries. Megawatts of power pulse into the compound through high-voltage lines, and on winter days steam rises from four-story-high silver cooling towers.

Google now has fifteen mega server farms like this worldwide, along with numerous smaller facilities. Microsoft, Facebook, Apple, and Amazon have similar server farms too, including several just up the Columbia River. Between 2003 and 2013, Google spent $59.6 billion dollars just on research, development, facilities, and equipment—three times (in constant dollars) what the U.S spent to build the atom bomb.[1] When Google's site first went live, it was hosted on just two computers on the Stanford University campus. But by 2009, with its new warehouse-scale computers online, a typical Google search touched thousands of computers, with the results returned in a fifth of a second.

Google's data centers represent a jaw-droppingly massive investment, larger than the GDPs of more than one hundred individual countries. Yet if folk theories of the internet are correct, Google's data factory in The Dalles should not exist.

We have been told—again and again—that the internet is a "post-industrial" technology. Online there is supposedly no need to spend millions on broadcast towers or printing presses or similar capital equipment.[2] With the industrial economics that homogenized print and broadcast media gone—so the story goes—barriers to entry fall and audiences radically spread out.

Google's data center at The Dalles stands in contradiction to this fable. Google's facility is exactly what it looks like: an industrial mill, a digital smelter refining not ore but information. Google's data factories are just as critical for it today as broadcast equipment was for NBC in an earlier era. The persistence of smokestack economies in the digital age should give us pause. If we have gotten something this basic wrong, what else have we missed?

This chapter, and the two that follow, aim to show how big sites got so big. A central concern is stickiness—the factors that allow sites and apps to attract and keep an audience (see chapter 1). Critically, many tactics that promote stickiness get cheaper per user as sites get bigger. The internet thus provides *economies of scale in stickiness*. Bigger, more popular sites and platforms thus find it easier to attract still more visitors, and to build up habits of readership. The economies of scale that shape countless traditional industries, from airlines to automakers, remain powerful in the digital economy. Understanding digital audiences starts with digital economies of scale.

This chapter does not attempt to provide an exhaustive list of every online economy of scale—that would require a much longer chapter. Rather, the goal is to highlight some of the most powerful and best-documented forces that skew the game toward the largest players. Size advantages alone are not the full story, as we shall see. But with so many strong economies of scale, of so many different types, in so many different areas of digital media, it is time to stop pretending that the internet is a level playing field.

Network Effects

In the early 1900s America was a hodgepodge of competing, incompatible telephone networks. The expiration of the Bell telephone patents had led to an explosion of telephone companies and cooperatives. Telephones had become cheaper, and telephone service was increasingly available even for those outside a city. In many places, though, multiple subscriptions were required to reach everyone with a phone. Those on non-AT&T networks also could not make long-distance calls.

Under the leadership of Theodore Vail, AT&T embarked on an effort in 1907 to consolidate the telephone system under its own banner. AT&T argued that users would be better off with a single integrated phone network. As Vail put it in the AT&T 1908 annual report,

> a telephone—without a connection at the other end of the line—is not even a toy or a scientific instrument. It is one of the most useless things in the world. Its value depends on the connection with the other telephone—and increases with the number of connections.[3]

In a wave of advertising AT&T declared its commitment to "one system, one policy, universal service." The campaign was a success, and it turned AT&T from one of America's most reviled companies into a well-liked, government-regulated monopolist.

The telephone system thus has become the canonical example of network effects or (more formally) positive network externalities. Such effects arise when the value of a good or service depends strongly on whether others use it too. Network effects are also referred to as "demand-side economies of scale." Even if per-customer costs stay steady, the product becomes more valuable as more people join the network.

There is increasing acknowledgment that internet services can follow the same pattern as the telephone system, especially for sites that depend on communication between users.[4] Facebook and Twitter, for instance, are useful only if other people use them. Network effects make it difficult to compete with established players. Many other microblogging sites have tried to compete with Twitter, but none has been able to reach critical mass.[5]

Acknowledgment of network effects is a welcome change from the rigid (though still common) belief that the internet is a leveling force. Unfortunately, talk about network effects has come with two common misunderstandings.

First, "network effects" is often, and inaccurately, used as a synonym for *all* economies of scale.[6] Not every size advantage is a network effect. A social network with no users is useless, while a search engine or an online app like Google Docs might still be valuable even before becoming popular. Confusing different sorts of scale economies leads to misunderstandings and ultimately bad policy.

Second, there is the persistent misuse of "Metcalfe's Law," a rule of thumb—and definitely *not* a real law—named after ethernet inventor Robert Metcalfe. As popularly understood, Metcalfe's Law claims that the value of a network increases with the square of the number of connected users. A network that connected a hundred users, for example, would be a hundred times more valuable than than a network that connected ten.

The endorsement of Metcalfe's Law has been repeated at the highest levels of public policy. Reed Hundt, former chairman of the Federal Communications Commission, declared that Metcalfe's Law, along with Moore's Law, "give us the best foundation for understanding the Internet."[7] Despite this, there has never been evidence for Metcalfe's Law in large real-world networks, and it has been regularly debunked for two decades.[8] Metcalfe's assumption that all ties are equally valuable is not true in a social context. People care more about talking to their family and friends and business associates than they do about talking to distant strangers.

But even if network effects have been overstated, sites and apps with a strong social component show remarkable stickiness. As of this writing, Facebook is the most popular site on the web, and it owns the two most popular apps (Facebook and Facebook Messenger) on both iOS and Android. Facebook's popularity is consistent with the large body of research on the power of social influence to change behavior.[9] Facebook's early expansion was partly driven by a "surround strategy":

> If another social network had begun to take root at a certain school, Thefacebook [sic] would open not only there but at as many other campuses as possible in the immediate vicinity. The idea was that students at nearby schools would create a cross-network pressure, leading students at the original school to prefer Thefacebook.[10]

The explicit goal was to maximize social pressure on prospective users.

On a smaller scale, network effects impact sites that rely on reader-created content. Some research on news sites shows that increasing user "engagement"—and especially comments—helps to make a site stickier.[11]

Those who post online want to have their words read by others. Sites without a critical mass of viewership have trouble attracting comments.

Some sites have considered commenting systems to be central to their business. For example, for years the Huffington Post had one of the largest and most sophisticated comment systems in the news business. The Huffington Post used thirty human coders on duty around the clock, coupled with computerized filtering technology, and handled more than eighty million comments during 2012.[12] The core filtering tech came from HuffPo's 2010 acquisition of the startup Adaptive Semantics, and the system learned over time which comments to filter, which to post, and which to send for human feedback.

These advantages and big investment make the ultimate fate of the Huffington Post's comment system sobering. In 2014 the Huffington Post gave up, and moved entirely to Facebook comments. In announcing the change, the Huffington Post noted the powerful gravity of network effects, explaining that the shift would "[bring] the discussions and debates to the places where you engage with them the most."[13]

Supply-side and demand-side economies of scale can thus be mutually reinforcing: sites with lots of commentators can afford better technology, and better technology platforms attract more comments. Yet few sites have been able to reach that virtuous circle. Even hugely popular sites like the Huffington Post have abandoned the Sisyphean task of policing comments, instead relying on big platforms (especially Facebook) to validate and track users. Relinquishing user comments to Facebook has reportedly boosted traffic and increased civility for many news sites, though at the cost of further empowering Facebook over content producers.[14]

ARCHITECTURAL ADVANTAGES

Network effects are certainly a concentrating force online, one factor that makes many sites stickier as they get larger. But they are far from the whole story behind why the Internet favors bigger companies. Debates about the internet still often start with talk about the medium's "openness," about how the "peer to peer" architecture of the internet treats all websites equally.

But such talk is increasingly obsolete. Changes on the internet mean that the architecture of large and small sites is no longer comparable. There is overwhelming evidence that large firms' architectural edge translates directly into a larger audience and more revenue.

To a rough approximation, internet firms produce goods from two primary inputs: lots of high-tech industrial equipment, and lots of software code. But as we know from long experience in traditional markets, both software production and equipment-heavy industries favor the very largest firms.

Industrial economics has long studied the "minimum efficient scale": the minimum size that, for example, a factory needs to achieve in order to have the lowest costs. With some important exceptions, the answer for industrial plants has long been that they scale up very, very large.[15] This is nothing new. Alfred Chandler's classic history of American capitalism, *The Visible Hand*,[16] is filled with examples of nineteenth-century entrepreneurs investing in single factories large enough to saturate the world market. The web combines the economic pressures that produced AT&T with the forces that produced Microsoft.

To understand how the internet looks different today than it did in the 1990s, it is useful to walk though the architecture of today's internet giants. We will start with Google. Because of its public statements, we know more about Google's efforts than those of other firms. Still, companies like Microsoft, Facebook, and Amazon have all made similar investments in server farms and high-scalability software platforms.

For all the talk about how the information economy is leaving "industrial economics" behind, Google's server farms have demonstrated the same economies of scale we have long seen in smokestack industries, where the largest plants are most efficient. Google does not say exactly how many computer servers it runs, but by early 2017 the company had fifteen mega data centers like the one in The Dalles, not counting numerous smaller facilities; past estimates have pegged the number of servers at 2.4 million as of early 2013.[17]

Running on these data centers is a dizzyingly complex software stack written by Google's engineers. One key early piece of this infrastructure was the Google File System, which allowed Google to store large "chunks" of data seamlessly across multiple different servers.[18] Google created its own storage and communication formats, and developed new tools for machines to share common resources without increasing latency.[19] Google's BigTable and MapReduce allowed it to store and process, respectively, datasets spread across thousands of separate machines.[20]

As the Google infrastructure has matured, its software architecture has grown even bigger and faster. Google's Caffeine and Percolator indexing tools have allowed for incremental processing and updating. New web pages now appear in the index as soon as they are crawled, dropping the average age of documents in the Google database by half.[21] The revised Google file system, codenamed "Colossus," has been reworked to provide increased responsiveness for "real time" applications like Gmail and YouTube. Google has even built new globally distributed database systems called Spanner and F1, in which operations across different data centers are synced using atomic clocks.[22] The latest iteration of Borg, Google's cluster management system, coordinates "hundreds of thousands of jobs, from many thousands of different applications, across a number of clusters each with up to tens of thousands of machines."[23]

In recent years Google's data centers have expanded their capabilities in other ways, too. As Google has increasingly focused on problems like computer vision, speech recognition, and natural language processing, it has worked to deploy *deep learning*, a variant of neural network methods. Google's investments in deep learning have been massive and multifaceted, including (among other things) major corporate acquisitions and the development of the TensorFlow high-level programming toolkit.[24] But one critical component has been the development of a custom computer chip built specially for machine learning. Google's Tensor Processing Units (TPUs) offer up to eighty times more processing power per watt for tasks like image processing or machine translation, another advantage Google has over competitors.[25]

These investments in the data center would mean little, of course, without similarly massive investments tying them to the outside world. Google's data centers are connected with custom-built high-radix switches that provide terabits per second of bandwidth. Google has made large purchases of dark fiber to speed traffic between its servers and the rest of the web. Frustrated with off-the-shelf equipment, Google has made its own routers, and in some cases even laid its own undersea fiber-optic cable.[26] Both moves have been mimicked by key competitors such as Facebook.

Google has also greatly expanded its peering capabilities. Peering is the sharing of internet traffic between different computer networks, and it requires a physical fiber optic interconnection. According to information Google posted on PeeringDB.com, the company had 141 public and seventy-nine private peering locations as of June 2013. Google's publicly acknowledged bandwidth, just from public peering locations, is 3.178 terabits—or 3,178,000 megabits—per second. For perspective, that number is equal to the entire bandwidth of all fiber optic cables running between the United States and Europe.[27]

The parallel investments of the biggest web firms have fundamentally transformed the internet's architecture. According to one report, the tipping point occurred between 2007 and 2009.[28] In 2007 a typical request for a web page would still go from a consumer's local ISP network (say a local cable broadband provider), up through regional networks, across the national internet backbones run by firms like MCI and AT&T, and then down through regional and local layers to the server hosting the content. Once the target server received the request, the process would reverse, with data packets streaming upward to regional networks, over the backbone, and then back down to the local user. This model was largely unchanged from the internet's original Cold War–era design.

By 2009, as big investments by large websites came online, traffic patterns had been transformed. Because the largest content producers had hooked fiber directly into local ISP networks, or even colocated servers in ISPs' data centers, the portion of data traveling over the national backbones dropped. Packets took fewer hops, and users saw their web pages and videos load faster, at least when they visited the largest sites. This shift of traffic to the edges is crucial for high-bandwidth, low-latency uses, like online video or interactive web applications. But it also challenges the notion that the internet is still a peer-to-peer network. Google might have its fiber hooked directly into Comcast's network, but small sites do not.

Google's hardware, networking infrastructure, and software stack all show how big internet firms become more efficient as they scale up. Google or Facebook or Microsoft or Amazon can deploy more storage, more computing power, and more bandwidth per dollar than smaller firms. Per computer, these big data centers are also much cheaper to run.

Large data centers have long been more efficient than smaller data centers. According to a 2012 industry survey, though, even large data centers have a typical power usage efficiency (PUE) between 1.8 and 1.89—meaning that for every watt spent on running the server itself, an additional four-fifths of a watt was spent on cooling and running the data center.[29] Google reported a PUE of 1.1 as of mid-2013. Facebook, whose servers are slightly newer and built according to similar principles, claims a PUE of 1.08.

The largest sites thus have roughly one-eighth or one-tenth the overhead electricity costs of traditional large data centers. In a business where electricity is the largest operating cost, that represents a powerful economy of scale. Even Google's investments in machine learning—discussed more in chapter 3—have helped here. Applying Google's DeepMind methods reduced cooling costs for data centers by 40 percent.[30]

Still, the key question is whether these infrastructural economies translate into advantages in stickiness—in attracting and maintaining audiences. Here we have substantial evidence that the answer is yes.

Many of Google's other advantages are closely tied to its edge in computing and networking scale. Exceptionally low computing and storage costs are essential for both personalizing content and for ad targeting (as we will see in the next chapter). The additional capacity offered by Google or other large companies has sometimes been part of the direct pitch to consumers. When Google launched Gmail in 2004, it provided users with a gigabyte of storage at a time when most other webmail sites offered just four megabytes. Google was able to offer 250 times more storage only because of its hardware and software investments. Many of those who switched to Gmail in 2004 still visit Google dozens of times a day to check their inbox.

Google's advantages in computing scale have also proven quite flexible. While web-scale data centers are an enormous upfront cost, they can be adapted to do many different tasks. Moreover, Google has benefited enormously from integration between its core web-scale technologies and the many applications it provides to users. As Google engineer Sean Quinlan explains,

One thing that helped tremendously was that Google built not only the file system but also all of the applications running on top of it. While adjustments were continually made in GFS to make it more accommodating to all the new use cases, the applications themselves were also developed with the various strengths and weaknesses of GFS in mind.[31]

Integration economies are classic economies of scale.

And, of course, Google's architecture is blazingly fast. This fact alone makes the site stickier.

As the introduction showed, even small differences in site responsiveness quickly grow into big differentials in traffic. In the words of Marissa Mayer, "Speed is the most important feature."[32] Every part of Google's infrastructure is designed around this "gospel of speed." As Google Senior Vice President Urs Hölzle explains, "'Fast is better than slow' has been a Google mantra since our early days, and it's more important than ever now."[33] For example, Hölzle reports that four out of five users click away from a page if a video stalls while loading.

Data from other websites shows much the same thing. Experiments with the Bing search engine showed that adding two seconds of delay immediately decreases page views by 1.9 percent and revenue by 4.3 percent. Microsoft quickly ended this experiment for fear of permanently losing customers.[34] AOL similarly reported that users with faster load times viewed more web pages: those with the speediest response times viewed 7.5 pages on average, while those with the slowest load times viewed only five.[35]

In response to this reality, every Google service must meet strict latency budgets. Many Google engineering offices feature "performance dashboards" on large screens showing constantly updated latency numbers across various Google services. As Hölzle puts it, "We have one simple rule to support this Gospel of Speed: Don't launch features that slow us down. You might invent a great new feature, but if it slows down search, you either have to forget it, fix it, or come up with another change that more than offsets the slowdown."[36]

Google has even created its own web browser, Chrome, which has surpassed Firefox and Microsoft Edge (previously Internet Explorer) in market share. Part of the motivation was to collect more user information for targeting ads and content. But according to Google's public statements, the single biggest reason for building Chrome was, again, speed—particularly faster speed with complex interactive websites. Most sites cannot build a new web browser, and then make it the most popular in the world, in order to speed up their site.

Google focuses on speed so intently that it now ranks *other* sites in its search results based on how quickly they load.[37] From Google's point of view, this makes perfect sense: speed *does* predict how much its users will like a website. Google wants people to use the web as much as possible, and sending users to a slow site increases the odds they will stop and do something else. But for smaller firms, the direct disadvantages of having a slow site are compounded by the speed penalty that Google assesses. Ranking sites by speed further advantages big sites over smaller ones.

Design Advantages

In March 2009, Google's chief designer, Douglas Bowman, left the company to take a job at Twitter. In a blog post, Bowman said that he was leaving because of the clash between his classical design training and Google's obsessive culture of data:

> Yes, it's true that a team at Google couldn't decide between two blues, so they're testing 41 shades between each blue to see which one performs better. I had a recent debate over whether a border should be 3, 4 or 5 pixels wide, and was asked to prove my case. I can't operate in an environment like that.[38]

Google's focus on data and metrics, according to Bowman, meant that designers were relegated to trivial problems. But Bowman also acknowledged that Google's approach had been extremely successful. In fact, Google's approach is part of a much wider industry shift. The profusion of online controlled experiments has produced a new model of design. And while small sites can (and increasingly do) use online experiments too, the model provides significant economies of scale for the largest firms.

Web design, like other research and development expenses, commonly produces large economies of scale. We have two decades of research showing that the design of a website can strongly influence site traffic and site revenue.[39] Once the initial design is finished, it is no more expensive to show users a beautiful and usable site than it is to show them an ugly or confusing one. In economic terms, design behaves like software because it is *encoded* in software: good design is expensive to produce, but essentially free to reproduce.

But Google's example also shows key differences between the online design process, particularly at the largest firms, and the design process elsewhere. For physical products, design happens at the beginning of the production process. Once initial design work and small-scale testing is completed, the assembly line is fired up, and consumers are presented with a finished, final product. Similarly, with media such as newspapers and magazines, the stories change, but the overall layout is largely static.

Many of the largest web firms now use large-scale online experiments as an essential design and testing tool. Companies that rely on the technique include Amazon, eBay, Etsy, Facebook, Google, Groupon, Intuit, LinkedIn, Microsoft, Netflix, Shop Direct, StumbleUpon, Yahoo, and Zynga.[40] The design process at these firms can now be constant, dynamic, incremental. Larger firms like Google or Microsoft now run hundreds of online experiments concurrently.

This testing infrastructure reframes the entire process of design. For large digital firms, design is not just about hiring and (as we saw above) retaining competent designers with a strong aesthetic sense and an understanding of usability principles. Increasingly, website and app design is about building a comprehensive testing infrastructure to optimize every element. As Google researchers report, "We evaluate almost every change that potentially affects what our users experience."[41] Design becomes a tracking and storage and data-crunching problem. Large digital firms can leverage their massive infrastructure and engineering expertise, along with their large user base, to build better sites than those of their competitors. As Microsoft's online experiment team emphasizes, "Building the infrastructure to do this cheaply and efficiently is the real challenge."[42]

It is thus unsurprising that testing infrastructure at large sites has grown in concert with the rest of large sites' hardware and software platforms. For example, the Google file system was intended to be employed just for indexing and crawling, but the company's research and quality teams soon clamored to use the system to store large datasets.[43] And as Google's platform expanded, it also focused on developing new tools for in-house researchers and testers. Today Google's Sawzall programming language, as well as its Tenzig and Dremel database tools, provides ways of analyzing the vast volumes of log data.[44]

Starting with a given design as a base, this testing infrastructure means that individual design elements have been heavily tweaked by testing, leaving few small changes that might increase traffic. But there is an important limit to this design approach: the local maximum problem. Even if a site tests countless small changes to its current design—every possible shade of blue, or exactly how many pixels should be placed between the site logo and the text that follows—users might actually prefer a completely different design altogether.

Still, research suggests that website usability is mostly "a first order problem."[45] The elements that go into a design are often easily separable. Making a good website usually does not depend on a complex interaction between design elements of the kind that is hard to discover with A/B testing.

Google itself seems to have belatedly taken a hybrid approach. One of Larry Page's first efforts when he became CEO in 2011 was to launch "Project Kennedy," a cross-company effort to unify and beautify Google's projects. In 2013, Google rolled out a new "design language" for its websites. As Google designer Matias Duarte explained, the new redesign tried to offer a more holistic vision, rather than a bunch of "little incremental changes."[46] This effort culminated in the unveiling of Google's "material design" language, which made user experiences on Android, ChromeOS, and the web simpler, more consistent, and more polished.[47]

Still, this process is more a refinement than a repudiation of Google's focus on testing. Designs are still extensively tested before widespread deployment. Google's oft-cited maxim "focus on the user, and all else will follow" is primarily about measuring and testing every part of the user experience. The predominantly data-driven approach may be more novel than more traditional design methods, but both approaches advantage large sites over their competitors. Smaller sites often do not have the hardware and staff to build this testing architecture, and they lack the statistical power to detect small effects.

Small changes to websites can lead to substantial bottom-line effects. Bing's Experimentation System is credited with adding hundreds of millions of dollars to Microsoft's bottom line. Just as important, though, were the large sums saved by catching damaging changes before they went live: "The system has also identified many negative features that we avoided deploying, despite key stakeholders' early excitement."[48] Ron Kohavi, now the head of Microsoft's online experiment team, relates an example of this from his time at Amazon.com:

> [I remember] how the Amazon Order Pipeline team wanted to introduce the new version based on the new app server, Gurupa, and [I] insisted that an A/B test be run: it failed with a 2 percent revenue loss. The team dug deep for two weeks, found "the" bug, and wanted to ship. No, you need to pass an A/B test was the message. The team ran it and it failed again. The new pipeline shipped after five iterations. It is not just new ideas that fail, but re-implementations of existing ones are not as good as we initially think.[49]

For established web firms, deploying a new product version that fails is one of the single largest business risks. A robust testing infrastructure can help mitigate those liabilities. At the same time, it can limit opportunities for upstart competitors.

Testing infrastructure has also shaped firms' strategic investment. As we have seen, Google's exponential spending increase on server farms and networking hardware was initially a large departure for the company. This multibillion-dollar risk would not have been undertaken without reams of evidence that it would pay off in more traffic and revenue.

ADVERTISING AND BRANDING

In 1896 a group of investors led by Adolph Simon Ochs bought the *New York Times* for $250,000. Prior to the purchase the *Times* had been on the verge of bankruptcy. Founded in the early 1850s, the *Times* had been more restrained and intellectual in its coverage than sensationalist competitors like the *World* or the *Journal*. The financial panic of 1893 had hurt all newspapers, but it had especially damaged the *Times*, which had dominated the market for financial advertising. At its nadir the paper had a daily circulation of just 9,000 readers.

What, then, did Ochs and his fellow investors actually buy? Surprisingly little. The newspapers' printing presses were old, run down, and not worth much. The linotype machines were rented. The newspaper had even been forced to rent offices in a building that it had originally owned. By the time Ochs purchased it, there was "virtually nothing [left] but the name and goodwill of the paper."[50]

The physical infrastructure of media distribution does matter, whether it relies on printing presses or server farms. Still, we should not forget that key assets in media organizations have always been, in a sense, virtual. A century later the editorial page of the *New York Times* stated that the internet had repealed the old aphorism that "freedom of the press belongs to those who own one." Yet, as the *Times'* history itself shows, physical printing presses were only part of the *Times'* ability to reach and grow an audience.

The story of the *Times* encapsulates two key features of media that remain relevant in the digital age. First, the *Times* had value, even in the late nineteenth century, as a paper more "serious" than its competitors. The *New York Times* brand conveyed a specific set of characteristics to its readers. Second, the *Times* had value as a marketplace for advertising. Media companies serve as a vehicle by which *other* brands establish and maintain themselves. Chapters 3 and 4 will look at how larger sites generate more ad revenue per user than comparable smaller sites. This section will focus on the first question: how larger sites are better able to build and maintain their online brands.

In the short term, a brand name is something that can be used with almost no additional cost. Adding a logo to a cheap handbag, or adding the *Wall Street Journal* masthead to a hastily rewritten press release, might immediately increase perceived value. But if Louis Vuitton started selling ugly vinyl handbags for five dollars a piece, the value of the brand would erode quickly. Companies spend vast sums of money building and defending their brands. For many firms their brands are their single most valuable asset.

Media have an especially intimate relationship with branding, because most media products are *experience goods*.[51] It is difficult for consumers to know how much they will like a given media product, such as a news article or a rock album, without consuming it first. Consumers go to the online New York Times or the Huffington Post or Reddit today because they found the site content interesting or entertaining the last time they visited. Experience goods tend to produce strong inertia effects, in which consumers develop strong brand loyalties.[52] When it is tough to judge quality in advance—that is, when search costs are high—consumers tend to stick to previous patterns of consumption.

The primary costs of maintaining brands are twofold: the costs of maintaining consistent quality (however defined), and the costs of advertising. But in economic terms it does not matter whether the quality difference is real or just perceived. As economists Carl Shapiro and Hal Varian write, "Customer *perceptions* are paramount: a brand premium based on superior reputation or advertising is just as valuable as an equal premium based on truly superior quality."[53]

Many business scholars have examined what drives these perceptions of site quality. Their work shows—consistent with the previous sections— that technical site traits such as download speed and navigability, as well as a site's visual appeal, are strongly associated with perceived quality.[54] All of these site performance and appearance traits, as we just saw, produce steep scale economies.

Moreover, many nontechnical traits associated with site quality similarly favor larger sites. Scale economies in online advertising can also come from *threshold effects*, with larger firms finding it easier to reach the tipping point at which ads are most effective. For example, standard advertising doctrine states that ads are most effective when they are seen multiple times, and that repetition is especially important for unfamiliar brands.[55] As we will see in the next chapter, this dynamic remains powerful online. Retargeting—in which prospective consumers are chased around the web by numerous ads for the same product—is more successful than showing an ad just once.[56] The need for a larger ad campaign disadvantages smaller firms.

In the abstract, then, there is plenty of reason to expect that branding is a powerful force for online traffic concentration. More direct evidence of just how powerful advertising effects are can be found in two key areas: the search engine market and the market for online news.

The search engine marketplace is an effective duopoly. Google and Microsoft's Bing now divide almost the entire market, with Google having twice Bing's share (including licensed Bing searches on Yahoo!). Yahoo!

spent billions of dollars on research, hardware, and acquisitions to build up a search business to compete with Google.[57] But in 2009 Yahoo! gave up, and signed a ten-year agreement with Microsoft to use Bing in exchange for 88 percent of Yahoo!'s search revenue. Microsoft's current search efforts began in earnest in 2005. The Bing search engine (previously MSN Search) had been dubbed a "black hole" by analysts; between 2006 and 2013 Microsoft lost $12.4 billion in their online division, of which Bing is the core.[58]

Despite enormous early financial losses, Microsoft built a search engine far better than Google itself was a decade ago, though, of course, Google's search engine is a moving target. Bing's search results have for years closely overlapped with Google's results, especially for popular searches. And as Bing has improved, the overlap has grown greater still.

Why did Yahoo! and Bing fail to dent Google's market share even as they dramatically improved in quality, and even produced quite similar results? One key reason is the power of Google's brand. Users' deep affection for Google is a striking feature of web use research. In a study on online trust, Hargittai, Fullerton, Menchen-Trevino, and Thomas found that many participants used highly emotional language, telling researchers that "I love Google" and that Google is "the best search engine."[59] Jansen, Zhang, and Mattila similarly report that "the depth of the positive sentiment [toward Google] is amazing," with several participants using the word "love," to describe their affection for the company.[60]

Similarly powerful results emerge from experimental studies. Jansen, Zhang, and Schultz showed that users strongly preferred Google-branded results over the same results attributed to other search engines.[61] Pan and collaborators used eye-tracking technology to show that users focused on just the top few search results.[62] This remained true even when the researchers reversed the real Google rankings, placing the last results first, something they attributed to users' built-up trust in the Google brand.

Microsoft has actually based a major advertising effort on this sort of A/B testing. Microsoft's "Bing It On" ad campaign, like the long-running Pepsi Challenge, asks users to compare unbranded results from both Bing and Google side by side. Microsoft claims that most users prefer Bing to Google, based on a self-funded study.[63] Outside research has not supported Microsoft's claims. Using blinded experiments, Ataullah and

Lank[64] and Ayres et al.[65] found that users deprived of brand labels still had a slight preference for the Google results. Tests by news organizations also found that Google slightly bettered Bing, especially for the less common searches that Microsoft conveniently excluded.[66] Still, both search engines overlap so strongly that Google's edge in any handful of searches is modest. Ataullah and Lank ultimately conclude that "While Google may outperform Bing in blind searching, trust in the Google brand is a much more significant factor in Google users' search preferences."[67]

Google's example shows how a brand built on an early technical lead can persist even after the quality difference between it and its competitors drastically narrows. In the online world, just as with cars or soft drinks or luxury clothing, branding tends to be persistent.

The sorts of strong brand effects seen with search engines also powerfully shape the online news market. Much recent work has focused on growing partisan self-selection in news. In the process, this work has shown that many online news consumers have robust—even fervent—brand preferences.

In a survey experiment using a nationally representative online sample, Shanto Iyengar and Kyu Hahn[68] took real-time news headlines and randomly attributed the stories to either Fox News, CNN, NPR, or the BBC. Republicans and conservatives showed a strong preference for Fox over all other news outlets, and an aversion to CNN and NPR. Liberals showed the opposite: a strong aversion to Fox, and a roughly equal enthusiasm for CNN and NPR. These brand preferences held not just for hard news, but also for soft news topics such as sports and travel.

Just as significantly, subjects were much more interested in reading stories attributed to major news outlets than the control group, which saw identical headlines without source labels. Established brand names drove traffic to news, while subjects largely ignored unbranded, anonymous news stories.

Natalie Stroud finds similar results in her book *Niche News*.[69] Using a modified version of Google news content, Stroud randomly attributed headlines to either Fox News or CNN. While the topic of the story mattered, there were nonetheless strong partisan brand preferences. Strong, durable branding effects are one more reason to expect online traffic to be persistently concentrated.

USER LEARNING

The preceding section shows how advertising builds familiarity with a product, and teaches consumers to associate a brand with (hopefully positive) attributes. All of this requires consumer learning, of a sort.

Yet websites also benefit from user learning in much deeper ways. Users prefer websites not just that they know, but that they *know how to use*. While brand-specific skills are a powerful force in many markets, the web provides an especially large role for brand-specific consumer learning.

Evidence for the importance of user learning comes from many areas of scholarship, including longstanding work on the so-called "digital divide." While early digital divide research focused on disparities in access, recent work has focused on large, and strikingly persistent, gaps in web users' skills. In this area the work of sociologist and communication scholar Eszter Hargittai and her collaborators has been especially important. Even as the web has diffused widely, Hargittai and her coauthors have shown that many common tasks remain difficult for most users.[70] Some have suggested that younger users will show fewer differences in digital skills, but the data has challenged these claims. Hargittai has shown that even many of these so-called "digital natives" struggle with basic online tasks.[71] A key coping mechanism is "reliance on the known,"[72] in which users stick to familiar routines and trusted name brands.

These findings dovetail with economics research showing that the buildup of user skills over time can produce strong brand loyalty among consumers.[73] Importantly, this can happen *even if* the competing products are identical in their quality and initial ease of use. As experienced users become more proficient, they tend to keep using products that they are already invested in. Companies with an established customer base thus find it easier to maintain market share.

Brand-specific skills are believed to be especially powerful in software markets.[74] Even comparatively simple software, like a word processor, can have a steep learning curve. For example, the marketplace transition from WordPerfect to Microsoft Word was extremely slow, because users' skills did not transfer from one product to the other.[75] Upstart software firms facing an established incumbent cannot succeed just by producing a slightly better product at a slightly better price. The new product has to be so dramatically better that it overcomes the costs of switching—most of which do not have anything to do with the new software's retail price. The costs in training and lost productivity and simple frustration usually far exceed the cost of buying the software itself.

But if the effects of brand-specific skills are well-known in traditional software markets, we should now expect these effects online. The web increasingly reproduces desktop software, from email programs to photo editing to games to spreadsheets to word processors. The growth of Ajax[76] and related technologies has shifted some processing from a distant server to the user's browser, allowing a web-based word processor to be as responsive as traditional software.[77] Other technologies have pushed in the opposite direction, shifting computation and storage onto remote web servers. As the difference between applications that run in the cloud and those that run on a local device shrinks, users are anchored to familiar sites just as they have long been tied to familiar software programs.

But even when interaction with websites is less complicated than learning a new software program, scholarship has found that the web can produce "cognitive lock-in." Johnson, Bellman, and Lohse provide the example of visiting a new grocery store for the first time.[78] It takes time to learn the physical layout of the store, the shelf location of the milk or mangoes or mayonnaise. After the first few visits, familiarity with the grocery store makes it increasingly attractive relative to competitors. Johnson and collaborators present evidence that the same dynamic exists in online shopping. Users spend less time at easier-to-learn sites, but these sites also produce more return visits and more purchases.

Work on cognitive lock-in helps explain a key puzzle. Some early economics work suggested that, by lowering search costs and switching costs for consumers, the web would lessen users' loyalty to particular outlets, and even produce "frictionless commerce."[79] Yet these expectations have been confounded by studies showing that consumers are *at least* as loyal online as they are in offline environments.[80] Subsequent work, consistent with that of Hargittai and collaborators, mentioned earlier, has emphasized the role of habit and routine. Kyle Murray and Gerald Häubl argue that the web produces what they term *skill-based habits of use*.[81] As users become more practiced and proficient, their browsing behavior becomes increasingly automatic. It becomes harder and harder to change their patterns of usage.

PATH DEPENDENCE AND THE DYNAMICS OF LOCK-IN

In early 2004 a student-created social networking site took over an Ivy League campus. Within a month most students on campus were posting photos and blogs and polls, sharing music and upcoming events, and commenting on their friends' activities. After conversations with Silicon Valley luminaries, such as Napster creator Sean Parker, the site expanded to many other campuses. The founder dropped out of school to work on the site full time. Soon the nascent social network had hundreds of thousands of users.

This is not the story of Facebook. Rather, it is the story of Campus Network, an early Facebook competitor that began at Columbia University. Started by Adam Goldberg, an engineering and computer science student, Campus Network (initially called CU Community) launched before Facebook. It began with a head start in features and functionality. Blogging and cross-profile discussion were built into Campus Network from the start, while these features came later to Facebook. In Goldberg's telling, Sean Parker urged Mark Zuckerberg to purchase Campus Network and to hire Goldberg.

So why was Facebook ultimately successful, while Campus Network ended up shutting down in 2006? Journalist Christopher Beam suggests several possible factors that may have outweighed Campus Network's early lead.[82] One is money. Facebook quickly pursued financial backing, while Campus Network turned down advertisers and declined to seek venture capital funding. This early capital allowed Facebook to hire more developers, to quickly add more features, and to rapidly expand into new markets.

Facebook was also simpler at first, letting users sign up with just a name, email address, and password. And Facebook was prettier. Wayne Ting, who was in charge of business and legal work for Campus Network, said the site looked like it was designed by "somebody who loves dungeons and dragons."[83] Perhaps, too, Facebook's Harvard origins provided additional cachet compared to Campus Network's Columbia heritage.

Ultimately, Facebook was able to expand faster. By the time Facebook had a million users it was four times the size of Campus Network, and growing more quickly. Campus Network had lost the race.

It is easy to draw the wrong conclusion from the early competition between Facebook and Campus Network. One might debate whether things would have been different if Campus Network had pursued venture capital, or if it had pushed to expand faster, or if it had just offered a less clunky interface. Perhaps so.

But the more profound lesson is that these advantages were small and largely arbitrary. Because Facebook was slightly better slightly earlier, and because it was lucky, it won the entire market. The web is not like economic sectors such as agriculture or logging or mining, where firms run up against hard constraints on their size. Digital firms online, much like software firms or telegraph companies, face few natural limits to their scale. Once a winner begins to emerge the market becomes highly inflexible. Early small events are magnified instead of being averaged away.

Economists commonly call this pattern *lock-in*. Lock-in emerges when the costs of switching grow large enough to outweigh any potential benefits. While the early stages of an emerging online niche are strongly dynamic, again and again once-open digital niches have locked in. Small differences in stickiness compound quickly.

Lock-in occurs not *despite* the fact that the web is constantly changing, but precisely *because* of its dynamic character. The evolutionary, constantly compounding character of web traffic is why digital niches lock in so quickly.

This chapter has documented many powerful but different forms of increasing returns on the web, each of which contributes to lock-in. Increasing returns come from more than just network effects—though those matter, especially for sites that allow direct user-to-user communication. Larger sites can be faster, and have more computing power and storage, while still costing less per user to run. Established sites benefit from branding, and (as we will see shortly) they can charge far more per user in advertising. Bigger sites are prettier and easier to use, and they provide larger, higher-quality bundles of content. And as users develop habits and site-specific skills they are increasingly anchored to sites that they already know.

But despite these increasingly obvious facts, the internet is often still portrayed as a magical fairyland of frictionless commerce and perfect competition. We still see news articles like a piece in *Forbes*, in which the headline blares "Anyone Anywhere Can Build The Next Google—There Are No Barriers." Executives at today's digital Goliaths still repeat the refrain that "competition is only a click away." Google chairman Eric Schmidt declared that the company should be worried because "somewhere in a garage [someone is] gunning for us. I know, because not long ago we were in that garage."[84] Former FCC chairman Tom Wheeler claimed in his book that the internet serves an inevitably decentralizing force—a sentiment that Trump administration FCC chair Ajit Pai has echoed (as we will discuss later on).

The notion of an intrinsically open, ever-competitive internet is still the central assumption behind U.S. communication policy, and the foundation of a substantial body of scholarship. But these claims are more and more at odds with reality. An internet on which *most traffic never touches the public backbone* is no longer a peer-to-peer network, nor one that (as FCC chairman Wheeler suggested) "pushes activity to the edges."[85] Unfettered competition never guarantees consumer-friendly outcomes in markets with strong economies of scale. Economics has long known that increasing returns can cause an industry to adopt a technology that later proves inefficient.[86] There is no guarantee that Facebook is a better site for consumers than, say, Campus Network would be today if it had survived.

Amid this discussion of lock-in online, one thing has been left out. In many markets, the largest barrier to switching is the hassle of finding and evaluating potential alternatives. How often do most people get an alternative quote for their car insurance? How often do they try out new brands of deodorant or toothpaste? How many consumers are really getting the lowest possible rate on their mortgage, or the highest interest rate on their savings account? Most of the time firms and individuals stick with products and services that are known to be good enough.

Search costs, then, can also produce lock-in. And these search costs will be the subject of the next chapter.

The Political Economy of Personalization

> It's becoming quite apparent to us that the world of playing the perfect
> music to people and the world of playing perfect advertising to them are
> strikingly similar.
> —Eric Bieschke, chief scientist at Pandora

In his 1995 book *Being Digital,* Nicholas Negroponte described a world
in which everyone had a virtual newspaper entirely tailored to his or her
personal taste. Negroponte proposed creating an intelligent, computerized "interface agent" that would "read every newswire and newspaper and
catch every TV and radio broadcast on the planet, and then construct a
personalized summary":

> It would mix headline news with "less important" stories relating to acquain-
> tances, people you will see tomorrow, and places you are about to go to or
> have just come from. It would report on companies you know. In fact, under
> these conditions, you might be willing to pay the *Boston Globe* a lot more
> for ten pages than a hundred pages, if you could be confident that it was
> delivering you the right subset of information. You would consume every
> bit (so to speak). Call it *The Daily Me.*[1]

Negroponte's vision of The Daily Me proved highly influential, partly
because it arrived just as the web was starting to transform the media landscape. The notion was endorsed by key technology industry leaders and
top public policymakers as well as scholars.[2] Much subsequent scholarship focused on media self-selection as functionally equivalent to The Daily

Me, with particular worry that the internet would allow a partisan "echo chamber."[3]

In recent years, improved filtering technologies and the emergence of social networking sites have produced something strikingly close to Negroponte's original vision. Online sellers such as Amazon.com and eBay pioneered this technology,[4] with other digital giants close behind. News sites such as Google News, CNN, and Yahoo! News now also rely heavily on learning algorithms. Facebook in particular has emphasized hyperpersonalization, with Facebook founder and CEO Mark Zuckerberg stating that "a squirrel dying in your front yard may be more relevant to your interests right now than people dying in Africa."[5] With the rise of the iPad and its imitators, Negroponte's idea that all of this personalized content would be sent to a thin, lightweight, "magical" tablet device has been partially realized, too.

Scholarship such as Siva Vaidhyanathan's *The Googlization of Everything* and Joe Turow's *The Daily You* has viewed the trend toward personalized content and ubiquitous filtering as a part of a worrying concentration of corporate power. Eli Pariser's bestselling book *The Filter Bubble* voices similar worries. But for journalism and media scholarship as a whole, as Barbie Zelizer has noted, there has been surprisingly little work on recommender systems.[6] To the extent that algorithmic news filtering has been discussed at all, it was long unhelpfully lumped with a grab bag of different site features under the heading of "interactivity."[7] Research by Neil Thurman and Steve Schifferes has provided a taxonomy of different forms of personalization and has chronicled their (mostly growing) deployment across different news sites.[8] Even Thurman and Schifferes's work, however, has said little about recommender systems because traditional news organizations lagged in deploying them. As this book goes to press, new journalism and communication scholarship has finally started to address this longstanding gap.[9] Still, much work remains to be done.

This chapter has two main aims. First, it offers a more detailed examination of the principals behind these recommendation systems than previous media scholarship. Recommender systems research has changed dramatically over the past decade, but little of this new knowledge has filtered into research on web traffic, online news, or the future of journalism. Much of the writing on recommender systems in these fields has been an unhelpful montage of hypotheticals and what-ifs. Elaborate deductive conclusions have been built from false foundational assumptions.

Second, this chapter examines the comparative impact of these technologies *across* media organizations, something that previous work has overlooked or misunderstood. Scholarship to date has focused on the impact of these technologies for an individual web user or an adopting media firm. But there has been little exploration of the wholesale effects of these changes not only *within* news and media organizations, but also with regard to *competition between them*.

This chapter takes a detailed look at the Netflix Prize—a contest with surprising lessons even for those who do not care about movies. As it turns out, the task of recommending the right movie is similar to recommending almost anything—predicting which songs users like, which ads they prefer, which news stories they engage with.

The Netflix Prize was the first large open-submission machine learning contest, and it produced big improvements in the accuracy of recommender systems. This contest remains perhaps the best lens through which to see the general principles of how recommender systems function.

The chapter goes on to examine how the general principles of targeting content apply to the broader attention economy. Two case studies are laid out in more detail: Google News, the algorithmic news pioneer, and Yahoo!, which has revealed much about how its behavioral targeting ad technology works. Taken together, these cases tell us much about who will win, and who will lose, as recommender systems assume a growing role in the delivery of media content.

These techniques, however, are not just for media organizations. The chapter concludes by looking at the Cambridge Analytica scandal, perhaps Facebook's biggest public relations disaster to date. As the author was the first to report,[10] Cambridge Analytica modeled Facebook user data using methods similar to those that won the Netflix Prize. Cambridge Analytica's example shows that data held by digital giants, coupled with now-standard machine learning techniques, can be an important tool to match citizens with online political messages.

But to understand the broader context, this chapter begins by talking more generally about the *economics of search*. Media targeting and personalization are part of a more fundamental problem in economics: how to efficiently match buyers and sellers.

THE COSTS OF SEARCH

In 1961 the economist (and later Nobel laureate) George Stigler published an article titled simply "The Economics of Information." Stigler's focus was on the effort needed to connect buyers and sellers. Potential buyers want to pay as little as possible, but it costs time to compare prices. Moreover, the savings earned by continuing to search get smaller and smaller the longer a search goes on. A couple shopping for a car are far more likely to save money after checking a second or third auto dealership than they are from checking prices at the ninety-ninth or the hundredth. Stigler argued that diverse and geographically big markets have especially high search costs.

How does one lower the costs of search? One answer is to localize markets, as has happened for thousands of years as merchants clustered in bazaars or town squares or shopping districts. Advertising is a slightly more recent attempt to lower search costs. Classified advertising in particular provides a mediated marketplace where buyers and sellers can meet.

Another solution, as Stigler explained, involves the creation of market makers: "specialized traders whose chief service ... is implicitly to provide a meeting place for potential buyers and sellers."[11] He suggested that such firms can take a variety of forms, from large used car dealers to trade journals to specialized information brokers. Stigler also predicted that the largest market-making firm is likely to eclipse any competitors: "Since the cost of collection of information is (approximately) independent of its use ... there is a strong tendency toward monopoly in the provision of information."[12]

Reading Stigler fifty years later, one is struck by how closely the logic above describes segment after segment of the web. If big, complicated markets have always tended to produce a single dominant information firm or a market-making monopolist, then the internet—the biggest and most complicated market in history—should produce these effects in spades.

Indeed it does. Take auctions. Auction houses are canonical examples of market makers. The art auction houses Sotheby's and Christie's localize markets, first segmenting art into subgroups by genre, time period, and region, and then holding auctions at regular intervals. Auction houses have many mechanisms to prevent *price dispersion*—or more plainly, to ensure that neither sellers nor buyers get ripped off. Substantial research goes into the sale catalogue, which describes each work and verifies its provenance. Insurance and security are substantial investments. Together, Christie's and Sotheby's account for the vast majority of high-end art sales worldwide. The duopoly has been prevented from merging only by antitrust laws—and even without a merger, the two companies have in the past colluded to set prices, leading to the criminal conviction of two top Sotheby's executives.

It is therefore unsurprising that a single firm—eBay—has come to dominate the online auction market. In addition to providing a centralized virtual marketplace, eBay has mechanisms to reduce price dispersion and ensure quality. Price history for similar items is easy to see, and eBay's reputation system and insurance policies help ensure that items bought will arrive as promised.

Yet other successful firms that dominate their online niche also turn out, upon closer inspection, to look like market makers or specialized information brokers. The market for books is large and complex for both publishers and readers. Amazon began by providing a virtual place for book buyers and publishers to meet, and giving targeted information to buyers about which books they were likely to enjoy. Netflix fulfills a similar role in the movie and television series marketplace (more on Netflix shortly).

But the most powerful extension of Stigler's framework goes beyond the sale of goods. The costs of search do not apply just to physical goods or market transactions. As Stigler emphasized, the key cost of search is not money but time. In this light, *Google itself is a market maker*, matching purveyors of information with information consumers.

Yet there are crucial differences between traditional market making and the algorithmic matching that has taken over the web. One key distinction is that—at scale—recommendation algorithms often outperform human experts. Among Amazon.com's early employees were about a dozen book critics and editors, who wrote reviews and suggested books. But as Amazon developed more sophisticated recommendation systems in the late 1990s, A/B tests showed that machine picks generated far more sales than the expert choices.[13] Continuing to use human experts was costing Amazon millions of dollars a year.

But the success of recommendation systems in some contexts raises a host of questions. How exactly do these systems work? How much do they change patterns of content consumption? Which sorts of firms, and which websites, are able to use them most effectively? The story of the Netflix Prize gives insight into all of these questions.

Netflix and Content Recommendation

In October of 2006, movie-rental service Netflix kicked off the Netflix Prize, a worldwide competition to improve its video recommendation algorithm. At the time Netflix rented DVDs to subscribers by mail. A typical Netflix user signed up wanting to see a short list of movies, which she watched within a few months. Whether the subscriber stayed or left thus depended on her ability to find *new* movies to watch.

Netflix offered a $1 million prize to the first team that could beat CineMatch, its in-house recommendation engine. Even more remarkably, Netflix actually released its data. Once the contest started, anyone could download a real-world dataset containing 100,480,500 one-to-five star ratings, from 480,189 anonymous users, for 17,770 movies. The contest would end up running for more than two-and-a-half years, and engaging the efforts of more than five thousand teams. In the process, it illuminated much that is usually hidden about the ways in which digital firms personalize the content that users see.

The central task of the contest was an example of *collaborative filtering*, using automated methods to infer a user's tastes from the preferences of other users. The key contest metric was root mean-squared error (RMSE)— a measure of how much, on average, a recommendation model misses the true value. If Joe Netflix Subscriber gives *The Empire Strikes Back* five stars, and the original CineMatch algorithm predicted that he would give it 4.5 stars, then the root squared error would be $\sqrt{(-.5*-.5)} = .5$. (Squaring the errors, and then taking the square root, means that the RMSE is always positive.)

The contest hoped to drop the error as low as possible. Predicting that every user would give a movie its average rating produced an RMSE of 1.054—a typical error of more than a star in either direction. Netflix's CineMatch offered an initial RMSE of .9525, about a tenth of a star better. Netflix described CineMatch as a relatively simple approach, "straightforward statistical linear models with a lot of data conditioning."[14] The contest winner, if any, would be the first team to drop the RMSE to .8572. Though this would still leave the model off by more than four-fifths of a star, this was twice the improvement CineMatch had managed on its own.

The contest showed rapid progress out of the gate. Within a week, several teams had equaled CineMatch; within three weeks CineMatch had been bested by 3 percent. These efforts revealed that CineMatch was actually a K-nearest neighbor (KNN) algorithm. If we wanted to predict Maria's rating for *Titanic*, for example, a KNN approach might start by finding the users who (1) saw *Titanic* and (2) agree with Maria's ratings of other movies—for example, those who also hated *Gladiator* but gave five loving stars to *A Beautiful Mind*. Once this "neighborhood" of similar subscribers is found, Maria's predicted rating for *Titanic* is just a weighted average of her neighbors' ratings. If Alex, Becky, and Chris are the users most similar to Maria, and they gave *Titanic* 1, 4, and 5 stars respectively, then Maria's predicted rating is just $\frac{1+4+5}{3} = 3.33$. KNN approaches dominated the early months of the contest.

The Netflix Prize attracted a wide range of participants from industry, the academy, and even some members of the general public. By late November, a team from AT&T Research Labs had also joined the competition. The team's key members were Yehuda Koren, a computer scientist and network visualization specialist, and Robert Bell, a statistician with a focus on machine learning. Bell and Koren called their team BellKor, and the duo would ultimately form the nucleus of the winning team.[15]

One goal of the open competition was to attract and aggregate insights from a far broader and diverse group than otherwise possible. As Netflix had hoped, one of the largest single improvements came from an unlikely source. In early December 2006, participants were surprised to see the name Simon Funk jump to third place on the leaderboard. Simon Funk was the pseudonym of Brandynn Webb, a computer scientist who had worked on artificial intelligence and pattern recognition.

While many teams were highly secretive about their methods, Funk explained his entire approach in a detailed blog post.[16] Funk had applied a factor analysis technique called singular value decomposition (SVD) to the Netflix data. SVD modeled the millions of movie ratings as the sum of a (smaller) number of unknown variables. As Funk explained on his blog,

> The end result of SVD is essentially a list of inferred categories, sorted by relevance. Each category in turn is expressed simply by how well each user and movie belong (or anti-belong) to the category. So, for instance, a category might represent action movies, with movies with a lot of action at the top, and slow movies at the bottom, and correspondingly users who like action movies at the top, and those who prefer slow movies at the bottom.[17]

While this is true in theory, interpreting factors can be difficult in practice, as we shall see.

SVD had rarely been used with recommender systems because the technique performed poorly on "sparse" datasets, those (like the Netflix data) in which most of the values are missing. But Funk adapted the technique to ignore missing values, and found a way to implement the approach in only two lines of C code.[18] Funk even titled the blog post explaining his method "Try This at Home," encouraging other entrants to incorporate SVD.

Nearly all of the top competitors did so. When the Netflix Prize was finally awarded, SVD methods were the the largest component of the models on the winning and second-place teams.

Still, it is unlikely that SVD techniques on their own would have been powerful enough to win the competition. One unexpected revelation of the contest was the advantage of blending different learning techniques together. As BellKor reported at the end of the first year, "Combining predictions from multiple, complementary models improved performance, with one model's strengths compensating for the weaknesses of others."[19] While SVD might be the single best technique, it would often miss relationships that would be obvious to a human observer, like recommending a sequel to a user who had liked the first movie in a series. KNN models were much better at finding clusters of closely related films.

By the end of the contest, teams were using megablends of hundreds of different models. And while latent-factor models like SVD and nearest-neighbors models made up the largest portion of the solutions, the final blends included a complex mishmash of different techniques, from principle component analysis to ridge regression to Restricted Boltman Machine neural network approaches. As AT&T's Chris Volinsky explained, "I don't think when we started that anybody expected that that would be the way to win the competition."[20]

The same premium on diverse approaches also led, eventually, to a wave of mergers among teams. The Netflix Prize rules, in addition the $1 million grand prize, called for the awarding of $50,000 yearly "Progress Prizes" for the team currently closest to the goal, providing that there had been substantial progress. The catch was that the winning Progress Prize team had to publish a full accounting of their techniques, allowing competitors to catch up.

As the end of the first year neared, BellKor had led narrowly since March. But with only a day left in the Progress Prize window, the fifth- and sixth-place teams combined their predictions, and the blended results vaulted them into second place. This unexpected move set off a flurry of last-minute activity (and forum debates about whether this new tactic was fair). The second- and third-place Dinosaur Planet and Gravity teams followed suit with a hasty merger of their own (When Gravity and Dinosaurs Unite), and the merged team submitted a final score that edged out BellKor's previous best. The BellKor team worked through the night, submitting two buzzer-beating entries that eked out a narrow victory in the Progress Prize.

At the end of the first year BellKor had managed an 8.43 percent improvement over CineMatch. But most of the easy progress had already been made. Over the next year the pace of improvement would be far slower. In early 2008, after the publication of BellKor's methods, several new teams appeared in the top twenty sites. In February, When Gravity and Dinosaurs Unite passed BellKor to take a narrow lead.

As the contest dragged on, it became clear that the BellKor team would be unable to win the prize on its own. So it, too, decided to seek the improvements that other teams had shown when they combined their efforts. As AT&T's official account later explained, "Teams that collaborated always improved over their individual scores *provided each team brought different methods to the table*."[21]

Bob Bell suggested a method by which teams could compare their results, without giving away all of their secrets. By adding statistically regular noise to their predicted ratings, teams could share their output and perform simple calculations to see how similar their approaches were. These results showed that the team BigChaos was the best merger candidate. BigChaos had a relatively low error rate, but, more importantly, its predictions were least correlated with the predictions of BellKor, suggesting a potential payoff to collaboration. After legal negotiations, the merger went through.

As it turned out, much of BigChaos's contribution came from using sophisticated neural networks to blend the results. As the AT&T team later wrote, "Where BellKor used simple, linear blending based on each model's individual performance, BigChaos had determined that the individual RMSE of a single method was not the best indication of how much that model would add to the blend."[22]

With the improvements from BigChaos, the combined team won the second Progress Prize in October 2008 by a comfortable margin. But progress soon stalled. Once again, the solution was to find another team to merge with. This time the candidate was Pragmatic Theory. Pragmatic Theory was particularly good at identifying unusual or even quirky predictors, like the length of a film's title, or users that rated films differently on Sunday than they would on Monday. On their own, these sorts of features predict little about users' ratings. In the context of the full model, however, they gave a small added boost in accuracy.

The teams initially disguised the merger by continuing to post separately. By adding noise to their results, they could see how close they were to the 10.0 percent finish line without alerting other teams to their progress. By June 2009, the newly merged team knew that they had reached their goal. On June 26, 2009, the team went public, submitting a 10.05 percent result under the name BellKor's Pragmatic Chaos (BPC).

The hectic conclusion of the Netflix Prize proved a replay of the first Progress Prize. The posting of a result with better than 10 percent improvement, as required by the rules, triggered a final 30-day period for all teams to submit their final answers. With nothing to lose, many teams rushed to join forces. The main competitor to the BellKor-led effort ended up being a super-group called The Ensemble, which ultimately comprised twenty-three different original teams or individual competitors, including the previously merged Dinosaur Planet and Gravity groups. The Ensemble improved rapidly in the last few weeks of the contest. In the final days, The Ensemble seemed to nudge past BPC on the public leaderboard. But since the leaderboard was based on public data, and the contest would be judged on a similar but unreleased private dataset, it was not clear who was really in the lead.

On September 21, 2009, almost three years after the contest opened, BellKor's Pragmatic Chaos was publicly announced as the winner. Only later was it revealed that The Ensemble had achieved the exact same level of improvement: an RMSE of 0.8567. BPC had won because of a tie-breaker in the fine print of the contest: BPC's final results had been submitted twenty-four minutes earlier. After years of effort, the contest had ended in a photo finish.

The Lessons of the Netflix Prize

Why should those interested in online audiences or digital news care about the Netflix Prize? One answer is that these recommender systems now have enormous influence on democratic discourse. In his book *The Filter Bubble* progressive activist Eli Pariser reported that posts from conservative friends were systematically excluded from his Facebook feed. This sort of filtering heightens concerns about partisan echo chambers, and it might make it harder for citizens to seek out opposing views even if they are inclined to. Increasingly, learning algorithms are also replacing editorial judgment and longstanding news norms.

Yet recommender systems should be of interest for an even more fundamental reason. Recommender systems do not just influence which articles users see, but also which sites they end up visiting in the first place.

Whether they are funded by advertising or subscriptions, websites require traffic to succeed. Sites live or die based upon their stickiness—their ability to attract readers, to make those readers stay longer when they visit, and to convince them to return again once they leave. Even slight differences in site stickiness compound quickly and rapidly create enormous differences in audience. Recommendation systems are one of the most powerful tools available for sites to keep and grow their traffic, and those who cannot deploy them are at a profound competitive disadvantage.

The key question is this: *which sorts of sites can build, and benefit most from, high-quality recommender systems?*

The Netflix contest provides a partial answer. Moreover, the Netflix Prize is likely the only chance we will have in the near future to look at the inner-workings of web recommendation systems using a large, public, real-world dataset. Netflix initially planned a successor contest to the Netflix Prize. However, facing a class-action lawsuit and an FTC investigation regarding user privacy, Netflix canceled the intended sequel.[23] Given these legal complications, other large digital firms have been wary about sponsoring similar contests or releasing comparable datasets.

The Netflix Prize is often discussed as an example of crowdsourced problem solving. The results of the contest, however, suggest that the advantages of recommender systems will accrue highly unevenly. The very largest sites have been able to build excellent content recommendation systems; the smallest sites have not.

Recommender systems favor large, well-resourced organizations. In order to inspire such a high level of participation, Netflix had to be willing to write a $1 million check. Large teams won the competition, and the winning team needed to merge with two other teams to cross the finish line. Even stronger evidence for this point comes from The Ensemble's nearly successful last-minute scramble to catch up. By combining the efforts of more than a dozen other teams, The Ensemble was quickly able to equal the results of BellKor's Pragmatic Chaos. Indeed, The Ensemble would likely have won if the contest had continued just a few days longer.

Building successful algorithms is an iterative and accretive process. It benefits from larger groups and diverse approaches, and thus provides inevitable size advantages. As the competition evolved, the models produced became absurdly complex. Managing this complexity also requires expertise and substantial staffing.

Similarly, the sorts of individuals who rose up the contest leaderboard also suggest limits to crowdsourced problem solving in contests like the Netflix Prize. Those who led the most successful teams were already prominent academic or corporate researchers. Even those who were initially unfamiliar names, such as Funk (Brandynn Webb) or the Princeton undergraduates who made up the Dinosaur Planet team, had formal training and relevant professional experience. The project benefited little from average citizens, but it benefited greatly from drawing on a broader and more diverse set of those with subject-area expertise. Netflix would never have been able to hire that level of expertise even at five times the contest budget. But if the research and positive publicity was worth it, the effort nevertheless required a seven-figure investment.

Not only do big sites have a large edge in terms of resources, but they also have an even more crucial advantage: *more data*. Building infrastructure to collect, store, organize, analyze, and constantly update data is an enormous investment. This is not something that a small startup could have done nearly as successfully, and not just because of the money, hardware, and expertise required. Data come from monitoring users, and startups do not have nearly as many users to monitor. As AT&T's team put it, "As the competition progressed, using more information almost always improved accuracy, even when it wasn't immediately obvious why the information mattered or how little the information contributed."[24]

The need for as much information as possible has broad implications. One fact often overlooked is that Netflix *already* had reached the overall level of accuracy they paid one million dollars for. As the contest FAQ explained,

> The RMSE experienced by customers on the Netflix site is significantly better than the RMSE reported for the training dataset. This is due both to the increase in ratings data but also to additional business logic we use to tune which of the large number of ratings to learn from ... let's just say we'd be seriously in the running for a Progress Prize, if we were eligible.[25]

In other words, even at the start of the competition, Netflix was able to do significantly better than the raw CineMatch results indicated. They did this both by adding more variables and by training on a larger dataset. The same techniques used to extract more information from a simple list of users and movie ratings work even better with data from (for example) user demographics or browsing behavior.

Subsequent statements from Netflix show that they have gone even further in this direction. Netflix's business has changed dramatically since 2006, as the company has gone from a DVD-by-mail model to a focus on video streaming over the web. In a blog post detailing their followup to the Netflix Prize, they explain that they now operate as if "everything is a recommendation," and that they extract information from almost every aspect of user behavior.[26] Most site features are now personalized based on this data. Netflix claims that optimized models and additional features provide them with a five-fold improvement over ratings data alone.[27]

Yet for learning algorithms more broadly, what constitutes *more information* is not always obvious. More data is not just about more variables. In the initial stages of the competition, several teams attempted to supplement the movie data with a host of other details about each movie: the director, actors, studio, genre, year, etc. In simple linear models, the inclusion of this data at first seemed to improve the results. But with more sophisticated latent-factor models and nearest-neighbor models, adding movie details did not improve the predictions *at all*, because the machine learning models had already implicitly included all of this information.

More information can also be found even without collecting more data, by transforming the existing dataset to extract new features. Koren, in a lecture a few months after the contest's end, declared, "One thing that we discovered again and again . . . is that understanding the features in the data, or the character of the data, . . . is far more important than picking the right model or perfecting the model."[28] The Netflix competition started off with a very limited feature set: just user, movie, rating, and day of rating. Jumps in accuracy involved taking that limited data and extracting new features, like temporal effects.

The moral here is somewhat paradoxical. Netflix released a massive dataset to find the best algorithm, but the algorithms themselves proved *less important* than the data. Similar lessons have emerged in other, quite different realms of machine learning. In research on natural language processing, Microsoft researchers examined how accuracy improved across several different algorithms as the amount of training data increased. Although these algorithms showed dramatically different performance on tests of one million words, as the researchers scaled up the training set— to ten million, one hundred million, and finally one billion words—the algorithms' performance became more and more similar. As Banko and Brill concluded, "These results suggest that we may want to reconsider the trade-off between spending time and money on algorithm development versus spending it on corpus development."[29]

The Netflix contest also highlighted several parts of the "black box problem." One disadvantage of complex learning techniques is that when a model is performing well, it is often not clear *why*. The success of latent factor models in the competition emphasized this issue. In theory, one might think of latent factor models as revealing human-interpretable categories like "action movie vs. non-action movie," or "serious vs. escapist," or "male-focused vs. female-focused." Sometimes the results that latent factor models give do seem to map easily to categories that humans already understand or expect.

But that is not really what happened with the Netflix Prize. The dimensions that popped out of the data do not map neatly to obvious predefined categories. Funk's first attempt at using an SVD model found that the most important dimension was anchored on one end by films like *Pearl Harbor* (2001), *Coyote Ugly* (2000), and *The Wedding Planner* (2001), while the other end of the scale was defined by films like *Lost in Translation* (2003), *The Royal Tenenbaums* (2001), and *Eternal Sunshine of the Spotless Mind* (2004).[30] These are very different sorts of films, yet it is tough to articulate a concise description of what separates these groups. As Koren later concluded, "It is very difficult to give names to these axes."[31] And if one latent-factor model is tough to interpret, how much harder is it to interpret the final blend of more than seven hundred models—many of which were themselves blends of different component models?

In one way, however, Netflix's example calls into question claims that filtering technologies will end up promoting echo chambers and eliminating serendipitous exposure. Such worries have been a centerpiece of scholarship on personalized news over the past decade (see earlier discussion). One of Pariser's key claims about what he terms the "filter bubble" is that it is ostensibly invisible to users.[32] Netflix, however, tries hard to make users aware of its recommendation system: "We want members to be aware of how we are adapting to their tastes. This not only promotes trust in the system, but encourages members to give feedback that will result in better recommendations."[33] Netflix also attempts to explain (in an oversimplified way) why specific movies are recommended, typically highlighting its recommendations' similarity to movies the user has already rated.

Even more important, Netflix shows that there is a performance boost for recommending *diverse* content, not just for predicting ratings accurately. Partly, this is because Netflix subscriptions are often shared among members of a household who may have very different tastes. But as Netflix explains, "Even for a single person household we want to appeal to your range of interests and moods. To achieve this, in many parts of our system we are not only optimizing for accuracy, but also for diversity."[34] The biggest, most blended models that drew on the most varied features performed best overall in the Netflix Prize. In hindsight, it is perhaps unsurprising that recommending a highly diverse basket of movies also ends up improving performance. But given concerns about "filter bubbles" and online echo chambers, a performance bonus for diversity challenges conventional wisdom.

Google News

The Netflix experience demonstrated several features of recommender systems that are likely to persist across many different websites and varied genres of online content. In recent years, several of the largest online websites have been willing to release greater details about their recommender systems, and the algorithms with which they personalize content for their users. Even more so than with the Netflix Prize, the information released by companies like Google, Yahoo!, Microsoft, and Facebook is only an incomplete picture of the whole. These companies are understandably wary about releasing information that would give their competitors an advantage or would compromise user privacy.

Nonetheless, recent disclosures do provide key details about how recommender systems are being applied in practice, and how they benefit some organizations over others. In particular, the results of A/B testing provide compelling evidence of just how important personalized content is for improving site traffic. Recommendation systems dramatically increase stickiness for the largest websites in ways small sites cannot replicate.

Consider the case of Google News, one of the largest news sites on the web, and a pioneer in replacing editorial judgment with algorithmic decision-making. In 2007, Google researchers released a paper detailing the company's internal work in news personalization.[35] In some ways recommending news stories is similar to recommending movies. Most users, most of the time, arrive at a news site without knowing which specific articles they would like to see. As Google's researchers put it, user attitudes are dominated by the demands to "show us something interesting."[36]

Yet news targeting also presents a series of unique problems, too. First, news articles provide a particularly severe example of the "cold start" or "first rater" problem. All personalization algorithms perform well with lots of information on both the items to be recommended and individual user preferences. With movies, for example, the accuracy increases for a user as he or she rates more movies, and as each movie gets reviews from a larger number of Netflix subscribers. News content, however, shows an enormous amount of turnover day to day, and even hour to hour. By definition news readers are most interested in content that is *new*, precisely the articles that lack substantial training data. Making the matter worse, it is quite costly—in both time and computing power—to constantly rebuild or retrain the recommendation framework to offer predictions for the newest content. Because site speed is one of the most important parts of the user experience, personalized results have to be returned to the user in no more than a couple hundred milliseconds.

The technical infrastructure that Google News requires is daunting: numerous large-scale data centers, more than one million server computers, enormous investments in fiber, even customized operating systems and file systems. Total development costs for this infrastructure, including both hardware and software components, ran into the tens of billions of dollars. Many recommendation algorithms are computationally costly to implement at scale, and some of Google's researchers' findings focus on achieving similar performance with less computation. Their initial paper details several slightly different algorithms, all in the same general family of methods as the K-nearest-neighbor algorithm described earlier.

The most dramatic results in the paper come from Google's testing of the extent to which these personalized recommendations improve traffic numbers. By interleaving personalized results with results based just on popularity, Google was able to control for the fact that higher-ranked items get more attention. The results were striking: overall, stories based on collaborative filtering had 38 percent more clicks than stories chosen just based on popularity.[37]

These early methods have now been superseded by even more effective forms of targeting. In 2010, Google released a second report on its targeting algorithms in Google News.[38] Here Google distinguished between the collaborative filtering approaches, which were the basis of its earlier work, and content-based approaches. Collaborative filtering looks at the similarity between users and between items, whereas content-based methods use text analysis to match users with the types of stories they have favored in the past. Content-based models proved better at recommending brand-new stories, and they better allowed for user differences. For example, Google reported that its first-generation collaborative filtering mechanism recommended entertainment news stories to all users, even those who had never once clicked on entertainment news: "entertainment news stories are generally very popular, thus there [were] always enough clicks on entertainment stories from a user's 'neighbors' to make the recommendation."[39]

Google's 2010 report details a hybrid model combining both collaborative and content-based approaches. When the recommendation system has few news clicks from a user, its predictions rely on collaborative methods, which focus on current popular stories. Once the system records a significant amount of click data, recommendations are based more and more on users' past behavior and demonstrated interests.

This hybrid model shows dramatic improvements over collaborative filtering alone, which (again) was itself far better than simply recommending to users whatever was popular. Compared to straight collaborative filtering, the hybrid model produced 31 percent more clicks on news stories, though this was largely the result of shifting traffic from interior sections of the site to recommended stories on the front page. Even more importantly, over the course of the study users who saw the hybrid model had 14 percent more daily visits to the Google News site. This is a clear demonstration of just how much improved recommendation systems can boost daily traffic.

Other computer science researchers have produced traffic bonuses with news recommendation engines. Hewlett-Packard researchers Evan Kirshenbaum, George Forman, and Michael Dugan conducted an experiment comparing different methods of content recommendation on Forbes.com. Here too, as at Google, the researchers found that a mixture of content-based and collaborative-filtering methods gave a significant improvement.[40]

Yahoo! and Behavioral Targeting

If Google's results are potentially worrisome for traditional news organizations, research from Yahoo! is perhaps even more dispiriting. Yahoo!, too, has been highly active in personalizing and targeting its news results. While Yahoo! itself has been circumspect about releasing details of its news targeting methods, journalistic accounts have similarly claimed big improvements in news traffic and click-through rates. Yahoo! reported that personalized targeting increased clicks on its news page's "Today" box by 270 percent.[41]

But if Yahoo! has been relatively discreet about its news targeting methods, research papers have pulled back the curtain on its targeted advertising abilities. The same technologies that provide users with the most clickable content also allow advertisers to match their messages to the most promising potential buyers. Understanding how this behavioral targeting works is crucial for understanding the political economy of online media.

There are three general types of online ad targeting. At the broadest level there is *property targeting*, in which ads are run on sites that feature related content or favorable demographics. Showing truck ads on an automobile site or a sports site is an example of property targeting. Second, there is a *user segment targeting*, which typically focuses on the age range and gender of the user: for example, showing ads for trucks to 25–40 year-old men across a wider variety of properties.

Both of these methods are crude compared to *behavioral targeting*. As the Yahoo! researchers explain, "The key behind behavioral targeting is that the advertisers can show ads only to users within a specific demographic of high-value (such as people likely to buy a car) and combine that with a larger number of opportunities (places to show ads) per user."[42] In this case the Yahoo! researchers used support vector machines, a common machine learning technique, to predict which users were likely to be good prospects. But it is almost certain that similar results would have been obtained with other learning techniques.

The key difference between the Yahoo! research and earlier targeting efforts (at least publicly acknowledged ones) lies in the type of training data. Typically, behavioral targeting models have looked at clicks on an online ad as the key metric. Yahoo! researchers instead trained their data on "conversions," sales that resulted directly from clicking on an online ad.[43]

Clicks on ads are uncommon, with typical click-through rates just a fraction of a percent. And if clicks are rare, conversions are only a tiny fraction of clicks. Increasingly, however, retailers have provided web beacons that beam sales information back to advertising networks or partner sites. Still, only a handful of organizations have the detailed user behavior and conversion data necessary to target in this way.

Yahoo!'s research demonstrates just how much purchase data matters. Pandey and collaborators performed A/B testing between models trained on conversion data and the same methods trained just on click data. In four tested real-world advertising campaigns, conversions increased between 59 and 264 percent. In every case there was a dramatic drop in advertisers' cost per sale. Advertisers ultimate goal, of course, is to get the greatest number of sales for the least advertising cost. The bottom line, as the researchers conclude, is that "we can improve the number of conversions per ad impression without greatly increasing the number of impressions, which increases the value of our inventory."[44]

The research also suggests that the greatest improvements accrue to the largest advertising campaigns. Since conversions are rare, only the largest campaigns have enough sales data to train the models effectively. This is especially noteworthy given that Yahoo! is one of the largest sites on the web, with an enormous online ad inventory. If only the largest campaigns on the largest sites are able to take advantage of these techniques, this has significant implications for the web as a whole.

What do these results mean for news sites? For starters, they show that standalone news organizations cannot perform behavioral targeting nearly as effectively as Yahoo! or Google. Many newspaper executives and print publishers have argued that local newspaper websites are valuable because they (supposedly) reach a local audience. The problem is that location targeting through property targeting is, by modern standards, extremely crude and inefficient. Nearly everyone who visits local newspaper sites also visits the most popular sites. Potential local customers can be found more cheaply and efficiently on Yahoo! or Facebook than on the local newspaper website.

Size matters for behavioral targeting. Even on Yahoo!, one of the largest online publishers, small advertising campaigns cannot be targeted as effectively as large ones. Few newspapers have conversion data, and no campaign on a mid-sized local news site has the scale that effective targeting requires. This means that newspapers must either partner with big sites or online ad networks—at substantial cost—or else subsist on much lower impression prices than their inventory would receive on a larger website. Neither alternative is attractive.

Recommendation Systems and Political Targeting

There is an important coda to the story of the Netflix Prize. Today svd and similar approaches are not just used to recommend movies or match consumers with product ads. Reporting by the author has revealed that techniques pioneered by the Netflix Prize have been adapted for online political targeting.[45]

Cambridge Analytica is a British political consulting firm best known for its role in the 2016 Donald Trump campaign and the 2015 Brexit campaign in the United Kingdom. For years Cambridge Analytica courted controversy—and garnered skepticism—by claiming that it used "psychographic" models that supposedly targeted voters based on personality traits.

In March 2018 the *Guardian* reported that Cambridge Analytica had downloaded tens of millions of Facebook profiles using a personality test app, as part of a partnership with Cambridge University researchers Aleksandr Kogan and Joseph Chancellor.[46] The revelation of this "data breach" sparked regulatory investigations on both sides of the Atlantic. Yet a key question remained: how exactly had these models built on Facebook data worked?

Based on the research in this chapter, I had a hunch that Kogan and Chancellor were doing singular value decomposition or something similar. I emailed Kogan to ask—and somewhat to my surprise, he replied.

"We didn't exactly use svd," Kogan wrote. Instead, he explained, "the technique was something we actually developed ourselves. . . . It's not something that is in the public domain." Yet he confirmed that his approach was a close cousin of svd. The same kinds of dimension reduction models that Funk had adapted for the Netflix Prize were the core of Cambridge Analytica's Facebook models.

Knowing the original approach of Cambridge Analytica's model answers some long-standing questions. If Kogan's account is accurate, the inferred categories that the model produces are not about personality per se.

Instead, they boil down demographics, social influences, personality, and everything else into a big correlated lump. Information about users' personality traits seems to have made only a modest contribution to the model's accuracy.

Still, this class of model is remarkably good at guessing personal details and political partisanship from seemingly trivial social media data, such as whether the user liked the Wu-Tang Clan or curly fries. Research by Mikal Kosinski, David Stillwell, and Thore Graepel showed that an SVD model made with users' Facebook "likes"—but *without* any demographic information—was 95 percent accurate at guessing race and 93 percent accurate at guessing gender.[47] Even more impressive, it was 88 percent accurate at distinguishing gay from straight men and 85 percent accurate at separating Democrats from Republicans. That level of accuracy is a floor, not a ceiling: any additional data boosts accuracy even higher. Kogan's model seems to have produced results comparable to this public research.

Modern campaigns depend heavily on voter databases to predict citizens' partisanship and their likelihood of turning out to vote. Only 28 percent of the users targeted by the Trump campaign on Facebook, however, were matched to the voter file.[48] SVD and similar dimension reduction techniques can make good guesses about users' political leanings even *without* data that is obviously personally revealing.

We should not exaggerate the effectiveness of these models, which are far from a crystal ball. Nonetheless, Netflix-style models were a real advantage for the 2016 Trump campaign. These techniques can condense information about individuals into usable form, even when that information is scattered across dozens or hundreds of different variables. Now that this approach is known to be effective, it is likely to be duplicated in countless other campaigns and with other kinds of digital trace data. Reaching users on Facebook and other large sites increasingly requires the kind of data mining that produced these digital giants in the first place.

LESSONS AND QUESTIONS

The rise of recommender systems as a key mechanism of content delivery is a tectonic shift in the media landscape, on par with the arrival of the rotary press or the emergence of the web itself two decades ago. Like these previous shifts, recommendation technology strongly favors some organizations over others.

What can we conclude from what we know about the inner workings of targeting and recommendation systems? Scholarship to date suggests six broad, interrelated lessons about which types of organizations are likely to win—and lose—in a world with ubiquitous algorithmic filtering.

First, and most important, recommender systems can dramatically increase digital audience. Web traffic is properly thought of as a dynamic, even evolutionary process. Recommender systems make sites stickier, and users respond by clicking more and visiting more often. Over time sites and apps with recommender systems have grown in market share, while those without have shrunk.

Second, recommender systems favor digital firms with lots of goods and content. There is only value in matching if the underlying catalogue of choices is large. Small outlets benefit little: users do not need help sorting through the content of a news site that produces only three articles a day. In the same vein, sites that have a wide diversity of content benefit most from recommender systems. Publications with a narrower scope—say, sites that focus just on technology news or entertainment gossip—derive less value from recommender systems.

Third, recommendation systems benefit firms with better hardware and more staff expertise. Even when the underlying techniques are relatively standard for the industry, deploying them in a production environment still takes substantial time, energy, equipment, and effort. Moreover, targeting techniques are often expensive in terms of CPU cycles and computing resources. Smaller organizations are unlikely to have the hardware and resources needed to deploy cutting-edge techniques.

The expertise and equipment needed to target content can also be used to target advertising. Personalization systems can provide dramatically better results for advertisers, generating more sales per dollar of ad spending while increasing the overall value of a site's ad inventory. As the Yahoo! research shows, some sites are far better at targeting than others. Sites that make more money in online advertising can use that revenue to produce even more content or to improve their sites, further increasing their advantages over competing organizations.

Fourth, recommender systems benefit firms with more data. The most popular and most heavily used sites have a significant advantage in building recommender systems over sites that are currently less popular. More signals, and a greater diversity of signals, significantly improve performance.

Fifth, personalization systems promote lock-in, making it costly for individuals to switch between sites and apps. Consider an occasional user of Google News who visits Yahoo! News or Bing for the first time. Initially, this user will see news content that is a significantly poorer match for her individual news tastes. Much of this apparent advantage is temporary: more time spent on the Yahoo! News site provides more information for Yahoo!'s targeting algorithms. From the user's perspective, though, personalization algorithms create barriers to moving from one provider to another.

Lastly, recommender systems promote audience concentration. This is the *opposite* of what most previous scholarship has assumed. Negroponte concluded that the The Daily Me would be a powerful decentralizing and dispersive force: "The monolithic empires of mass media are dissolving into an array of cottage industries . . . the media barons of today will be grasping to hold onto their centralized empires tomorrow."[49]

While Negroponte's technological vision was prophetic, his economic logic was precisely backward. There is a long tradition in media scholarship that ties homogenized, broadcast media with media consolidation.[50] Mass broadcasting provided large economies of scale, whereby the same sitcom or news broadcast could be seen in hundreds of millions of homes simultaneously.

But most observers have failed to understand that *personalization* can produce the same result as broadcast standardization. One large website, by learning its users' tastes, can match users to their preferred content far more efficiently than hundreds of small "cottage industry" sites. Economies of scope—where the efficiencies come from providing a broad mix of different products—generate concentration just as surely as economies of scale do. The Daily Me provides media organizations with unprecedented economies of scope, and increasingly they succeed not by being "monolithic," but by being all things to all users.

The Economic Geography of Cyberspace

With Bruce Rogers

Every cheapening of the means of communication, every new facility for the free interchange of ideas between distant places alters the action of the forces which tend to localize industries.
—Alfred Marshall, *Principles of Economics*, 1895

In the late 1970s, a young economist by the name of Paul Krugman began publishing a series of articles about international trade. Krugman's work was motivated by a puzzle. For more than a century-and-a-half, economists had explained trade largely through theories of comparative advantage. David Ricardo (1817) explained this idea through a parable about cloth and wine. Since the English climate is terrible for growing grapes, Ricardo argued, Portugal should end up with the vineyards and Britain should end up with the looms.

This was true, Ricardo said, even if Portugal was better at *both* weaving and winemaking: if relative advantage won out, trade would make both countries better off. Ricardo's logic was compelling, as anyone who has actually tasted English wine can tell you. And with some modifications, it was the main framework for understanding international trade for a century-and-a-half.[1]

But in the post–World War II era, it became increasingly clear that Ricardo's theories explained less than they used to. As trade barriers fell, the bulk of international trade turned out to be between countries with similar economies—similar climates, similar natural resources, similar levels of industrialization. Even more puzzling, these countries were often engaged in intraindustry trade, or even trading exactly the same type of goods. This clearly could not be explained by comparative advantage. What was going on?

Krugman's answer was a model with three central assumptions. First, the model assumed that firms had economies of scale—that larger firms were more efficient. Second, it was assumed that consumers had diverse preferences—that some buyers would prefer to drive a Volkswagen even if they could afford a Cadillac. Lastly, the model assumed that there were shipping costs.

With these key assumptions, Krugman was able to produce patterns of trade that looked much like those in the real world.[2] The model also produced other, initially surprising results that mirrored real world patterns. For example, it predicted that countries with the largest domestic markets would end up being net exporters—something that turned out to be true.

This chapter is about building simple economic models of online content production. The style of these models owes much to the so-called "increasing returns revolution" that began in the industrial organization literature,[3] and then found expression in the "new trade theory" and in the "new economic geography" scholarship that Krugman's work exemplified. This parallel is no accident. If economic geography studies the production and consumption of goods in space, much of this book is about understanding *where content will be produced and consumed in cyberspace*. There is a clear analogy between the industrial agglomeration we see in the real world, and the traffic concentration we see online.

The central building blocks of our simple web traffic model are threefold:

- First, we assume that there are strong economies of scale online, both for content production and advertising revenue.
- Second, we assume that users have at least modest preferences for diversity.
- Third, we assume that it takes time and effort for users to seek out online content—that users face *search costs* or *switching costs* in navigating the web.

By this point in the book none of these assumptions should be controversial. But combined, they add up to a vision of the web that is starkly different from the one that continues to shape public policy: in this model, portal sites emerge spontaneously and have substantial market power, most content is produced and/or hosted at the largest sites, and niche dominance is the norm rather than the exception. It is an internet, in short, in which competition is deeply unequal.

Economic models have recently become a highly public front in the war over net neutrality and internet regulation. In one of his first high-profile speeches after being confirmed as FCC chairman, Ajit Pai denounced the supposed lack of economic analysis behind the FCC's 2016 pro-net neutrality Open Internet Order.[4] The notion that the Obama-era FCC ignored economic analysis, in the Open Internet Order or elsewhere, is questionable at best.[5] But if economic modeling is to be the currency in which policy is argued, we should at least start with the type of increasing returns models that best capture the logic of the digital economy.

The statistician George Box's famous aphorism—"all models are wrong, but some are useful"[6]—certainly applies to the models in this chapter. Economists often talk about these types of models as "fixed" or "static" models, but they are better thought of as sped-up or time-compressed dynamic models, in which things that happen fast are presumed to be nearly instant. As we will see, this acceleration helps show the often strange incentives of online content production. Understanding the incentives of both users and producers, in turn, helps explain otherwise baffling features of digital life.

Importantly, the results here are less sensitive to key assumptions than some past writings. Classic models from the broadcast era depended on strong assumptions about consumers' media preferences, and much writing about the internet has assumed that diverse users' preferences are the primary force fragmenting digital audiences.[7] Our models here, though, produce similarly concentrated results for *either* strong or weak preferences. Weak preferences give no reason for users to spread out, but strong preferences just end up sending users to portals, aggregators, and search engines. If digital media diversity requires Goldilocks preferences—not too strong, but not too weak—then it is unlikely to be stable.

Yet before we delve into model building, several topics touched on earlier require a fuller treatment. We will start by discussing online aggregation and the economics of bundling. We will then lay out what we know about media preferences, and why larger sites now get more money per visitor than small local producers.

BUNDLING AND AGGREGATION

While chapter 2 and chapter 3 talked at length about the advantages that large sites possess over small sites, one crucial advantage has been deferred until now. Large sites have an edge, in part, because they construct large bundles of content. *All* of the web's most successful sites are aggregators—bundlers—of one form or another.

Many types of firms offer their products in packages, a practice known as *bundling*.[8] Early economic research on bundling suggested that the producers were simply taking advantage of economies of scale in production or distribution. As we saw earlier, these sorts of scale economies are common. Still, Adams and Yellen's[9] pioneering work showed that bundling made sense *even without* these sorts of scale efficiencies.

To see how, consider the case of Microsoft Office, one of the world's best-selling bundles of software (table 4.1).[10] Alice, Bill, and Chris all have different prices they are willing to pay for different parts of Office. Alice will pay $100 for Word, $45 for Excel, and nothing for Powerpoint. Bill will pay a $100 for a spreadsheet, $45 for a presentation program, and nothing for a word processor. Chris will pay $100 for PowerPoint, $45 for Word, and nothing for Excel.

In this simplified example, Microsoft can make more by selling Word, Excel, and PowerPoint as a package. Instead of selling one copy each of Word, Excel, and Powerpoint for $300 total, Microsoft sells three bundles for $435.

This model has been extended to media markets too. As Jay Hamilton's research shows, the same logic applies to media goods.[11] Two subscribers of the *Wall Street Journal* may read the paper for very different reasons, but newspapers can make more subscription revenue by bundling these different types of news together. Media subscriptions capture not just variation in interest across media sections or stories, but also variation across time. Few people read the paper closely every single day. Some have argued that newspapers were the "original aggregators,"[12] combining disparate varieties

TABLE 4.1
A Simple Example of Bundling

	Alice	Bill	Chris	Total
Word	$100	$ 0	$ 45	
Excel	$ 45	$100	$ 0	
PowerPoint	$ 0	$ 45	$100	
Total w/o Bundling	$100	$100	$100	$300
Total w/ Bundling	$145	$145	$145	$435

Note: A simplified example of bundling, showing how technology firms can earn more by requiring users to buy different pieces of software as a package instead of piecemeal. In this example Microsoft can earn $435 by bundling Office together, but only $300 if the component software is sold separately. This example is loosely adapted from Shapiro and Varian, 1998; see also a similar example of bundling in Hamilton, 2004.

of content into a single product. What's true in print is also true for goods like cable television, which is almost always bought as a bundle or series of bundles.

Bundling works, in part, because it serves as a form of *price discrimination*. Companies would love to charge people different prices for the same exact product—ideally, as much as each consumer is willing and able to pay. Bundling takes advantage of the law of averages. It is easier to guess what a consumer is willing to pay for the package deal—for *all* of Microsoft Office, or *all* of the *Wall Street Journal*—than it is to guess what she might pay for the individual parts. Bundling thus provides "predictive value" for firms figuring out what price to charge.[13] Willingness to pay for the bundle varies less than willingness to pay for the component parts.

Bundling is an especially powerful strategy with information goods, such as media or software. With real goods and services, extra items in a package deal cost the producer more. A two-for-one deal on laundry detergent means that Tide pays more in production, shipping, and packaging. But with information goods, the marginal cost approaches zero.[14] Once the movie is released, or the software is finished, it costs little extra to provide somebody with a digital copy. If the software code for a website is well designed, it can cost almost nothing to serve an additional user.

Bundling has other advantages, too. Barry Nalebuff[15] suggests that bundling discourages competition. Bundling forces an upstart firm to enter several markets at once—a much tougher proposition than just entering one. This is especially true in markets that have strong economies of scale: new competitors have to get big to be efficient, and getting big enough to compete in many markets simultaneously is a daunting challenge.

So far, so good. Still, research on bundling has focused on the amount of money firms can extract from consumers. But if bundling helps explain how much *money* firms can extract from consumers, a similar logic also helps explain their ability to extract *time*. Taking seriously the idea that attention is a scarce resource has important consequences in this case.

Most content consumed online is not paid for directly by those who view it, challenging the traditional explanation of bundling. For websites, bundling is a winning strategy because it maximizes the number of users who spend at least a little bit of time on their site. A larger user base leads directly to higher per-user revenue, thanks to better ad targeting (as we saw in chapter 3) and reduced audience overlap (more on this momentarily). More users also leads to lower average costs, thanks to economies of scale.

From an individual's perspective, too, seeking out bundled content makes sense even when she does not pay for what she reads. Bundling provides predictive value for a site visitor spending his or her limited time budget. For an individual visiting an aggregator site, bundling reduces the risk that the trip has been in vain. If there is nothing interesting to read in the entertainment news, then perhaps sports or business news or the style section will have something worth reading. Sites that can provide users with their information needs, without requiring them to spend time and effort searching other sites, keep users engaged for longer. Recommendation systems (chapter 3) compound this advantage.

THE NEW ECONOMICS OF ADVERTISING

Understanding the basic logic of bundling is crucial to understanding the political economy of the web. But there is another key building block that needs to be acknowledged: bigger sites get more ad revenue per user than smaller sites. Despite efforts to push digital subscriptions (see chapter 7), digital advertising continues to dominate other online revenue streams. A site that doubles its readership will more than double its ad revenue—a game-changing break with traditional media.

The fact that *local* per-person advertising rates were higher than *national* per-person rates was arguably the defining feature of twentieth-century media. National broadcast advertising was expensive, but cheap per viewer reached. For example, General Motors' success has been attributed partly to efficiencies in national advertising.[16] This is the reason we see ads for national brands when watching the Super Bowl, but not ads for local restaurants. As Yoram Peles argued in the broadcast era, "It appears that there is an indivisibility in the advertising media, so that it is worthwhile only for big companies to advertise through some mass media."[17] By the same token, neighborhood newspapers traditionally had higher ad rates than metro papers, and local TV stations higher rates than network broadcasters. The expectation that this will remain true on the web inspired much of the hype around hyperlocal media (more on hyperlocal in media chapter 6).

Online advertising turns a century of advertising economics on its head. As we saw earlier, online revenue is hyper-concentrated on the largest players, with the Google-Facebook duopoly alone controlling more than 70 percent (and counting) of U.S. digital ad revenue.[18] There are several reasons that the internet has reversed the revenue curve, some of which we discussed in chapters 2 and 3. Much of the local-advertising advantage came from the power of local newspaper monopolies. As Philip Meyer writes, "In their efforts to find one another, advertisers and their customers tend to gravitate toward the dominant medium in a market. One meeting place is enough. Neither wants to waste the time or the money exploring multiple information sources."[19] But it is now large web firms—not local newspapers—who enjoy the premium from reduced duplication of audience. Local newspapers no longer have the widest reach even in their own market.

In addition to lower audience duplication, big sites are *also* far better at measuring how well digital ads work. Even multimillion-dollar digital ad campaigns, with tens or hundreds of millions of impressions, are often unable to make reliable inferences about their own effectiveness.[20] Google has developed powerful statistical methods to help address this problem, but these techniques need data on how similar campaigns performed—information only Google has access to.[21] And of course, as we saw in the last chapter, digital giants are better at ad targeting. The largest targeted ad campaigns, on the largest digital platforms, produce far more sales than simple untargeted ads.[22]

The ultimate result is an enormous disparity in ad pricing. Advertising prices are often measured in CPM, or the cost per thousand impressions (with *M* being the Latin numeral for *thousand*). Hard numbers on ad prices are difficult to come by—a fact that by itself says much about the power of the largest digital platforms, which usually succeed in keeping most ad sales data private. But as of 2012, Google's CPM for banner advertising was estimated at $95.[23] For newspaper sites, by contrast, CPM was only $12 to $15 for advertising sold directly. While this sounds discouraging for newspaper sites, the reality was worse: few such sites came close to selling the majority of their inventory. The balance of unsold advertising space was typically sold as "remainder" or "remnant" advertising on different ad networks, most often at a price between $1 to $2 per thousand impressions. A surprising number of smaller newspaper sites still offer only "run of site" banner advertising, in which the ad appears on all pages, or a random selection thereof. Further more, mobile or video ads are often crude or nonexistent on many smaller newspapers' sites. The *per user* advantage for large sites is even greater than the *per impression* numbers above, because users tend to stay longer on big sites.

Both real-world data and theoretical work, then, show that large sites earn more per user, an assumption we will build into the models to follow. To be conservative, though, we will remain agnostic about exactly how large that advantage is—only that large sites earn at least a bit more per user.

What We Know about Preferences

The last, crucial building block for our models has to do with the character of media preferences.

Many continue to assume that media preferences are inherently diverse—and thus that the internet will create radical diffusion of audience attention. Assumptions about diverse preferences lead to the "Waiting for Godot" belief that audiences will eventually democratize (see chapter 1), or to Negroponte's assertion that the internet would dissolve the mass media (see chapter 2), or to Andrew Sullivan's claim that the internet allows for "the universe of permissible opinions to expand, unconstrained by the prejudices, tastes or interests of the old-media elite."[24] If the economics of broadcasting produced bland, homogenized content,[25] the internet is supposed to produce the opposite. Chris Anderson's writings on the "long tail" similarly assume that consumers have strong, diverse content preferences that will finally be satisfied in the digital era.[26]

Yet the empirical case for diverse media preferences is surprisingly modest. Early work on the economics of media often assumed that people had strong genre preferences for radio or television shows.[27] Yet empirical work soon found that genre preferences were rather weak.[28] As one influential British study concluded, it is not true that "programs with similar content appeal to some particular subgroup of viewers."[29] Viewers' likes are not strongly influenced by genre—though their *dislikes* are often grouped.[30]

Some might see the lack of strong genre preferences as an artifact of the broadcast era. Much the same pattern, though, emerges in the Netflix Prize data (see chapter 3). Teams expected most improvement to come from better matching users' preferences with the characteristics of each movie, but these effects turned out to be remarkably modest. Some movies get higher average scores from nearly all users, and some Netflix users are more generous with awarding stars. These general biases that work across all users, or all of an individual's ratings, accounted for *three times* as much variance in ratings as user-movie interaction effects.[31]

Still, there is good evidence that media preferences *do* affect politics more than in the recent past. As Markus Prior shows in *Post-Broadcast Democracy*, roughly 40 percent of the U.S. public prefers entertainment over news.[32] These preferences mattered little in the broadcast era, when there was little choice of programming. The "switchers" who abandoned news for entertainment fare in the post-broadcast era show significant drops in political knowledge and their likelihood of voting.

Similar findings emerge in news readership data from the web, where preferences increasingly drive news consumption (or lack thereof). Pablo Boczkowski and Eugenia Mitchelstein document a "news gap" between the news stories that editors highlight as important, and stories that actually receive the most attention.[33] The size of this news gap is larger on some news sites than others, though, and it shrinks in election season.

In recent years the *ideological* preferences of users have been a major topic of research. Many scholars have found that a sizable minority of citizens prefer like-minded news content.[34] Though only a fraction of citizens prefer partisan news, those who do are among the most involved and partisan citizens—thus amplifying the impact of partisan media sorting.[35]

Much remains uncertain about the character of media preferences. We still know far too little about their true origin. Some recent work, too, has begun to explore the extent to which preferences can be altered or cultivated.[36]

In general, though, a few broad points are clear. Some citizens, some of the time, for some types of content, *do* differ significantly in their media preferences. There is little evidence for the radically divergent media preferences that underlie many claims about the democratizing power of digital media. Still, user preferences are clearly more important in today's media environment than they were a generation ago. And continuing uncertainty means that we should show how different assumptions about media preferences change—or *do not* change—the conclusions of our models.

A SIMPLE MODEL OF DIGITAL CONTENT PRODUCTION

With these building blocks in place, it is time to start constructing our formal model. The full model, including mathematical detail, can be found in the Appendix. But the outline of the model, and its most important conclusions, can be understood without any math.

We will build the simplest model first, and then make the model progressively more realistic (and complicated) by relaxing some initial assumptions. As a general rule, though, increasing realism strengthens the position of the largest sites.

We will start with some number of websites, and some number of consumers. The consumers get utility—which is to say, enjoyment or satisfaction—from consuming site content.

Each site produces its own distinct *variety* of content. Our consumers have preferences for some varieties of content over others. For example, they might prefer serious versus escapist content, or perhaps liberal-leaning news instead of conservative-leaning news.

Users get more utility from consuming content *closer to their ideal preferences*. Conservative users would thus enjoy watching Fox News more than CNN, but they enjoy CNN more than liberal-leaning MSNBC. For simplicity we will consider content variety to be one-dimensional, but the model works with multidimensional preferences, too. The distance from the ideal could be measured in two or more dimensions: a liberal who prefers entertaining content might consider the *Daily Show* nearly perfect, but find Fox News doubly far from her ideal because it is both conservative and serious.

This content has to come from somewhere, so each site hires writers. The more writers they hire, the faster the content is produced: a site with twenty writers has a production rate twice as fast as a site with ten writers. Similarly, sites can pay different amounts to their writers. Writers paid higher wages create higher-quality content.

How much utility users can receive from each site is thus a function of three things: the *quality* of the site, the *quantity* of content the site produces, and how close the site's specific content *variety* is to one's ideal.

Consumers each face a budget constraint, which is the amount of time they have to enjoy the web. We will start by assuming that all users have the same time budget. Additionally, there is a fixed cost to the user's attention—which we will call a *switching cost*—each time she navigates to a different site.

Switching costs are an important part of what makes this model work, so it is worth saying more about what we mean by them. The key is that *it costs consumers to switch from one site to another*. This might be search costs as traditionally understood in economics, the time and effort to find another interesting site (see chapter 3). Alternatively, we might conceive of these costs through the lens of cognitive psychology, which has found that it takes effort for people to switch tasks.[37] The "don't make me think" school of web design,[38] or Jeff Bezos's focus on reducing "cognitive overhead" in digital media,[39] similarly suggest that decision-making is costly for users. Any of these explanations are consistent with our model.

With perfect information, consuming digital content resembles the task of deciding which stores to shop at. An all-knowing consumer could visit numerous boutiques to purchase exactly the variety and quality of goods he wants, or instead save time and gas by going to a department store. A single trip to Walmart is more convenient, but requires compromises on quality, quantity, or variety.

If consumers are trying to maximize their enjoyment, our model websites want to maximize profit: revenue minus costs. In keeping with our findings in previous chapters, we will assume that revenue is an increasing function of the total content consumed at a site. Sites' production costs have two parts: a fixed cost and labor costs, which are the number of workers times the wage rate. As we assumed earlier, content *quantity* is proportional to the number of employees, and *quality* is proportional to the wage rate.

The combination of quality, quantity, and variety determines how much of a site's content users are willing to consume. As with the assumptions we have made thus far, users have a clear preference ordering for all websites. *Rational users will consume sites in order*, from their most to least favorite, paying the search cost at each transition until their time budget is exhausted.

That is the skeleton of our model. But though the assumptions that go into the model are straightforward, they already produce some surprising results. Let us consider some examples.

Example: Two Sites and One Consumer

For our first example, consider the simple case where there is just one consumer and two possible websites, which we will call Site A and Site B. Site A is closer to the consumer's preferences. In fact, let us assume that Site A produces *exactly* the variety that our sole consumer most prefers.

The model shows that even perfect preference matching might not matter. If Site B produces high-quality content fast enough, it can earn *all* of the consumer's limited attention. Sites that can make sufficient investments in quantity and quality can draw consumers past sites that are closer to their ideal preferences.

This itself is an important result. As we have already seen, debates about the future of media have often claimed that small online outlets will beat big media companies by producing niche varieties of content. Our model suggests, instead, that even modest search costs or quality/quantity advantages can make competition lopsided.

Our simple model also reproduces a central tenet of internet wisdom: the key role of fresh content. The importance of new, previously unseen content every time a user visits is a central component of site stickiness (more on this in chapter 7). Sites cannot be a destination unless they produce a steady stream of new stories. Even in this simple model the rate at which new content is generated is a key predictor of success.

Our model tells us, too, about the pressures on content quality. Somewhat surprisingly, it suggests that most websites have a strong incentive to *drive down* their content quality. Economies of scale are attached to volume, not quality. High-quality content costs more without necessarily producing any additional revenue.

Websites thus maximize profit when consumers read a lot of mediocre, inexpensive content. Quality needs to be high enough to prevent competitors from emerging—but no higher. Provided that readers have large time budgets, websites will seek to hire lots of cheap, low-wage writers. In short, the model has already produced the logic of the content mill.

Example: Two Sites and Many Individuals

For our second example, consider the situation where there are two websites and many consumers. Suppose that consumers' preferences are spread evenly across the spectrum of possible content.

A couple of consequences are quickly clear. First, the strength of preferences becomes critical. Consider what happens if preferences are weak. Any user will still consume any variety of content, provided the quantity and quality are high enough. In the case of weak preferences, then, both sites will attempt to locate in the center of the preference space. This is a very old economics finding across many different kinds of markets, dating back to Harold Hotelling's work nearly ninety years ago.[40] Locating in the center means that sites have minimized the distance to the average user's ideal point.

Even more importantly, if revenue grows faster than production costs, more content production will mean larger profits (or at least smaller losses). Sites will strive to get bigger and bigger: hiring more writers always produces a greater payoff. If writers are all paid the same wage, each additional writer for a site provides more profit than the last.

Provided there are no upper limits on production, the highest possible revenue occurs when all users spend their entire attention budgets on a single site. If this level of production is profitable, then there is a stable monopoly: *all* consumers will spend their *entire* budgets on one site. This is the only site consumed; no other sites will be profitable. Our consumers even prefer this arrangement, because they do not have to waste their time budget changing sites.

Example: Strong Preferences for Variety

For our third example, let us see what happens when consumers' preferences for variety become stronger. In the previous example, one dominant site could use its size and quality advantages to monopolize the audience.

But suppose that some individuals get *zero* utility from content varieties far from their own preferences. Consider a conservative news consumer who ideally prefers Fox News. Our conservative consumer might be coaxed to visit ABC News if quantity and quality are high enough. He will never visit MSNBC or DailyKos, though, because he gets no enjoyment at all from their content.

Our model can reproduce this result by giving consumers a limited *preference window*. While there is still a bonus for content closer to their own preferred variety, consumers will examine content only within a given distance of their own ideal. To keep things simple, we'll also assume consumers' preference windows are all of the same width.

As long as all users' preference windows include the midpoint of the variety spectrum, a monopoly will still emerge. But as preference windows narrow further, it becomes impossible to capture everyone's full attention. The narrower these windows become, the more opportunities there are for additional sites to enter the market—further fragmenting users' attention.

In the real world, the extent to which consumers have strong variety preferences varies across different content categories. As we saw earlier, many scholars have found that a sizable minority of political news consumers prefer news from like-minded sources. But in this regard political news is unusual. Variety preferences are weaker in other news domains, such as weather or sports or entertainment. Entertainment content preferences show more overlap than disagreement. Democrats and Republicans alike watch their sports on ESPN. Many digital content categories show little or no evidence for diverse preferences.

Extending the Model: Bundling and Aggregation

We can also consider preferences for variety in a different way as well. Thus far we have limited sites to producing a single category of content. But what happens if some sites can produce more than one category of content? As discussed earlier, most traditional media are bundles of disparate content types: news, entertainment, sports, comics, cat videos, and so on. Bundling complicates the model, requiring a couple of additional assumptions to find an equilibrium, but in general it strengthens the hand of the largest sites.

Consider a simple case of bundling with three different sites:

- A site that produces only news.
- A site that produces only entertainment content.
- A *portal site* that produces *both* news and entertainment.

For this extension, we will make preferences even simpler: users either get perfect preference matching from all content in a category, or they get no enjoyment at all from the category. We will assume, too, that users get slightly less utility from a content category as they consume more. The first entertainment article consumed provides more enjoyment than the tenth, and the tenth article provides more enjoyment than the hundredth.

As before, assumptions about the distribution of audience preferences are crucial. For starters, we will assume that a third of the audience likes only news, another third likes only entertainment, and the final third likes *both* news and entertainment.

Despite the even spread of preferences, the portal site captures *all* of the audience. With economies of scale, the portal site can produce more content and/or higher-quality content in both categories at once. Even the news-only and entertainment-only consumers end up at the portal site, though they get zero utility from half of the content.

Surprisingly, though, portal sites can dominate even if the overlap between user preferences is small. We can vary the portion of users who like both news and entertainment. We can even construct extreme cases in which a tiny amount of overlap allows portal sites to win out. Even if 49 percent of users like only news, 49 percent like only entertainment, and 2 percent like both, the portal site will still attract all of the audience. To be sure, the advantages in this case are smaller compared with more evenly spread preferences—and likely quite fragile since they are so close to the tipping point. Yet as this limiting case shows, even low levels of preference overlap can be an advantage for portal sites.

Overall, then, the models thus far suggest grim conclusions for smaller digital publishers. How solid are these findings? One measure of robustness is how much we need to alter the model for small sites to survive.

Varying the amount of time users have to surf the web is one change that might improve the fate of small publishers. Some users would be given little time online, others middling amounts of time, and still others an almost unlimited time budget. This assumptions of varied time budgets is broadly consistent with real-world web traffic, in which users with less time—such as those surfing at work—spend a greater proportion of their time on big sites. Big events such as elections similarly increase the market share of big news sites more than those of smaller niche outlets, such as political blogs.[41]

In this case, then, time-poor users with varied preferences will visit only portal sites. By contrast, users with near-boundless time will include niche sites in the tail end of their browsing.

Adding this complication can provide a narrow path for niche sites to survive—but it makes it hard for them to *thrive*. Even with favorable assumptions, these niche sites still have fewer users and lower potential profits than large portals.

Extending the Model: National, Local, and Hyperlocal

Bundling provides discouraging predictions about the economics of small-scale digital content. Even worse: local news is just a special case of bundling. The model predicts local publishers will struggle to survive, while national publishers hoard most of the attention and profits.

Consider two digital newspapers, in two different cities, which produce both local and national content. National content appeals to readers across the country, while local news appeals only to those in the same city. Users vary in their relative preference for local vs. national news, and in the amount of time they have to spend online.

Importantly, one of our cities—let's call it Gotham—is larger than the other city, which we will call Midway. The *Gotham Gazette* is thus larger than *Midway Meteor*.

Start by making switching costs high—so high, in fact, that there is no cross readership *at all* between the two newspapers. High switching costs essentially return us to the print era, when local newspapers enjoyed regional monopolies. With no competition, both newspapers produce both local and national news. But because the *Gotham Gazette* is bigger, it earns more per reader, and produces more and higher-quality national news.

Then consider what happens as switching costs fall: *Midway Meteor* readers start switching to the *Gotham Gazette* for their national news. Readers with the highest time budgets, or those who have a strong preference for national vs. local news, make the switch first. If switching costs drop low enough, the *Gotham Gazette* will cannibalize most of the *Meteor*'s national news readers.

Real news markets over the past decade have mirrored the results of our model. In 2004 only about 12 percent of U.S. reporters lived in New York, Washington, D.C., or Los Angeles. By 2014, though, that proportion had jumped to about 20 percent and counting.[42] More than 40 percent of digital journalism job listings are now located in the New York or D.C. metro areas.[43] Far from announcing the "death of distance,"[44] digital media has made news production *more* geographically concentrated.

The same forces that have diminished metro news apply even more strongly at the neighborhood and hyperlocal level. To see how, add a third level of news to the model above: national, local, and now hyperlocal. Imagine a hyperlocal news site in Midway, the *Old Town Observer*. If the model holds, this hyperlocal site will earn less per reader than the larger *Meteor*. As we will see in later chapters, that prediction is consistent with the chronic struggles of hyperlocal news.

Extending the Model: Search Engines

The model could be extended in another important way as well. It can accommodate a new, special kind of website: a *search engine*.

A search engine reduces switching costs. When surfing from one site to another, users can visit the search engine and pay only *part* of the normal switching penalty. In this context any site that helps users find new content is considered a search engine. Google and Bing are search engines, of course—but by this definition so too are platforms like Facebook or Twitter or Apple News. Crucially, search engines—just like other websites—are assumed to have economies of scale in revenue.

At first glance, search engines seem to expand users' horizons. With the same time budget, users will range further afield in their search for content. Diversity of consumption increases as switching costs go down, with smaller sites in particular benefiting from this shift. This mirrors patterns seen in real-world data. Small sites get a far larger fraction of their audience from search engines than large sites do.[45] Similarly, when Google shut down the Spanish version of Google News in 2015, traffic to smaller news outlets fell precipitously, while the audience at the largest outlets was not significantly affected.[46]

Yet search engine benefits to smaller outlets are not the whole story. In economic geography, a common pattern is that transportation hubs can end up becoming manufacturing centers. If the goods have to pass through the shipping hub to reach the consumer, it's often cheapest to produce them in the transport hub in the first place. (We'll see an example of this in the next chapter).

The model predicts a similar result online. All else being equal, the best place to host content is *wherever the largest audience already is*. Successful search engines thus face strong incentives to produce—or at least *host*—content themselves. Most search engines have taken this path, starting with the early efforts of Yahoo!, AOL, and MSNBC. Even Google, which initially stood out for resisting this trend, is now the largest host of digital content in the world through its ownership of YouTube.

The model helps explain the push by Facebook, Google, and Apple to directly host news content created by others. The spring 2015 introduction of Facebook's Instant Articles was an important shift in the media landscape. Instead of Facebook just linking to articles on other sites, the full text of Instant Articles would appear directly in users' news feeds. Facebook promised news partners more traffic, as well as a 30 percent cut of ads that Facebook sold against publishers' articles. Google's Accelerated Mobile Platform (AMP) and Apple News are also attempts by digital giants to directly host others' content. By shifting content directly onto Google's servers, news providers get faster load times and a privileged position in search results. Apple's revamped News app, introduced in September 2015, similarly moved content from news partners to Apple servers.

Search engines, then, do not provide a solution to media concentration—they just re-create the original problem in a new form. Successful search engines face strong incentives to directly host content. Increasingly, all of the digital giants are acting to do just that.

Increasing Returns in the Digital Economy

In 2008, in his Nobel prize lecture, Paul Krugman recounted the intellectual journey that had led him to the podium in Stockholm. Despite the influence of his work, Krugman acknowledged that his research had been partly superseded by events. Growth in international trade since 1990—such as growing trade between China and the West—was a return to the old comparative-advantage pattern. The economic advantages of industrial concentration, too, seemed to have waned. The U.S. auto industry, once clustered in a single region, has spread out to include most of the American South, and even much of Mexico. The "increasing returns revolution" in trade and geography, Krugman admitted, now described "forces that are waning rather than gathering strength."[47]

From a broader perspective, though, the increasing returns revolution is more important than ever. The internet economy now accounts for more than 5 percent of the total economy in developed countries.[48] The multitrillion-dollar digital economy is still growing at roughly 8 percent a year, far faster than the rest of the economy. The increasing returns models developed for economic geography help explain many of the apparent paradoxes of digital life. And these models show that widely held assumptions about the internet, taken together, add up to some surprising conclusions.

Our formal model provides some surprising insights. It suggests, first, that *even perfect preference matching is not enough to ensure an audience*. High quality, perfectly matched content can still end up ignored if other sites produce more content more quickly. This result follows irresistibly from strong online economies of scale, and it helps explain why a constant flow of fresh content is essential for audience building. (More on this in later chapters.)

Perhaps even more unexpectedly, the model shows that diverse content preferences can actually *concentrate* audiences rather than spreading them out. Many scholars and commentators still claim that strong, diverse preferences will eventually spread out digital audiences. Many still view the triumph of hyperlocal content as inevitable, despite failure after failure of real hyperlocal sites. Yet our models suggest that this thinking is backward. Portals sites and aggregators can get *stronger*, not *weaker*, when individuals prefer an extremely diverse media diet.

The model also casts light on the logic of content farms and aggregators. Websites maximize profit when they show a broad audience a mountain of cheap content. *Low-quality* content on a big site can earn more than the *high-quality* content on a small site. Journalists are regularly outraged when a big aggregator's hasty rewrite of a story brings in more money than the original version. This model explains why this unfairness is both predictable and difficult to remedy.

The model also forces us to rethink the role of search engines, which prove to be a double-edged sword. On the one hand, they can push traffic out to smaller niche producers of content. At the same time, though, search engines and portal sites have powerful incentives to produce—or at least *host*—content of their own. The logic of industrial economics, in which shipping centers often become manufacturing centers, reappears in the digital realm.

The simple models of content production, then, are helpful in understanding the underlying logic of digital media production. Yet these models do have limits: by speeding up the time scale, this chapter has skipped over important details of how digital audiences evolve over time. The day-to-day dynamics of audience growth will be the subject of the next chapter.

The Dynamics of Web Traffic

With Bruce Rogers

[A] small company had to court disaster. It had to grow like a weed just
to survive.
—Tracy Kidder, *The Soul of a New Machine*, 1981

Somewhere around 1790, New York City grew to 32,000 inhabitants, and
passed Philadelphia as the largest city in North America. New York's early
emergence as America's metropolis was driven by both new technology
and natural advantage.[1] While shipping in the 1700s had mostly followed a
point-to-point pattern, larger ships and speedier passage across the Atlantic
meant a shift to a hub-and-spoke model with New York as the cheapest
shipping hub. New York's harbor was deeper than Philadelphia's, and less
likely to freeze in winter. The Hudson River provided better access to the
interior of the continent, an advantage that grew when the Erie Canal
connected New York with the Great Lakes and the Midwest.

But once New York was America's biggest city, it *stayed* the largest city
even when its initial advantages were decades or a century gone. New York's
edge as a transportation hub made it a manufacturing hub as well. The
sugar refining, publishing, and garment industries dominated the city's
life in the nineteenth century, and each settled in New York partly because
it had the lowest shipping costs.

The persistence of New York as America's largest city is a classic case of
the economics of agglomeration. New York of the 1790s was tiny by today's

standards. But it was larger than other urban centers, and that *relative* size meant that it could grow faster than competing cities. It was able to sustain its position despite the progressive settling of the old Northwest, and then the American West, and the more recent population shift to the Sun Belt. Even as the U.S. population has grown a hundred fold, New York's relative position has been unchanged.

But while New York has been a model of consistency, other cities have not been as lucky. A few of the largest cities, many medium-sized cities, and *lots* of small cities have seen big drops in their relative size. Among large cities, Detroit is unusual for both its rapid growth and steep decline. The sudden arrival of the automobile industry took the city from 285,000 in 1900 to 1,563,000 in 1930. Today Detroit has 700,000 residents, two-fifths of its peak population. But as we look at smaller and smaller cities, we find more and more cities that, like Detroit, have seen big percentage changes in their population.

The unbroken success of New York, and the decline of Detroit, may seem a strange subject for a chapter about internet traffic. But digital audiences do not follow the patterns we are used to seeing in broadcast ratings or print circulation. The old metaphors and metrics lead inevitably to mistakes. The internet has not just broken media business models, it has broken our cognitive models as well.

This chapter aims to build better models of web traffic, and in the process to solve some longstanding puzzles. Early writings assumed that the internet would be a media Robin Hood, stealing audience from large broadcast and print outlets and giving it to the little guys.[2] Actual audience data, however, has always painted a different picture. Web traffic is roughly power law distributed, in which a highly concentrated "head" of the web is coupled with a long, diffuse "tail" of tiny sites. These power law–like patterns have provoked vigorous debate about whether the web is dominated by new or old elites.[3]

Amidst this debate crucial questions have remained unanswered. First, *where did these power laws come from*? After all, as we saw in chapter 1, the World Wide Web was specifically designed to prevent this sort of inequality. Some scholarship has suggested that rich-get-richer effects are the culprit.[4] But power law patterns can be produced by many *different kinds* of rich-get-richer loops, and also by some processes that are different altogether.[5]

Second, and just as important, *how stable* are these winners-take-all patterns? The "Waiting for Godot" crowd (chapter 1), and the Silicon Valley advocates of "disruption" and Schumpeterian "creative destruction," argue that today's concentration will be short-lived. Even progressive-leaning net neutrality advocates have made similar claims, suggesting that if the internet's architecture can be kept open, the "natural" tendency toward decentralized audiences will reassert itself.

This chapter challenges these claims. Most work to date has focused on *either* the concentrated head of the audience distribution, or the long tail of small outlets—alternately treating one or the other of these categories as exceptions. In contrast, this chapter builds new models that scale seamlessly from the largest websites down to hundreds of smaller ones. This approach does a better job of capturing the whole elephant, rather than just the tusks or the tail. We build and test these models with a rich dataset from Hitwise, a web measurement firm.

As we shall see, digital audience growth follows predictable patterns. These patterns look much like the growth of cities over time, or the fluctuations of stocks on an equity market (more on that shortly), or even the growth and decline of biological species. This chapter borrows mathematical models and techniques from other disciplines to demonstrate these patterns, with the full mathematical details provided in the Appendix. As with the previous chapter, the focus here is on understanding the principles and intuition behind the models.

Our data show that the audience of large sites is much more consistent than that of smaller sites. Even more important, the day-to-day fluctuations in traffic make the *structure* of the web stable. For example, the traffic that the twenty-first or fifty-fifth sites receive is consistent over time, even as the specific sites that rank twenty-one or rank fifty-five change daily. This previously unacknowledged paradox—structural stability coupled with enormous *in*stability for individual sites—is key to understanding digital media.

Within the tech industry it is common to talk about "churn," the constant turnover in site traffic and site rankings. This chapter is one of the first rigorous examinations of traffic churn, and the first to show how the structure of churn itself—the compounded daily perturbations in traffic—sustains the inequality in digital audiences.

WEB TRAFFIC AS A STOCK MARKET

If we want to understand churn in digital audiences, we must start by considering similar types of problems in other fields. And that means we need to learn about *stochastic dynamical systems* (*SDS*)—which is a fancy way of saying *systems that change randomly over time*.

Fortunately, SDS is a long-established field with a powerful toolkit. If want you want to study rabbit populations, say, SDS is the approach you need: ecology and microbiology have used these tools for decades.[6] Countless other areas also depend on SDS fundamentals, from signal processing[7] to biochemistry,[8] economics,[9] and epidemiology.[10]

For our purposes, one well-known stochastic dynamical system is especially relevant: equity markets. In some specific and surprising ways, web traffic behaves *nearly exactly* like a giant stock market. Reviewing some basic facts about how stocks fluctuate explains many apparent contradictions of digital audiences.

Let's start with perhaps the most fundamental fact: stock markets are concentrated.

Systems that evolve over time often produce power law or (synonymously) scale-free distributions. Power law patterns have been reported in the citations received by scientific papers,[11] the intensity of wars,[12] the wealth of individuals,[13] and—as the chapter opening suggested—populations of cities.[14] The stock market is no exception, with the total value of each firm's stock—their *market capitalization* or market cap—forming a rough power law.[15] Out of roughly ten thousand U.S. public companies, the top twenty-five stocks account for about a quarter of the total market value. The top one hundred account for nearly half.

It is not just that the stock market approximates a power law or similar distribution—it is that the *entire structure* of the market is amazingly consistent. Compared to the bottom half of the market, the relative value of say, the 55th or 99th or 1001st ranked company varies little from day to day. We can't predict exactly *which* stock will be in any given rank—if we could, we could make a lot of money! But the rank structure is strikingly consistent even in extreme cases, such as the days before and after a stock market crash. And the structure has persisted across decades and even centuries. In the early 1900s the New York Stock Exchange was only slightly less concentrated than it is today with thousands of more public companies.[16]

Crucially for our purposes, *we know* what creates this durable stock market structure: patterns in the way stock prices fluctuate. All stock prices fluctuate constantly—but some stocks jump around far more than others.

Consider two companies: a tiny tech startup that has just gone public, and big blue-chip firm like General Electric. Which of these companies is going to have a more stable stock price?

The obvious answer is GE. The vast majority of startups fail, often quickly. Firms with healthy stock prices almost *never* fail quickly, with the rare exceptions typically due to fraud (prominent sudden failures like AIG or Enron fit this pattern). The flip side of big-company stability is that small firms have more room for growth. A lucky startup can grow its revenue ten- or a hundredfold. As we move from large to medium-sized to small to tiny companies, stock prices become an order of magnitude more volatile.

As Robert Fernholz's work shows, these compounded fluctuations in stock price actually create and sustain the power law structure of the stock market. The concentration emerges, surprisingly, from the simple fact that big stocks are (much) more stable. Stocks from firms that are lucky enough to grow are more likely to keep their gains—after all, bigger stocks are more stable. Stocks from unlucky firms that lose value face an even greater risk of loss going forward.

This stock market behavior provides crucial context for our study of digital audiences. *We should expect the same size-equals-stability pattern with digital audiences* that we see with equity markets. As we showed in chapters 2 and 3, big sites have both "hard" advantages in technical infrastructure (servers, code base, fiber, etc.) and "soft" advantages from human capital (branding, user learning, consumer habit, even a greater volume of user data). Yet large sites also face limits that smaller sites do not. eBay already dominates online auctions. It can't grow by taking market share from its competitors, because it has already decimated them. Already-big sites are buffered from traffic losses, but they also have less rapid upside potential.

But if web audiences show this size-stability pattern, then several things follow. First, larger sites should show far more audience stability over any time scale—in daily, weekly, monthly, even yearly traffic data.

Second, online audiences should be roughly power law distributed, something we already have plenty of evidence for. Third, crucially but less obviously, this power law pattern should be stable. The traffic at a given rank should be consistent even as individual sites change rank. Fourth, the relative stability of big versus small sites should even determine the overall level of concentration—which is to say, the slope of the power law.

High-Resolution Data

These novel ways of thinking about digital audiences can be tested, thanks to a rich dataset provided by Hitwise. Hitwise is a multinational web traffic measurement firm, with a client base of hundreds of companies from Honda to Heinz. Large internet firms such as Google, Amazon, and eBay have also been among Hitwise's clients.

Hitwise's data differ from those gathered by Nielsen and comScore, its two largest competitors, which both rely on opt-in panels of users with monitoring software installed on their computers (more on comScore's data in the next chapter). In part Hitwise relies on panel data too, particularly for the gathering of demographic information. However, the bulk of Hitwise's data is supplied by internet service providers (ISPs). Traffic data is collected by Hitwise's ISP partners, and then sent to Hitwise in anonymized, aggregate form. Because few of these users realize that their traffic is being recorded (albeit anonymously), Hitwise data are less subject to selection and observer effects. While some details are proprietary, Hitwise's broad claims about its methodology and privacy protection have been confirmed by outside auditors.[17]

The dataset provided by Hitwise contains three years of daily web visits. Traffic is measured in *visits*, an industry-standard metric defined as one or more clicks on a website with less than thirty minutes between clicks.[18] Visits are a better metric for cross-site comparison than page views, which can be quite sensitive to site architecture. Site redesigns that spread the same content out over a different number of pages can sharply inflate—or deflate—the number of page views a site receives. Time spent on a site is another possible metric, but measuring it well across all websites requires installing monitoring software on users' computers, leading to selection problems.[19] Other measures of traffic, such as "audience reach," or "unique visitors," generally do a dismal job of measuring sites' real audience (more on that in chapters 6 and 7).

The Hitwise data list the market share of the top three hundred sites for every day from July 1, 2005, through June 30, 2008, in two Hitwise categories: all nonadult websites, and news and media sites. Though Hitwise tracked roughly eight hundred thousand sites in a typical month in this period, the top three hundred sites received nearly half the total traffic, and the top ten sites alone received a quarter of web visits (a fraction that has continued to grow steadily since). The five thousand sites in Hitwise's news and media category are even more concentrated. The top three hundred media sites account for 80 percent of traffic on a typical day, with the top ten sites receiving 30 percent of all news visits.

Importantly, the Hitwise data contain *relative* traffic information: only the proportion of visits to each site is known, not the total number. This data alone does not tell us whether the entire market is growing or shrinking, though other sources show that web traffic grew significantly over this period. The rapid overall growth in web use during this period makes the stability in traffic share we see even more remarkable.

This data can also tell us about the overall distribution of online attention. It is often suggested that web traffic is power law distributed, though only a few pieces of scholarship have tested this claim with a representative dataset.[20] Figure 5.1 plots June 2008 traffic for all sites with a market share of at least one-thousandth of one percent (0.001%), a traffic threshold that captures 65,553 sites. The traffic distribution forms a nearly perfect straight line on the log-log plot, consistent with a power law distribution (for a fuller discussion see the Appendix).

TRAFFIC CHURN

Does the behavior of web traffic match that seen in stock markets or similar systems? To a surprising degree, the answer is yes. There are two main ways to measure site churn: by rank and by audience share. We will start with rank.

One important metric is *leakage*, the likelihood that a site drops out of the top three hundred sites the next day. Figure 5.2a plots, by rank, leakage both for all nonadult sites (in black) and for news sites (gray). As

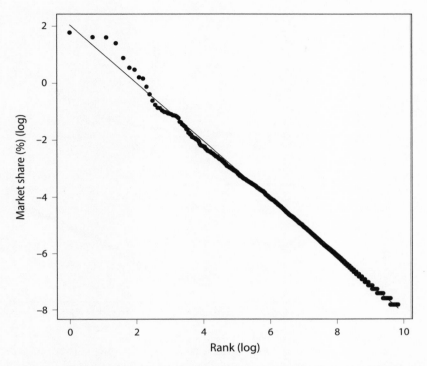

Figure 5.1 A plot of the Hitwise data audience share by rank, with both axes on a logarithmic scale. The body of the data closely follow a straight line, a common characteristic of power laws and closely related distributions.

we would expect, leakage for the most popular sites is nonexistent, and only becomes significant at ranks of 200 and below. Leakage increases in a consistent, roughly exponential fashion as one moves from rank 200 down to smaller and smaller sites. Sites that go missing are overwhelmingly those closest to the cutoff, with sites right at the rank 300 margin leaking slightly more than half the time.

Other rank-based metrics measure how often sites switch places. If a site is the fourth most visited on the web, we say that the site *occupies* rank 4. Figure 5.2b plots, by rank, the fraction of days on which occupancy changes. For both the overall traffic group and the news sites we see that those in the top ten rarely trade places, but sites ranked below 25 switch ranks almost daily. Because smaller sites are much closer together in terms

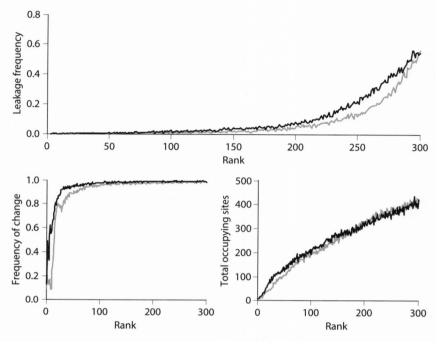

Figure 5.2 This figure shows change in site ranking over time. Data from all nonadult websites in black; news sites plotted in gray. Top (a): The likelihood that a site falls off the top 300 list the next day, by rank. Left (b): The percentage of days that the site at a given rank is different from the day before. Right (c): The total number of websites occupying each rank during the three-year period.

of market share, it is far easier for them to change places. Table 5.1 shows the median difference in market share for pairs of sites near the top of the market. Since sites below rank 20 are less than a hundredth of a percent apart, small audience shifts are far more likely to produce changes in rank.

Figure 5.2c records a related metric, the total number of sites that occupy each rank during the three years of data. The data show a steady, roughly linear relationship between rank and the number of occupying sites. Note that figure 5.2c adds up only those sites that have never previously appeared at that rank, while figure 5.2b includes all daily occupancy changes. For example, if the top site were Google on even days and Yahoo! on odd days, figure 5.2b would record a change 100 percent of the time, while figure 5.2c would record only two occupying sites. The lowest ranks

TABLE 5.1
Audience Gap between Sites at Adjacent Ranks

Ranks	1–2	5–6	10–11	15–16	20–21
Median Difference	.542	.531	.239	.024	.007

Note: This table shows the audience gap for sites in selected adjacent ranks. While more than half a percent of overall audience separates the first and second ranked sites, those ranked 20 and below are separated by less than a hundredth of a percent.

record more than four hundred occupying sites in both the news and all nonadult websites categories, a testament to just how extreme churn is among smaller sites.

Volatility by Traffic

In addition to looking at changes by rank, we can also look at how the size of a site's current audience predicts future volatility. Focusing directly on traffic helps explain the consistent patterns in rank (in)stability seen above.

Measuring and understanding change over time is always the key to understanding dynamical systems. We are particularly concerned with proportional growth rates—the percentage change in traffic from one day to the next—instead of raw traffic numbers.

Several facts need to be borne in mind when considering growth rates. First, growth rates here can be negative as well as positive. In casual conversation, growth refers just to increase, but for dynamical systems, growth can be *negative* as well as positive. Indeed, in dynamical systems, growth rates usually *are* negative at least half the time.

Second, we will focus on the *logarithm* of these growth rates, because we care mostly about compounded traffic gains or losses. Using logarithms turns a *multiplication* problem into an *addition* problem, greatly simplifying our analysis.

Third, as discussed earlier, we cannot observe sites that leak out of the top three hundred. This skews the distribution of the observed growth rates for the smallest sites, but does not change any of the findings discussed later in the chapter.

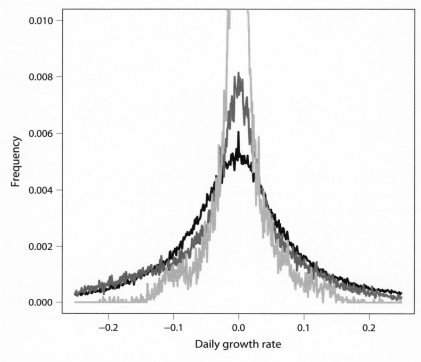

Figure 5.3 This figure shows the distribution of daily log growth rates for large, midsize, and small sites in our data. All three sets of sites show a clear bell curve, with the distribution much more dispersed for midsized and (especially) smaller sites. Fully observed data would show even fatter and more symmetrical left-hand tails for the smallest sites, since they are most affected by leakage.

For many dynamical systems, changes over time are normally distributed on a log scale. Consider a basket of randomly selected stocks. Over time, the log changes in stock price will form a bell curve, with a skinnier curve for larger firms, and a fatter curve for smaller ones. For firms of all sizes, too, the bell curve will grow fatter and fatter as time passes, though the changes will stay (log)normally distributed.

Do web audiences show the same patterns? Figure 5.3, which shows day-to-day changes on a log scale, is strong evidence that the answer is yes. The largest sites are in light gray, mid-tier sites in medium gray, and the smallest sites in black. What emerges are three rough-but-unmistakable bell curves, albeit with slightly heavier tails than perfect (log)normal distributions. Daily changes are proportionally smaller among the largest sites, bigger among mid-tier sites, and largest of all among sites with the least audience.

Figures 5.4a (left) and 5.4b (right) give an even fuller account of audience change over time. Figure 5.4a graphs *daily* changes in traffic on a log scale. The previous day's traffic is on the x-axis, and the next day's traffic is on the y-axis, for all days in our sample. Sites that showed no change fall on the 45° line bisecting the graph. The data form a funnel surrounding the 45° line, with audiences growing far more volatile as sites get smaller.

Figure 5.4b presents the traffic change over a year rather than a single day. Remarkably, the same pattern holds even over a far longer time scale: the bell curve has grown fatter for sites big and small, but the same funnel-shaped pattern is clear. Because this data is on a log scale, a spread twice as wide represents an order of magnitude difference.

At any time scale, then, individual site traffic is subject to a *funnel of churn*. The smaller a site, the more volatile its traffic. As time passes, too, the funnel gets wider. No website can be certain of its future traffic, but smaller sites face radically greater uncertainty.

SIMULATING WEB TRAFFIC

The preceding sections have shown an apparent paradox. On one hand, the data show enormous—though statistically regular—volatility in audience numbers, especially for sites below the top ten or twenty. On the other, the power law structure of digital audience is stable over the time we observe. Web traffic looks like a game of musical chairs, in which sites frenetically switch between ranks with relatively fixed audiences.

But what if these facts are not contradictory at all? Perhaps the distribution of web traffic is not stable *in spite* of the constant fluctuations of individual sites. Perhaps the funnel of churn actually *produces and maintains* the power law patterns in web traffic, and with it the structural stability of online audiences.

Most readers are familiar with the normal distribution, the bell-shaped curve that results from adding lots of small, independent variables together. But in recent years researchers have realized that power law and lognormal

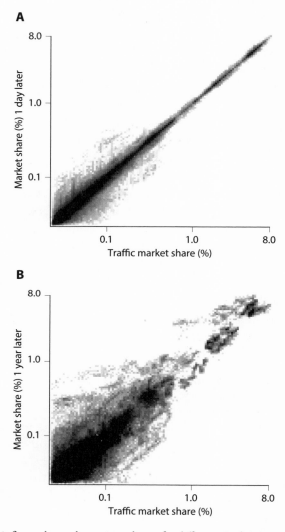

Figure 5.4 This figure shows change in audience for different-sized sites over a day (a: top) and a year (b: bottom). The top graph shows a clear funnel-shaped pattern of churn, with smaller sites far more likely to either lose or gain traffic. The bottom figure shows that the same pattern emerges even over a year-long time scale.

distributions—arguably even more common than bell curves in the social and natural sciences—have a somewhat similar origin. If a bell curve is the result of *adding* lots of small variables together, a log-linear distribution comes from *multiplying* lots of small, independent variables together. Power laws are so ubiquitous because they are the "attracting" distribution for many different types of growth processes.[21]

The hypothesis, then, is that power laws in online audience are the attracting distribution for the growth rates we observe. The evidence shared in this chapter is suggestive of, and consistent with, similar dynamical systems such as the stock market. Still, there is typically no way to "prove" that a specific power law was produced by a specific mechanism.[22] The best practice is to use simulation, showing that our proposed mechanism can produce results similar to the real-world data.

Which is exactly what we do next. We construct a simulation of web traffic to test the link between traffic churn and power laws in digital audience. The model is as simple as possible—so simple, in fact, that it ignores any information except each site's present rank. The goal is emphatically not to produce the fullest or most "realistic" simulation of web traffic. Instead, it aims to identify the minimum mix of ingredients necessary to approximate the audience structure we see in our data.

We thus create a model with three hundred simulated sites, each of which changes randomly each day depending on its current rank. We know that daily traffic changes follow a rough (log) normal curve, albeit one with heavy tails and a slight downward skew. One option would be to estimate the parameters of this bell curve with a normal distribution or something similar. Out of an abundance of caution, though, we avoid this approach. Instead of presuming that the data are normally distributed or otherwise well behaved, we rely on bootstrap-style sampling from the actual data.

On each simulated day, we rank the sites from 1 to 300 in terms of market share. For each site a growth rate is sampled depending on its current rank. The site at rank 125, for example, gets a growth rate pulled randomly (with replacement) from one of the 1,095 daily changes we saw for rank 125 in the real data. This new growth rate is used to compute a new market share. Market weights are then sorted from largest to smallest, and the process repeats.

Our simulation must account for two other issues. First, some sites will lose enough market share to fall off the list, and other small sites will bubble up into the top three hundred. After the market weights are sorted, we pick a cutoff for the market share of the three hundredth site, based on the average values from our observed data. Sites below our cutoff are considered to have left the list, and new sites are added to maintain the three-hundred-site mark. Here again we use a bootstrap-style approach: newly entering sites are given market shares chosen randomly (with replacement) from entering sites in the real-world data.

Second, we must choose the traffic for each site on day one. Simulations of this kind often depend heavily on the choice of starting values, so for robustness we pick three different initial conditions. In condition one, we start the simulations with site traffic equal to the last day of our sample, essentially running the simulation forward from our last time point. In condition two, we try an ultra-egalitarian approach, starting every site with equal traffic. All sites start with the median traffic seen in the real data, and they are given a starting "rank" randomly for the first day. Lastly, in condition three, we spread starting values evenly between the 5th and 95th traffic percentiles—essentially spacing sites linearly from ranks 15 to 285.

For all three starting conditions we run one thousand simulations, with each running for 1,500 simulated days. More than four years of simulated traffic makes this a very challenging test. Figure 5.5a shows the average of these one thousand simulations, by rank, at the end of 1,500 days. Viewed on a standard scale, it is clear that all of the simulations did indeed produce extreme, log-linear audience distributions. The results hug the margins of the graph, typical of power laws or similar distributions. Particularly noteworthy is the equal traffic condition. Even when sites are given *exactly the same traffic*, the observed growth rates quickly converge to a highly concentrated log-linear distribution within just a month or two of simulated data, an unexpectedly strong result.

Figure 5.5b, on a log scale, shows in greater detail how the simulations differ from the data. Initial condition three—which starts with far more high-traffic sites than the real data—is an outlier, while initial conditions 1 and 2 are more bottom-heavy with a surplus of smaller sites.

A better way of presenting this data is seen in figure 5.6, a sedimentation plot with four columns. The first column is the actual data, and the second

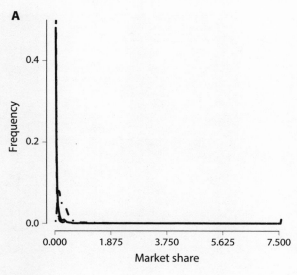

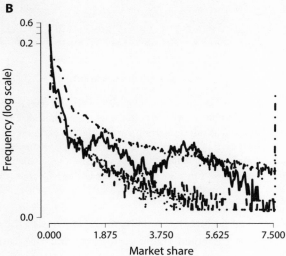

Figure 5.5 Average values from one thousand simulations at the end of 1,500 days, from both the observed data (black line) and the three simulations (dashed lines). The real data are roughly sandwiched between the results of simulations with different initial conditions.

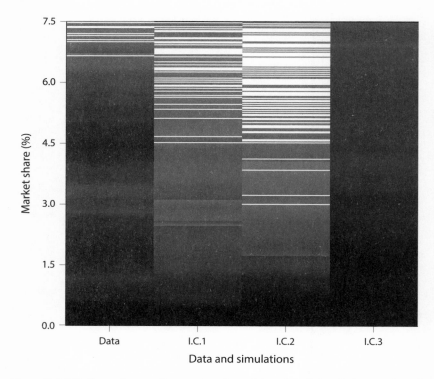

Figure 5.6 This figure shows sedimentation plots of the original data (leftmost column), and of the three initial conditions: starting from the last data of real data (IC 1), giving all sites equal traffic (IC 2), and a uniform starting distribution (IC 3). IC 3 produces far more large sites than the real data. IC 1 and IC 2 instead overrepresent the very smallest sites, and over time the largest sites in their simulations pull away from the market—an interesting result that mirrors the growing dominance of Facebook and Google in recent years.

column presents simulations that start from the last day of the actual data. The third column is the equal traffic condition, and the fourth column starts with sites evenly spread between the 5th and 95th traffic percentiles.

Market shares between maximum and minimum values in our data— 0.02 and 7.5 percent market share—are divided into three hundred equal-sized bins. These bins then record tally marks for each site. The number of tallies is represented in gray-scale: white means 0 tallies for that market share bin, black means many (roughly 150,000 or so for the smallest market shares).

Both the simulation starting from the last day of the observed data (column 2) and the equal traffic condition (column 3) show the top of the market starting to pull away from smaller sites as the power law gets progressively more extreme. The flat distribution used for initial condition 3 explains the nearly uniform shading of the last column. IC 3 produces more large sites than the actual data, and once these sites are large they tend to stay big.

If allowed to run forever all models of this type eventually fail. No model can capture all the important features of the data, and even tiny misspecifications grow exponentially because they are multiplied together at every time step. In this case, too, we have deliberately omitted complications that would constrain the model. We eliminate all correlation across days and across websites, and do not even ensure that the total market share stays equal to 100 percent on every day for fear of putting a finger on the scale.

Yet when these models do fail, interestingly enough, they all do so in a way that mirrors real-world changes in web traffic. When allowed to run for three thousand simulated days or longer—more than eight years—all of the models become more concentrated than our data. While the bottom half or two-thirds of the market remains relatively stable, the very largest sites pull away from the rest of the market.

THE MORE THINGS CHANGE, THE MORE THEY STAY THE SAME

The data in this chapter provide a novel look into the deep structure of the web. Web traffic may be random, but it is not chaotic: there are strong regularities in the way that web traffic fluctuates over time. These patterns force us to rethink much of the supposed wisdom about what a "dynamic" and "constantly changing" internet means for politics, business, and the public sphere.

This chapter's key findings can be summed up in three stylized facts. First, large sites show much more stable traffic than smaller sites. The smaller a site's audience, the more variable its future traffic.

Many still proclaim that the web is a rapidly changing environment, that barriers to entry are low, and that popular new sites emerge often. Our data show that this is false. It is rare for a site to enter or leave the top ten. Indeed, these data capture the last major shift in the top websites, the decline of MySpace and the rise of Facebook. No change since has come close.

Second, the overall *distribution* of web traffic is relatively stable. Web traffic resembles a game of musical chairs: sites may change places, but the market share of the site at rank 11 or rank 52 (for example) remains remarkably constant. By the same token, the collective market share of the top hundred sites remains the same, even as the sites in the bottom part of that list change daily.

Third, the concentration in audience emerges from the day-to-day differences in audience growth. Even when we eliminate everything else—when we destroy correlation structure within and between days, give sites no memory of previous traffic levels, and simulate just by rank—the structure of churn reproduces the log-linear traffic patterns seen in the real data. The funnel-shaped pattern in daily traffic zigs and zags can, by itself, produce and sustain these power law patterns.

To date, it has been an open question as to whether online audiences will spread out over time. Our data and models provide strong evidence that the dispersionists are wrong. Even the most ardent members of the wait-and-see crowd do not invest their retirement on the notion that big blue-chip stocks will all be whittled away. The fact that new companies are constantly entering the stock market, and that others are dying, is hardly evidence that all blue-chip firms will be destroyed by an army of tiny startups. Quite the opposite: the concentrated structure of the stock market is *created* by this constant market churn.[23]

The same mathematical patterns define the stock market–like dynamics of web traffic. Claims that online audiences will diffuse outward make a crucial and unacknowledged assumption. Knowingly or not, they are claiming that the funnel-shaped pattern of churn we see today will be different in the future. We should not accept this hidden assumption without evidence.

At the same time, though, understanding the funnel of churn opens up new approaches for policymakers and media leaders. Fixes that make *smaller* sites stickier relative to *bigger* sites would decrease online concentration, and make the slope of the power law less steep. Repeated calls for "innovation" and "entrepreneurship" and "experimentation" have failed to give clear metrics for success. By contrast, a focus on the dynamics of web traffic, and on sites' relative stickiness, provides a more promising way forward. We will return to this theme in chapters 7 and 8.

This chapter also connects naturally with earlier discussions of lock-in. Much media scholarship has taken a qualitative approach to understanding media lock-in, looking at the early choices and built-up advantages that made firms like Western Union or AT&T or NBC dominant for decades.

This chapter provides a quantitative, large-N approach to the same problem. Indeed, the slope of the power law is a good measure of *how strongly locked-in an online niche is*. For niches with extreme slopes—such as search engines or online auctions—lock-in is similarly extreme. Less concentrated niches, by contrast, make it easier for new sites to bubble to the top. As the web expands the number of media outlets to be considered, scholars must adopt analytical tools that scale up.

The size-equals-stability pattern that creates the structure of the web is mathematically simple, even elegant. But in numerous ways this pattern contradicts most of the conventional wisdom about digital audiences. At the very top of the web, these findings cut through self-interested rhetoric about competition being "only a click away." They predict enormous difficulty for upstart local or hyperlocal news outlets, which by definition are tiny. The structure of traffic churn challenges optimistic claims that the web tomorrow will have more outlets and more voices than the web today. Traffic churn is also driving many of the changes in contemporary journalism, from the frenzied "hamster wheel" news production to "spreadable" media to the rise of news aggregators.

All of these themes will be taken up in the next few chapters. A dynamic and constantly changing web, it turns out, is not an egalitarian one.

Less of the Same: Online Local News

In newspapers, the basic rule was survival of the fattest. And the trick was to be bigger than the other guy because at that point you had more help-wanted ads, you had more automobiles for sale, you had more people if you lost your dog who might find it if you ran a classified ad. And you got more dominant because to many people—this kills people in the news business—the most important news in the newspaper are the ads.

—Warren Buffett

One Saturday morning in 2007, with his kids in the car, Google executive Tim Armstrong had an idea.[1] Stopped at a traffic signal, Armstrong saw cardboard road signs advertising events in his affluent Greenwich, Connecticut, neighborhood. But once home, Armstrong could not find a similar digital listing of neighborhood news.

So Armstrong co-founded a neighborhood-focused news site of his own. Called Patch.com, the site was soon synonymous with so-called hyperlocal news. Patch's neighborhood sites were usually run by a single full-time editor, who might produce five or six content items daily.

Patch was acquired by AOL in 2009, not long after Armstrong was hired to be AOL's new CEO. Patch became a centerpiece of AOL's bid to refashion itself as a content provider rather than a dial-up ISP. Patch expanded feverishly, and at its zenith it had nine hundred neighborhood sites and approximately 1,400 employees.[2] The price tag for the effort was three hundred million dollars, comparable to AOL's high-profile purchase of the Huffington Post.

But throughout, Patch encountered skepticism from the business media and AOL's own shareholders. Traffic lagged badly, and ad revenue was dismal. In 2012, in an effort to fight off an activist investor group, Armstrong promised that Patch would be profitable by the end of 2013. But even with a brief traffic surge from Hurricane Sandy, profitability remained far out of reach. In August 2013, Armstrong announced that a third of Patch sites would be closed. Armstrong even tacitly admitted that some of Patch's own editors did not use the site, telling all of his employees that "if you don't use Patch as a product and you're not invested in Patch, you owe it to everybody else at Patch to leave."[3] In January 2014, AOL finally sold majority ownership of Patch to Hale Global company for undisclosed terms. Overnight, the company went from 540 full time employees to ninety-eight.[4]

Despite the high-profile failure of Patch, Armstrong and a legion of hyperlocal evangelists still believe in a bright future for hyperlocal media. In an unrepentant interview in December 2013, Armstrong insisted that the Patch model would have worked if it had been given more time.[5] Jeff Jarvis, a prominent hyperlocal advocate, declared that "execution problems" and unfounded fears of "hyperlocal cooties" had doomed an otherwise sound idea.[6]

Armstrong and Jarvis and other hyperlocal news boosters are wrong. The problems with hyperlocal news—and even not-so-small local news sites—are far worse than they let on. Patch is a limiting case, the most extreme version of the problems that old-fashioned local news faces on the web. And while not everyone will mourn the decline of Patch, we should all worry about what its failures tell us about the local news that democracy depends on.

No part of the American media environment is as little understood as internet-based local news. The relative importance of internet news overall has grown steadily; Pew studies have found that nearly twice as many Americans regularly get news from the internet as they do from print newspapers.[7] But even as the web is a larger slice of the American news diet, systematic data on digital local news has been scarce.

Even very basic questions have remained unanswered. How many online local news outlets are there in a typical media market? Are successful local news sites new, or just online versions of traditional media? How much competition is there in online local news? Just how much attention do local news websites receive?

Online local news is also a crucial test case for the theories and models that are at the heart of this book. Hopes for hyperlocal news are founded on the idea that internet audiences will inevitably diffuse toward smaller and smaller niche sites, including niche sites defined by locality. In contrast, this book has argued that size matters greatly online. As we have seen in chapters 3 and 4, the largest sites earn far more per visitor than small niche sites. Our theories suggest that newspaper and television sites should have substantial advantages over upstarts: they have established brands and habits of readership, more usable websites, and larger and more attractive bundles of content. A poor showing by local digital news sites would be worrying for democracy, but consistent with this book's hypotheses. By contrast, if most media markets have diverse, thriving networks of local digital news sites, that would challenge this book's central claims.

The internet's potential to expand local news voices matters, too, for public policy. Online media diversity has featured prominently in FCC and congressional debates about broadcast ownership regulation.[8] The federal courts have similarly focused on the disputed ability of the internet to provide greater viewpoint diversity for local news.[9] In addition to the FCC, policymakers in Congress and at the Federal Trade Commission have studied the internet's ability to sustain local journalism even as newspapers struggle financially.[10] This chapter began life as a commissioned report by the FCC, as part of their quadrennial review of media ownership regulation.

Despite the importance of online local news, there has been little systematic evidence about the local news environment on the web. This chapter aims to change that. Using comScore panel data that track a quarter of a million internet users across more than a million www domains, this chapter examines online local news within the top one hundred U.S. television markets. It identifies and analyzes 1,074 local online news and information sources across these one hundred markets, studying their audience reach, traffic, and affiliation (or lack thereof) with traditional media. The chapter also looks at concentration in local online news markets, and conducts a census of internet-only local news sites that reach more than a minimum threshold of traffic.

The breadth and the market-level granularity of the comScore data makes this study the most comprehensive look to date at internet-based local news. The portrait that emerges contradicts claims that new online outlets are adding significantly to local news diversity. New, digital-native news organizations are nearly absent from this traffic data. Local news on the web is fundamentally about consuming *less* news from the *same* old-media sources. Understanding the local news landscape online has profound implications for policymakers, journalists, and local self-governance in the twenty-first century.

Data on Local News Online

This chapter relies centrally on data provided by comScore, a large U.S. web measurement firm. comScore tracks the browsing behavior of a large panel of internet users with user-installed software, and its coverage is exceptionally broad: as of July 2010, the firm reported tracking traffic to 1,049,453 web domains. Research prior to this study overwhelmingly used aggregate U.S. web-usage data, in which only the largest local sites in the largest local markets could be studied. For this study, full data from February, March, and April 2010 were purchased by the FCC for the one hundred largest U.S. broadcast market areas, and provided to the author as government-furnished information.

These one hundred markets contained a monthly average of 253,953 comScore panelists. Because comScore strives for a nationally representative sample, the number of panelists varies according to a market's size, from 19,998 in the greater New York City market (the largest in the sample) to 647 in the Burlington-Plattsburgh market, which straddles the Vermont-New York state border (the smallest by panel size, and one of the smallest by population). The median market by panel size, Little Rock-Pine Bluff in Arkansas, had 1,606 panelists. In most cases sites are tracked at the domain level: all pages on Example.com would be considered together as traffic to a single site. With particularly popular sites, however, comScore tracks different parts of the domain both individually (for example, images.google.com and maps.google.com) and collectively (all Google-owned properties together).

Thanks to the breadth and detail of the comScore data, this study provides the first comprehensive, nationwide look at the state of local news on the web. The comScore data offer several key traffic metrics within each broadcast market. These include *monthly audience reach*, which is the portion of panelists that visits a website at least once in the calendar month; the number of *monthly page views* that a site receives; *monthly minutes*, which measure the time spent on a site; and the number of monthly panelist *sessions* that a site accumulates, measuring the number of times that a person accessed one or more of a site's pages with no more than thirty minutes between clicks. For each market, comScore's listings include all sites visited by at least six of that market's panelists. Sites that have five or fewer visitors are not reported.

The full details of the procedure to determine which sites are counted as local news outlets can be found in the Appendix. But the intuition behind our method is simple: local news, by definition, draws a larger audience share within its home market than it does nationally. A local news website covering Seattle will have a larger audience share in the greater Seattle area than it will in Tulsa or Toledo. This fact, along with the richness of the comScore data, allows us to distinguish local from national news outlets.

More on Web Metrics

Before delving more deeply into the analysis of local news traffic, we should elaborate a bit more on traffic metrics and methodology. Much discussion of the digital news audience focuses on "monthly audience reach" or equivalently "monthly unique visitors," statistics that count users who view at least one of the site's pages in a given month. Newspaper organizations in particular are fond of monthly audience reach, perhaps because the audience reach figures are closest to old estimates of print circulation.

In fact, monthly audience reach is a much shallower statistic not remotely comparable to audited circulation numbers. The number of sites that a typical user will visit over the course of any thirty-day period is huge, and any individual visit means little. Those who visit a site once, spend less than thirty seconds, and then immediately click away still count as visitors. Most news sites have a high "bounce rate," in which users visit a single page and then leave. A study of the twenty-five most popular national news outlets by the Project for Excellence in Journalism highlighted this pattern. Most unique visitors to these top sites—77 percent on average—are "extremely casual users" who visit just once or twice a month.[11] For many sites the portion of casual users exceeds 90 percent.

Despite the connotation that these users have been "reached," then, most unique visitors make no real connection with a site and spend almost no time there. With print, we do not count those who glance at newspaper headlines at a newsstand as readers. With television, we do not count those who flip past CNN while channel surfing as news viewers. But in the online world, similar behavior gets rolled into inflated monthly audience reach numbers.

Even when looking at the same metric, though, comScore data are significantly different from the data that websites collect themselves. Overcounting of unique visitors is a widespread problem that comScore's data help address.

For those that publish on the web, browser cookies are one option for audience measurement. When users log in, web publishers can set a browser cookie that—at least in theory—can be used to track a user across different computers, different browsers, and different locations. Relatively few visitors choose to log in, though, and most readers use multiple devices or even multiple browsers over the course of a month. When cookies are not tied to a specific registered user, every computer and every browser counts as a unique reader. Simply clearing cookies, or browsing in "private" or "incognito" mode to escape a paywall, creates the same problem. Industry reports estimate that the unique-visitor-to-actual-person ratio is four to one or higher on many sites.[12] This problem has persisted even as real-time analytics platforms like Chartbeat and Omniture have allowed sites to gather increasingly rich data on user behavior.

Another option for counting unique visitors is to look at the IP addresses of users. Though less common, this method increases overcounting even more. Over the course of a month, an itinerant user with a laptop and an iPhone can count as dozens of unique visitors under this standard. This method also allows for undercounting, too, as multiple users in a coffee shop or a business may share an IP address.

comScore, by contrast, measures audience reach by installing software on users' computers. While there are methodological challenges with recruiting and maintaining a representative sample, comScore's data should not suffer from the overcounting of audience reach endemic to other data sources.

The number of unique visitors a site receives thus tells us little about a site's usage pattern or its relative audience. Audience reach numbers have the additional complication that they are not additive. Two sites with 5 percent audience reach don't add up to 10 percent, because we cannot know how much their audiences overlap. Precisely *because* audience reach includes even the shallowest interactions with a site, though, monthly reach numbers let us cast the net as wide as possible in searching for local news sources.

Compared to audience reach, page views and time spent on a site tell us much more about a site's contribution to the overall media landscape. These two metrics are the main focus of the rest of the chapter. However, both need to be understood within the overall landscape of digital media usage.

A site with tens of thousands of monthly page views may sound extremely popular. But in fact, page views are plentiful: users viewed 2,700 pages a month in our sample on average, or roughly ninety pages a day. Facebook alone—the most visited site by page views—accounted for 10 percent of page views (270) in the median market in our comScore data, with Google properties accounting for another 188 page views.

Most page views are short. Our comScore data show that a page view lasts twenty-six seconds on average; 98 percent of page views last less then two minutes, and 99.8 percent last less than 10 minutes. Pages views are most helpful when used comparatively, in understanding the relative audience that two sites have. The page-view numbers we are most interested in are fractional—the portion of the total online audience, or the portion of news traffic, or the portion of just local news traffic. It should be remembered that each of these fractions has a *very* large denominator.

One disadvantage of page views as a metric, however, is that they can be impacted by site architecture. Changes in the page layouts can increase—or decrease—the number of page views recorded. Some news sites are notorious for spreading short articles or photo slide shows over multiple pages in an attempt to maximize page views. Studies of page-view traffic need to be supplemented by metrics of time spent. As we will see below, though, page views and time spent on a site tell a nearly identical story about the audience for local news.

Page views and time spent on a site are important for another reason as well: advertising. Even as many sites have renewed their efforts to put up paywalls, most online news revenue comes from selling online ads. Ad sales by the impression or the click are closely tied to page views. Video advertising on the web is more complicated, but is often sold by the second. The page views and minutes that accrue to news sites are thus a decent proxy for the amount of advertising space that local news sites control.

comScore data offer big advantages over other sources, particularly many news sites' self-reported traffic numbers. If we want to study a broad cross-section of web usage, particularly across dozens of local media markets, there is no real alternative to panel data from firms like comScore and Nielsen. However, this sort of data also has limitations that should be kept in mind.

A key question in any panel survey is how representative participants are of the general population. comScore reports that they use "an array of online recruitment techniques to acquire the members of [comScore's] panel." Calibration panels recruited offline, census data, and monthly phone surveys are used to weight online-recruited panelists in proportion to the general population. In several validation studies, the weighted comScore traffic estimates have differed by less than 5 percent on average from estimates compiled from other independent sources.[13] Still, many details of comScore's approach remain proprietary and cannot be evaluated independently. Online-recruited panelists may overrepresent avid web users: the more pages someone visits, the more likely she is to see a recruitment ad. Even if weighting the panel failed to correct for this, however, an excess of highly-active web users would tend to bias audience reach statistics upward rather than downward.

The comScore data have other limitations, too. Importantly, the comScore panel data used here do not measure usage from mobile devices. Mobile traffic was small in 2010, when the data were collected, but it has grown rapidly since. The growth of mobile browsing and news apps has hurt local news badly overall—a topic that we will discuss at length in chapter 7. But omitting mobile usage, again, means that local news audience share is even lower than this data suggest.

comScore's workplace panel is also smaller and likely less representative than its home panel. Much digital news consumption takes place during working hours,[14] but few workplaces allow the installation of comScore's tracking software. It is possible that home and workplace news consumption patterns differ in ways this dataset cannot capture.

THE BASICS OF ONLINE LOCAL NEWS CONSUMPTION

The broad landscape of online local news is easy to summarize. Local news is a tiny part of web usage: collectively, local news outlets receive *less than half of a percent* of all page views in a typical market. Newspapers and television stations dominate what local news can be found online. Only a handful of local news websites—seventeen out of 1,074, all detailed later—are unaffiliated with traditional print or broadcast media. Across the one hundred markets, our methodology finds the following:

- 395 television station websites
- 590 daily newspaper websites
- 41 weekly news publication websites (nearly all alt-weekly newspapers)
- 31 radio station websites
- 17 web-native local news websites unconnected to print, television, or radio outlets

There is surprisingly little evidence in this data that the internet has expanded the number of local news outlets. And while the internet adds only a pittance of new sources of local news, the surprisingly small audience for online local news helps explain the dire financial straits in which local news organizations find themselves. A summary of the the web traffic data can be found in table 6.1.

Let us start with the discussion of audience reach, the broadest and shallowest metric of web use. Measured by unique visitors, the largest local news site in each market reached 17.8 percent of local users on average, with a standard deviation of 6.3 percent. However, the audience reach numbers drop quickly as one moves down the rankings: the second-ranked site averaged 11.6 percent, the third-ranked site 8.7 percent, the fourth-ranked site 6.0 percent, and the fifth-ranked site 4.3 percent. Because comScore does not provide individual-level data or the overlap between various sites'

TABLE 6.1
Summary of Online News Outlet Data

	Mean	Std. Dev.	Min.	Max.
No. of Web-Native Local News Outlets	.19	.44	0	3
No. of Local Online News Outlets	10.5	4.2	4	28
Local News Page Views / Capita	13.8	10.0	1.8	90.2
Local News Minutes / Capita	10.6	7.6	1.3	63.4
Local News as Pct. of All Page Views	.51	.27	.06	3.4
Local News as Pct. of All Online Minutes	.54	.39	.06	3.2
Nonlocal News Page Views / Capita	60.0	30.8	28.0	370
Nonlocal News Minutes / Capita	59.0	16.4	23.4	126
HHI in Page Views	2749	1297	921	9003
HHI in Minutes Spent	2943	1444	939	8955

Note: Summary of the data on online news sources across our one hundred broadcast markets. Most local markets have no internet native news sources, challenging the common assumption that the internet is expanding the number of local news outlets.

visitors, it is impossible to calculate the portion of the audience that visits at least one local news site.

Statistics for audience reach can be greatly deceiving when used to measure how much traffic news sites get overall. As noted earlier, the large majority of unique visitors to national news sites are made up of users who visit just once or twice a month.[15] In fact, more detailed traffic metrics show that the total audience for local news outlets is uniformly small.

Online local news sites received only 11.4 monthly page views per person in the median market. Even with a few high-end outliers, the overall average rises to just 13.8 monthly page views, or roughly three pages per web user per week. These numbers represent just 0.43 percent of the total monthly page views in the median market (with the overall average slightly higher at 0.51).

Local news sites were between 0.30 and 0.62 percent of all monthly page views in half of the markets, equivalent to between 8.3 and 17.0 page views

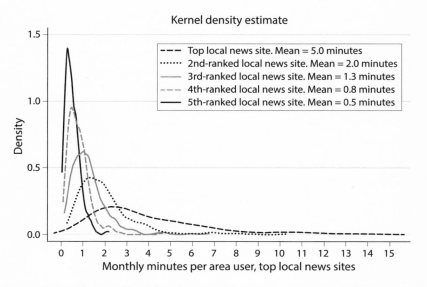

Figure 6.1 Distribution of local digital news audience in monthly minutes per capita. Not only do audiences spend little time on local news sites, numbers usually fall dramatically below the top-ranked local site. Fourth- and fifth-ranked local news sites average less than a minute a month per internet user.

per person. The largest outlier by far is Salt Lake City, where local news—and especially the television site KSL.com—gets more than 3 percent of all page views. At the other end of the spectrum are Colorado Springs–Pueblo, Las Vegas, and Los Angeles, which give less than 0.15 percent of their page views to local news sites on average. All three average less than four monthly local news page views per web user.

A similar story can be seen with time spent on news sites rather than page views. In the median market only 9.1 monthly minutes per user went to local news sites, just 0.45 percent of time online. More than half of that time, on average, goes to the local market's top-ranked site.

These numbers are illustrated graphically in figure 6.1, which shows the distribution of time spent on local news outlets. Time spent falls precipitously from a market's top-ranked site—averaging five monthly minutes per user—to the fifth-ranked site, which averages just thirty seconds. Half of markets had local news at between 0.33 and 0.63 percent of online minutes, or between 6.3 and 12.4 minutes per capita. Measured by page views or minutes, local news outlets get just a tiny portion of citizens' attention.

Are these grim numbers because of low news consumption overall, or because local outlets are losing out to national news? The comScore data show that the answer is "both." Looking at all news sites—both those in the "News/Information" category and all the additional news sites identified earlier—we find that the average market sends seventy-four monthly page views to news sites of all stripes. This works out to roughly sixty page views for nonlocal news sources and fourteen for local ones. The figures for minutes spent are even smaller. In the average market, users spend sixty minutes per month on nonlocal news websites, but just eleven minutes on local ones.

These numbers are consistent with previous findings from other data sources that news sites receive just a few percentage points of web traffic.[16] Still, the small proportion of local news is surprising. Less than one in five news page views goes to a local news source.

How Many Outlets? Of What Type?

Even if local news is a small part of web content, knowing where that content comes from matters. How many such sites are there in a typical broadcast market?

Markets in the sample average about ten-and-a-half online local news sources. On a typical month, that breaks down into 6.1 newspaper sites, 3.8 local television sites, 0.3 radio stations, and less than 0.2 web-native news outlets. The markets with the largest numbers of outlets are Chicago (19), New York (20), Minneapolis (20), Cleveland (21), and Boston (with a whopping 28). Larger population broadcast markets have more digital news outlets, even after adjusting for market share. More populous markets *do not* show greater consumption of local news as measured by time or page views, however—a finding we will return to later. The markets with the fewest outlets in our survey were Baton Rouge, Louisiana (4), Fort Smith, Arkansas (5), and El Paso, Texas (5).

Importantly, the biggest differences in the number of outlets come from varying numbers of newspapers. Eighty-eight out of the hundred markets have three, four, or five television station websites, including stations with just cable distribution. Most have no radio or internet-only outlets that meet our minimal audience threshold. That leaves differences in the number of newspapers to account for the rest of the variance. About half of the markets have either three or fewer newspapers or more than eleven newspapers. As we would expect, several of the markets with only two print news sources—Richmond-Petersburg (Virginia), Baton Rouge, Tucson (Arizona), El Paso, Colorado Springs-Pueblo, Fort Smith—compete for the fewest number of outlets overall. The two markets with the highest number of newspapers—Hartford-New Haven, Connecticut (14) and Boston (21)—both boast a profusion of papers tied to small New England towns. Most of the newspapers found are published daily. However, forty-one newspapers in our sample are weekly publications—almost all alternative weeklies published in one of the larger metro areas in our sample.

If there are more print than television online news sources, their collective online audiences are closer to parity. Put together, newspaper sites average 0.25 percent of their markets' monthly page views, versus 0.20 for television sites. But television sites do better in terms of minutes spent. Television and newspaper sites have identical averages: 0.25 percent of minutes each. This modest improvement is likely due to online video, which produces longer than average page view times.

Local News Competition on the Web

As the audience numbers in the previous section show, local news is a small niche in the broader web. But within that niche, most local news markets are quite concentrated. Consider the top newspaper and top TV station site in each market. The top paper earns 0.15 percent of all page views on average, while the top television station adds another 0.16 percent. The outlet with the highest audience reach overall—always a TV station or newspaper—averages 0.22 percent of all local page views. These means are skewed upward by a few outliers, but the top newspaper and TV station sites together get 56 percent of local news page views in the median market.

Traffic for the smallest outlets we examine is minuscule by comparison. In an average month in our sample, sixty-three sites (out of 1,074 total) attain an audience reach between 1 and 1.2 percent, barely above our cutoff.

These sixty-three sites average less than 0.008 percent of all local page views (with a standard deviation of 0.0012). This means that the average top-rated local site has *275 times* as many page views as the smallest included sites. These numbers mean than any sites *too small* to be included in our survey account for only a tiny fraction of the local news audience. At this rate, even a dozen sites missing right below our cutoff threshold would still leave local news with less than half a percent of all page views.

Evidence of concentration shows up in more systematic metrics as well. The most commonly used metric of market concentration is the Herfindahl-Hirschman Index (HHI). The HHI is the sum of the squared market share (in percent) of all of the firms in a given market; it has possible values between 0 and 10,000. According to Department of Justice and Federal Trade Commission rules, markets with an HHI between 1,500 and 2,500 are classified as *moderately concentrated*, while markets with an HHI greater that 2,500 are classified as *highly concentrated*. The HHI statistic serves as an initial screen for heightened scrutiny, while the full test examines other factors—such as entry conditions—that might allow a firm to produce a "significant and non-transitory increase in price."[17]

If we consider local online news markets separately from print and broadcast markets, we find a surprising level of concentration. Whether we use minutes or page views to measure market share, the HHI indicates that most online local news markets should be within the envelope of closer regulatory scrutiny.[18] Averaged across our three months, the median market has an HHI of 2,479 with page views and 2,593 with minutes spent online. Ninety-five of the one hundred markets have an HHI above 1,500 measured by page views, and ninety-six reach that level with online minutes. Markets do show high month-to-month variance in HHI, with a median monthly swing of ±296 points in page views and ±340 points in minutes spent. But the overall picture is clear: most online local news markets are dominated by just two or three news organizations.

A CENSUS OF ONLINE-ONLY LOCAL NEWS OUTLETS

A central goal of this chapter is to catalogue online news sites that are not affiliated with traditional media outlets—and that therefore have a strong prima facie claim to be adding to media diversity. Perhaps the single most surprising finding in this study is just how few such outlets there are.

Out of the 1,074 online local news sources this study identifies, only seventeen are genuinely new media outlets rather than just online outposts of print or broadcast outlets. The dearth of new internet outlets allows us to list these sites in their entirety. In descending order of local audience reach, here are *all* of the internet-only news outlets that show up in our survey:

- The online-only local news site with the largest audience reach is SeattlePI.com. Once the online home of the *Seattle Post-Intelligencer* newspaper, the site remained active even after the *P-I* stopped its presses and laid off nearly all of its staff in 2007. In the comScore data, the P-I website achieved reasonably broad reach but only shallow usage. Audience reach was between 7.7 and 12.7 percent, while the share of monthly page views (across all types of websites) was between 0.026 and 0.046 percent.
- Chattanoogan.com, an online newspaper based in Chattanooga, Tennessee, is one of the earliest online-only local news projects in the country. Chattanoogan.com was founded in the summer of 1999, in the wake of the sale of the *Chattanooga Times* to the larger *Chattanooga Free Press*; the consolidation made Chattanooga a one-newspaper town. Chattanoogan.com garnered between 6.3 and 8.6 percent monthly reach, and between 0.06 and 0.08 percent of monthly page views.
- TucsonCitizen.com is the site of the former *Tucson Citizen* daily newspaper. The site survived the closure of the paper in May 2009, with the revamped site having a heavy focus on political opinion. The site received between 2.6 and 6.3 percent audience reach in Tucson during the period studied, but just 0.003 to 0.007 percent of page views.
- KYPost.com is an online newspaper serving northern Kentucky. Formerly the website of the *Kentucky Post* daily newspaper—a regional variant of the *Cincinnati Post*—the website continued on after the print versions ceased publication in December 2007. KYPost.com achieved between 2.1 and 3.3 percent audience reach in Cincinnati, and between 0.007 and 0.005 percent of the market's page views.
- OnMilwaukee.com is an online publication based in Milwaukee, Wisconsin, that marries local arts and events coverage with some local

news. It received between 2.5 and 3.1 percent reach, and between 0.002 and 0.003 percent of page views.

- GoWilkes.com is a local news and information site focusing on Wilkes County, North Carolina. It has only modest reach, getting between 2.1 and 2.8 percent of local users. Surprisingly, however, it has a heavy page-view count, accounting for between 0.26 and 0.60 percent of page views in the Greensboro-High Point-Winston Salem market area.

- FingerLakes1.com serves the Finger Lakes region in upstate New York. The relatively simple site contains both local events coverage and a listing of local news stories. It earned between 1.0 and 3.1 percent reach and between .11 and .22 percent of page views in the Rochester market.

- LorainCounty.com of Ohio is a local news and directory site founded by two brothers; the site's history as a news source stretches back to the mid-1990s. It received between 1.0 and 2.2 percent audience reach and 0.004 and 0.008 percent of local page views in the Cleveland market.

- GWDToday.com serves Greenwood, South Carolina. The site's design is unpolished, but its reporting staff does produce original local reporting, often several articles a day. The site had a market reach between .7 and 1.8 percent, and a page view share between .005 and .010 percent in the Greenville-Spartanburg-Asheville market.

- SanDiego.com declares that it has "evolved from a destination-focused travelers portal" into an "online community partner for locals and visitors alike." Travel links and resources are the most prominent site features, though it does provide a small amount of local news. The site had an audience reach of between 1.1 and 1.7 percent in San Diego, along with a minimal page view share of between 0.001 and 0.003 percent.

- SOMD.com is a local site focused on southern Maryland. While it features mostly local events and listings, it does include some local news, much of it from content partners and law enforcement press releases. The site's audience reach in the Washington, D.C., market was between 1.0 and 1.2 percent, with page views between 0.005 and 0.008 percent of the market total.

- iBerkshires.com is a small news and local information site that serves western Massachusetts. The site appeared only in our February data, with a reach of 1.2 percent and 0.008 percent of page views in the Albany-Schenectady-Troy market.

- SanJose.com is a "city guide" that focuses on dining and events, but also provides some local news. The site had a market reach of between 0.8 and 1.3 percent, and a page-view share between 0.0007 and 0.0015 percent.
- MinnPost.com, a nonprofit news site, describes its mission as providing "high-quality journalism for news-intense people who care about Minnesota." Though it has often been discussed as a potential business model for local news, its traffic in our data is minimal: between 0.5 and 1.3 percent of audience reach in Minneapolis-St. Paul, and from .0009 to .0012 percent of page views.
- VoiceofSanDiego.com is a nonprofit news organization focusing on investigative reporting. Traffic numbers are low, however: reach was .48 percent in February (with 0.0005 percent of San Diego pages), 1 percent in April (with 0.0008 percent of pages), and too low to measure in March.

In addition to the above sites, the data included two sites that have since been shuttered. PegasusNews.com was a local site in Dallas-Fort Worth, which combined local news from staff writers with mostly syndicated content. The site was eventually sold to the *Dallas Morning News*, and shut down in 2014. SDNN.com, a San Diego News Network "community hub," also counted as an online news site during the period studied, but shut down in mid-2010.

Some patterns in this data are obvious. The internet-only sites that average more than 3 percent monthly reach are websites of newspapers that ceased print publication, or—in the case of Chattanoogan.com—were founded in the aftermath of a newspaper closure. While these sites may help maintain a bit of news diversity that would otherwise be lost, their persistence is not evidence of expanding local news options.

The poor showing of MinnPost.com and VoiceofSanDiego.com may be especially surprising to some. While MinnPost and VoSD have been celebrated examples of a new breed of local and regional online news organizations, numerous other local online news sites are missing altogether in the above listing—including many other sites once mentioned as promising experiments. The fact that traffic to these "model" outlets is minimal across the board is sobering for the future of journalism.

These results are so discouraging, and so contrary to prominent claims about hyperlocal media, that I performed a deeper dive into the data. Perhaps these outlets are present in the data, but miscategorized, or slightly below the 1 percent traffic threshold set as a consistent cross-market bar.

I thus assembled a larger list of internet-only news organizations, checking to see if any are included in the comScore data. This deeper search looked for specific site names regardless of category or traffic level, as long as comScore's six-visitor minimum was met. Sites based outside one of the top one hundred broadcast markets were excluded, as (of course) were outlets focusing on national rather than local news. The catalogue of relevant online local sites was drawn from the *Columbia Journalism Review's* News Frontier Database, from Michelle McLellan's listings at the Reynolds Journalism Institute, and from a list put out by the Harvard Kennedy School's Hauser Center. The final list of local online-only news organizations included the following:

- The Arizona Guardian (Phoenix)
- Baristanet (New York)
- The Bay Citizen (San Francisco-Oakland-San Jose)
- Capital (New York)
- California Watch (San Francisco-Oakland-San Jose)
- Chicago News Cooperative (Chicago)
- The Colorado Independent (Denver)
- The Connecticut Mirror (Hartford-New Haven)
- Florida Center for Investigative Reporting (Miami)
- The Florida Independent (Miami)
- The Gotham Gazette (New York)
- InDenver Times (Denver)
- Investigate West (Seattle)
- The Iowa Independent (Des Moines-Ames)
- The Lens (New Orleans)
- Maine Center for Investigative Reporting / Pine Tree Watchdog (Portland-Auburn)
- The Michigan Messenger (Detroit)
- The Minnesota Independent (Minneapolis-St. Paul)
- New England Center for Investigative Reporting (Boston)

- The New Haven Independent (Hartford-New Haven)
- New Jersey Newsroom (New York)
- Oakland Local (San Francisco-Oakland-San Jose)
- Open Media Boston (Boston)
- Portland Afoot (Portland, OR)
- The Rapidian (Grand Rapids-Kalamazoo-Battle Creek)
- Rocky Mountain Investigative News Network (Denver)
- The Sacramento Press (Sacramento-Stockton-Modesto)
- The San Francisco Appeal (San Francisco-Oakland-San Jose)
- The SF Public Press (San Francisco-Oakland-San Jose)
- The Seattle Post Globe (Seattle)
- Spot.us (San Francisco-Oakland-San Jose)
- The St. Louis Beacon (St. Louis)
- The South Los Angeles Report (Los Angeles)
- The Texas Tribune (Austin)
- The Tucson Sentinel (Tucson)
- Twin Cities Daily Planet (Minneapolis-St. Paul)
- VTDigger.com (Burlington-Plattsburgh)
- Wisconsin Center for Investigative Journalism (Madison)

The results of this deeper survey are striking. The Minnesota Independent showed up in just the April Minneapolis-St. Paul data, with six visitors (out of 3,201 panelists). In the same market, the Twin Cities Daily Planet also marked nine visitors in April, though none were recorded in February or March. The San Francisco Appeal earned eight visitors (out of 5,540 panelists) in February, six visitors in April, and too few to measure in March. The Gotham Gazette was in the New York sample for March and April, though not February; it received twelve visitors both months, out of 19,998 NYC market panelists. All of these numbers are far below our traffic threshold.

None of the other thirty-five outlets appeared even once in the comScore data.

Another site largely absent in our data is Patch.com itself. Patch shows up just four times in our data: all three months in the New York market, where it received between thirty-seven and fifty visitors, and in the San Francisco market, where it received nine visitors in April. The New York media market is where Patch.com started, and it has its densest listing of hyperlocal sites there. Even in New York, however, the numerous Patch sites collectively did not achieve 1 percent audience reach. Contemporaneously published reports suggest that the typical Patch story got only a hundred or fewer page views.[19] If these reports were accurate, they put most Patch sites far below our expected detection threshold.

The broad comScore coverage also allows us to piggyback onto in-depth studies of local journalism in the digital age. First, the Institute for Interactive Journalism (J-Lab) authored a 2010 study of the online news ecosystem in Philadelphia. They identified 260 local blogs, including "about 60 [with] some journalistic DNA in that they report news, not just comment on it."[20] While J-Lab did not provide a full listing of these sites, they single out several as particularly successful examples.

The Philadelphia media market provides the fourth-largest panel in the sample, making it dramatically easier to find low-market-reach sites here than almost anywhere else. PlanPhilly.com shows up just in the February data, with seven visitors out of 7,967 panelists. None of the other online news sources show up at all.

The Project for Excellence in Journalism (PEJ) also conducted a detailed look at Baltimore's online news environment in "How News Happens: A Study of the News Ecosystem of One American City."[21] PEJ found ten unaffiliated digital news sources based in Baltimore. Half were hosted on larger sites such as Blogspot or Twitter, meaning that they were not visible in our data. Sites hosted on independent domains included BaltimoreBrew.com (founded by former *Baltimore Sun* staffers), BMoreNews.com, ExhibitANewsBaltimore.com, InsideCharmCity, and InvestigativeVoice.com (run by former *Baltimore Examiner* employees). None of these sites appeared in the comScore data.

How are we to make sense of these null findings? First, it is worth remembering just how much traffic one visitor in the comScore panel represents. As a rule of thumb, one comScore panelist approximates— *very* roughly—six hundred real-life audience members. The New York City television market, for example, has an online audience of slightly more than 11 million people, which comScore tries to track with a New York panel of 19,998. Assume for a moment that the sample construction is perfectly random: in that case, a site that averages three thousand unique, within-market visitors a month will still appear in our data less than half the time. Since our data have a traffic threshold for each market, local sites with some cross-market reach can receive even more traffic without being likely to appear.

Measuring the size of tiny groups with panel methods is a known problem in the social sciences. In these cases, even small amounts of bias or measurement error can exceed the size of the group to be estimated.[22] While the comScore data set may be enormous by the standards of national surveys, it still cannot make precise audience estimates for the smallest websites in the smallest local markets. Still, the fact that such sites are too small to measure is a powerful substantive finding in its own right. Our data can provide strong bounds on their maximum audience.

REGRESSION ANALYSIS

Local news may be a tiny subset of the content that citizens consume, but the comScore data do show that markets differ in both the number of online local news outlets available and the traffic that local news receives. How systematic are these differences? For example, in which kinds of media markets do we find web-native news outlets? What factors predict greater local digital news consumption? And are there consistent patterns in which local news markets are most concentrated? To shed light on these questions, I performed regression analyses on our one hundred local markets, combining the comScore data with additional data provided by the FCC.

A full list of variables used in the regression analysis can be found in the Appendix. The data are analyzed using two different sorts of regression models. First, negative binomial models are used to estimate both the number of web-native news outlets found in a given market, and the number of local online news outlets of all kinds. Second, OLS regression models are used to analyze local news consumption and the level of market concentration.

In all cases, the analyses use robust standard errors clustered by market. Repeated observations of the same market across months are certainly not independent, reducing our effective sample size. Because our sample size is small, only the largest and most consistent relationships are likely to be statistically significant.

Table 6.2 presents the results of the negative binomial models. These models, which assume that the dependent variable is a positive integer, are a better choice for count data than OLS regression.[23]

Let us start with the number of web-native news outlets found in a given market. Greater numbers of internet-only news sites are found in markets with lower per-person print circulation. The relationship is highly statistically significant, and it persists even if we exclude markets where print newspapers have stopped print publishing while maintaining their websites. While these online-only sites are unlikely to close gaps in coverage, internet-only news sources are more likely be be found where print newspaper readership is lower.

The model also suggests that markets that are both large and heavily Hispanic have fewer internet-only news sites, though the result is not quite statistically significant. No other variable comes close to statistical significance.

The story looks somewhat different when examining the total number of online local news outlets, a category dominated by sites of daily newspapers and television stations. First, there is strong evidence that larger markets have more news outlets. With a t-score > 5, this finding is nearly impossible to have been produced by chance alone. Still, the effect size is only moderate: adding four million people to a market would, on average, predict only one extra local news site.

There is also a strong association between the total number of online outlets and the number of newspaper companies operating in the market. This is consistent with our earlier analysis showing that most variance comes from different numbers of newspaper sites.

As with the analysis of internet-only news outlets, there is a complicated relationship between the racial and ethnic makeup of a market and the number of online news outlets we find there. The coefficients for the portion of Hispanic and black residents are both positive, though only the latter is significant. However, there are also strong and highly significant interaction effects. The model finds fewer online outlets in cities that are *both* large *and* heavily minority. There is perhaps a hint that markets with more elderly people have fewer local online outlets, though the result is not significant ($p < .13$ in a two-tailed test). None of the other explanatory variables approach statistical significance.

TABLE 6.2
Regression: Number of Local Online News Outlets

	Web-Native Local News Sites	Total Online Local News Sites
TV Market Population	.0007 (.0005)	**.00026** **(.00005)**
Broadband Pct.	1.80 . (2.84)	.045. (.277)
Newspaper Circ./Capita	**−2.92** **(1.36)**	.135 (.129)
Daily Newspapers	.142 (.321)	−.030 (.035)
Newspaper Parent Companies	−.0049 (.0887).	**.031** **(.009)**
Commercial TV Stations	−.088 (.086)	−.005 (.012)
Locally Owned TV Stations	. .094 (.258)	.044 (.029)
Minority-Owned Stations	−.063 (.452)	−.012 (.040)
Newspaper-TV Cross-ownership	. .209 (.529)	−.045 (.091)
Radio-TV Cross-ownership	.186 (.218)	−.003 (.029)
News-Format Radio Stations	−.064 (.066)	−.0047 (.0055)
Hispanic Pct.	1.56 (2.55)	.462 (.291)
Hispanic Pct. × Market Pop.	**−.0016** **(.0009)**	**−.00043** **(.00008)**
Black Pct.	−.656 (3.76)	**1.35** **(.52)**
Black Pct. × Market Pop.	−.0014 (.0015)	**−.0008** **(.0002)**

TABLE 6.2
(*continued*)

	Web-Native Local News Sites	Total Online Local News Sites
Income	.123	.002
	(.108)	(.010)
Age 65+	−2.92	−1.46
	(11.2)	(.95)
February	**.223**	.012
	(.101)	(.008)
March	.223	.014
	(.118)	(.006)
Constant	−3.07	1.77
	(2.05)	(.25)
$\ln(\alpha)$	−14.5	−18.6
	(.63)	(.38)
α	.0000	.0000
	(.0000)	(.0000)
N	294	294

Note: This table presents results from a negative binomial regression model, analyzing both the number of web-native local news outlets and the total number of online local news outlets. Standard errors (in parentheses) are robust, clustered by media market.

These data also allow us to examine the consumption of local news, measured both by page views and minutes. Here we return to standard OLS linear regression models (table 6.3).

A particularly consistent predictor of local news consumption, in both page views and minutes, is the portion of the population that is Hispanic. Communities with a proportionally larger Latino population consume less local news than otherwise comparable cities. Moreover, interaction effects between market size and ethnic composition amplify this finding. Not only do heavily Hispanic markets have lower local news consumption on average, but also local news traffic in *larger* heavily Hispanic markets is lower still. The portion of market residents who are African American does not produce similar findings.

TABLE 6.3
Regression: Online News Audience and Concentration

	Page Views	Minutes	HHI Page Views	HHI Minutes
TV Market Population	−.0002	.0003	**−.525**	−.403
	(.0016)	(.0014)	**(.279)**	(.318)
Broadband Pct.	16.6	17.3	896	2174
	(13.0)	(11.2)	(1453)	(1573)
Newspaper Copies/Capita	4.63	1.92	−581	−975
	(3.31)	(2.83)	(550)	(652)
Daily Newspapers	1.21	.590	47.7	98.5
	(.88)	(.744)	(114)	(156)
Newspaper Parent Companies	−.134	−.070	−9.20	43.0
	(.421)	(.317)	(55.7)	(60.4)
Commercial TV Stations	−.091	.217	−.53	−18.9
	(.386)	(.317)	(57.8)	(64.8)
Locally Owned TV Stations	3.11	**2.13**	52.1	37.9
	(1.95)	**(1.27)**	(170)	(173)
Minority-Owned Stations	1.60	**2.20**	125	254
	(1.23)	**(1.18)**	(234)	(264)
Newspaper-TV Cross-Ownership	**3.96**	1.68	**1115**	**1201**
	(2.41)	(1.62)	**(514)**	**(559)**
Radio-TV Cross-Ownership	.521	.095	125	94.2
	(.921)	(.656)	(156)	(164)
News-Format Radio Stations	.516	.247	57.3	25.4
	(.399)	(.269)	(35.9)	(39.1)
Hispanic Pct.	**−10.5**	**−7.15**	−586	−27.8
	(5.5)	**(4.14)**	(953)	(1049)
Hispanic Pct. × Market Pop.	−.0058	−.0061	.345	.045
	(.0024)	(.0021)	(.327)	(.373)
Black Pct.	2.26	1.09	−507	−1589
	(10.3)	(7.38)	(2705)	(2543)
Black Pct. × Market Pop.	−.0046	−.0028	1.02	.82
	(.0040)	(.0041)	(1.03)	(1.16)

TABLE 6.3
(*continued*)

	Page Views	Minutes	HHI Page Views	HHI Minutes
Income / capita	**−.670**	**−.480**	−10.8	−28.4
	(.334)	**(.254)**	(44.9)	(46.6)
Age 65+	−109	**−75.9**	−9670	−8643
	(71)	**(45.2)**	(7207)	(7239)
February	**1.52**	**1.80**	−81.0	77.9
	(.54)	**(.53)**	(85.7)	(101)
March	−.088	**.608**	−67.0	78.1
	(.35)	**(.35)**	(68.6)	(93.1)
Constant	**26.2**	**16.0**	**4435**	**4456**
	(10.8)	**(7.2)**	**(1233)**	**(1292)**
R^2	.374	.323	.269	.225
Root MSE	8.26	6.47	1155	1323

Note: This table presents results from OLS regression models that predict local news audience. The first two models analyze comScore audience numbers in page views and minutes. The third and fourth models analyze local online news concentration in page views and minutes, respectively, using the Herfindahl-Hirshman Index. Robust standard errors clustered by media market are in parentheses.

The model also suggests that media ownership patterns predict the level of local news consumption. The presence of a minority-owned television station is associated with greater local news usage in both page views and minutes, though only the number of minutes is statistically significant. Many of these minority-owned stations are in large, heavily Hispanic markets (such as Miami-Fort Lauderdale or Los Angeles). Similarly, the presence of locally owned TV stations also predicts higher levels of online news consumption, though here, too, only the number of minutes spent is statistically significant.

The level of TV-newspaper cross-ownership also seems to matter. Markets with cross-owned newspaper-television firms show an extra four monthly page views per person going to local news sites ($p < .10$, two-tailed). Findings for local news minutes are similar though not significant.

Curiously, markets with greater per capita income are estimated to consume local *less* news online than comparable poorer markets. This finding emerges with both minutes and page views, and it is statistically significant for both measures. Markets with more residents age sixty-five or older also show lower local internet news consumption, though the results are significant only with time spent.

Lastly, we look at predictors of local news market concentration online as measured by the HHI. Concentration in minutes and in page views is examined, and both metrics tell a very similar story. Overall, market concentration findings are less than in the preceding models. Most of our predictors do not approach statistical significance, with two exceptions.

First, all else being equal, more populous markets have lower levels of estimated concentration. This result is significant with page views, and approaches significance with minutes spent.

Second, markets with newspaper-television cross-ownership show dramatically higher levels of concentration in both minutes spent and page views. There are nineteen such markets in our data, and the estimated effect size is enormous: with TV-newspaper cross-ownership the model predicts an 1115-point jump in the HHI in page views, and a 1201-point jump in the HHI by minutes spent. Both metrics are statistically significant.

On (Not) Expanding Local News Voices

Has the internet significantly expanded the number of local news voices? The answer that emerges from the comScore data is a firm "no." We can say least about online news sources that receive less than a few thousand unique visitors monthly, and are thus unlikely to appear in our data. But we do not need data on the tiniest sites to know that local online news falls far short of the hopes that continue to be placed on it.

Most television markets have fewer than a dozen local news websites— with two or three sites getting nearly all the digital audience. Those sites that do comparatively well are overwhelmingly newspaper and local television station websites, rather than new and independent sources of local news. Only sixteen of our top one hundred markets have an unaffiliated internet news source that reaches our 1-percent audience threshold.

Even the exceptions prove the rule: the four most successful internet-only news sites were all related to the closure of a traditional print newspaper. The fact that sites like SeattlePI.com continue with a skeleton crew is welcome, but it does not represent an expansion of media diversity. Online local news markets resemble downsized versions of traditional media news markets, with the same news stories produced by the same newspapers and television stations.

Even more surprising than the small number of outlets, or the lack of new web-native news organizations, is just how small the local online news market is. Discussions about the newspaper crisis often start with the claim that online news has a revenue problem, not a readership problem. We are told repeatedly that "audiences are bigger than ever"[24] and that the problem with newspaper sites is that "lots of people came, but lots of advertising didn't."[25] We will address these sorts of foolhardy or simply false claims at greater length in the next chapter.

The comScore data show that this diagnosis is wrong. The central problem facing local online news sites is that their audiences are small—proportionally far smaller than even many publishers and journalists seem to realize. Metrics such as monthly audience reach are often falsely inflated, and deceptive even when measured accurately. A news startup is hailed as a success if it gets ten thousand page-views a month, even though many individual citizens view thousands of pages a month each, and even though page views last less than thirty seconds each on average. Online local news has a revenue problem in large part *because* it has a readership problem.

Arguments that the internet has expanded the number of local news voices, or allowed new web-based news outlets to fill gaps in news coverage, find little support in this data. In deciding *Prometheus v.* FTC (2004), the court's majority worried that online local news sources might just be repackaged versions of television and newspaper content. The comScore data show that this is indeed the case.

Some have found evidence of consumer substitution between online and traditional news sources.[26] For national news, and particularly for commodity news content, this finding might hold. But the comScore data make it difficult to sustain the same argument with regard to local news content. We find almost no examples of web-native news sites that are straightforward substitutes for the product of a television station or a newspaper. The lack of traffic these sites receive is strong evidence that citizens themselves do not think that they are comparable to television and newspaper websites.

The low levels of traffic to local news sites should color our assessments in other ways as well. The small audience for local news online makes it implausible that a midsized or smaller media market can support numerous online-only news organizations with adequate staff and resources. The story of hyperlocal journalism thus far is mostly a long list of failed experiments.

Moreover, the situation for most local digital news sites has been getting *worse* since the data in this chapter was collected. The analysis in this chapter remains, as of this writing, the only comprehensive study of online news at the media market level. But recent work shows that the struggles of digital local news have only grown. Iris Chyi and Ori Tenenboim, in a longitudinal study of fifty-one major newspapers, find that more than half saw their digital audience decline between 2011 and 2015.[27] The rise of mobile news in particular has been disastrous, a theme we will take up at length in the next chapter.

Lastly, offline media concentration carries over into online media markets. Most local news markets on the web are dominated by just a few firms. If online local news were to be considered as a separate market, half of the one hundred largest markets would qualify as highly concentrated under Department of Justice and Federal Trade Commission HHI guidelines, and nearly all would be considered at least moderately concentrated.

Perhaps the most striking example of offline media structure intersecting with local news on the web is seen with newspaper-television cross-ownership. In cities where a firm owns both a newspaper and a television station, we find an estimated jump in the Herfindahl-Hirschman Index greater than one thousand points. While the underlying causal relationship deserves more study, these numbers make a strong argument for regulatory caution. Restrictions on media cross-ownership do not just matter in print and on the airwaves: they impact news diversity on the web as well.

All of these findings are especially worrisome given recent decisions by the FCC as this book goes to press.

The FCC's December 2017 decision to roll back net neutrality rules has garnered a firestorm of public controversy. But for local media online, the decision made a month earlier to eliminate rules on media cross-media ownership will have a just as big of an impact. Critics saw the rule change as a gift to conservative-leaning Sinclair Broadcasting. Chairman Ajit Pai dismissed such concerns, claiming the old rule "doesn't reflect a world in which we get news and analysis throughout the day from countless national and local websites, podcasts, and social media outlets."[28]

But Pai is wrong: it is flatly not true that there are "countless" local digital news outlets. We know, *because we counted them.* The internet has added almost no new voices to the local media landscape, while weakening most existing newspapers and TV stations. Now the FCC's order threatens to weaken them further, and in the process create local media monopolies in small markets across the country. How local media can survive—even with these added challenges—is the subject of the next chapter.

Making News Stickier

Nobody thinks for a moment that he ought to pay for his newspaper....
The citizen will pay for his telephone, his railroad rides, his motor car, his
entertainment. But he does not pay openly for his news.
— Walter Lippmann, *Public Opinion*, 1922

The American Republic was born on the pages of local newspapers. For
more than two centuries, local papers have produced most U.S. journalism,
and employed most of the country's reporters. The arrival of the internet in
the mid-1990s brought worrisome omens, but it did not—at first—seem
to change much. So when the newspaper decline finally arrived in 2008,
along with the worst recession in generations, its swiftness and severity
took even many pessimists by surprise.

In 2007 there were 57,000 newspaper journalists in U.S. newsrooms;
seven years later there were just 32,900, when the most widely used newsroom census was stopped. U.S. newspaper ad revenue was $65 billion in
2000, but had plunged to just $18 billion by 2016.[1] One of the biggest
news stories of recent years has been the future of the news itself.

A parade of public figures—journalists, editors, media and technology
executives, scholars, and public officials—have offered a laundry list of
contradictory proposals to save journalism. News organizations have been
told both to get bigger (through consolidation) and to get smaller (by going
hyperlocal). Some have demanded that newspapers put up paywalls, while
others have urged newspapers to shut down their printing presses, become
all-digital organizations, and embrace the open web. Others have proposed that journalism should give up trying to make a profit at all, relying

on government subsidies, philanthropy, new nonprofit journalism models, or even blogs and citizen-created content. Still others have recently suggested that a so-called pivot to video could make digital journalism sustainable.

These proposed "solutions" are deeply worrisome. Not only are they inadequate or unworkable, but they also prove that most media leaders deeply misunderstand the digital audiences who are supposed to be their future. Any real solutions have to begin with a basic understanding of how traffic compounds or decays over time, and the ways in which *all* kinds of websites—news sites included—are able (or not) to translate that traffic into revenue.

This chapter thus offers a different perspective on the future of news, grounded on the models of web traffic and online revenue we laid out in chapters 4 and 5—and the grim reality of local news audiences that we saw in chapter 6. The problem of stickiness, of generating compounded audience growth, is the most urgent problem facing journalism today. If journalism needs an audience to succeed, then most digital publications are failing.

This dearth of digital readers is especially dire with local newspapers. As we saw in the last chapter, the notion that a host of local and hyperlocal news startups will fill in the gaps created by the retreat of local newspapers is a fantasy. Like it or not, preserving local journalism is thus mostly a question of helping local newspapers adapt to the digital age.

A dynamic perspective on web traffic leaves room for both hope and skepticism. On one hand, our traffic models show suggest that the biggest problems facing local papers are both *different* and *more severe* than is generally acknowledged. On the other, they suggest concrete ways to increase traffic, and metrics to judge whether changes are working. Dynamic models of web traffic let news organizations move beyond vague calls for "innovation" and "experimentation," while actually providing metrics for success.

Compounded audience is the most powerful force on the internet. The success of local news in the twenty-first century depends on this compounding process, on measuring stickiness and optimizing for it. First, though, newspapers have to acknowledge some uncomfortable truths.

THE MYTH OF MONETIZATION

For all the difficult challenges faced by local newspapers, one of the biggest threats is of their own making. Many newspaper leaders have been eager to construct self-serving fables that obscure the grim fundamentals. The most popular and dangerous of these tall tales is what we might call the Myth of Monetization.

There is a large audience for online news, we are told—it is just hard to get these readers to pay. Industry leaders have declared over and over that the total newspaper audience, digital included, is larger than ever. Such talk is usually justified with references to unique visitors or audience reach, shallow and sloppy statistics that—as we saw in the last chapter—often overstate the true audience by a factor of four or more.[2]

When we look at better metrics, though, a bleaker picture emerges. All of the major digital measurement firms tell similar stories about how people spend their attention online. Web users spend a lot of time with Google and on Facebook and pornographic sites. They visit Yahoo! and Bing, they shop, they read their email.

Against this broad backdrop, news sites get only about 3 percent of web traffic. Even worse, a huge majority of that audience goes to national news outlets instead of local news organizations. As chapter 6 showed, only about one-sixth of news traffic—half a percent overall—goes to local news sources. With local traffic split between newspaper sites and television stations, local papers are left with just a quarter of a percent of time spent online—only about five minutes per capita per month in web user attention. Local newspaper traffic is just a rounding error on the larger web.

The bottom line is that newspapers cannot monetize an audience they do not have.

The problems with the myth of monetization do not stop there. Local sites have long asserted that their digital audiences were especially valuable because they were locally targeted. Such talk misses just how sweeping the digital revolution has been. The internet has turned traditional advertising economics on its head: it is hard for *any* small digital audience to be valuable to advertisers, no matter how locally concentrated that audience is (see chapter 3).

This book has called this the *advertising inversion*. Local media in the United States long thrived on the fact that, per person, local audiences were more valuable than national audiences. In the age of big data, however, this logic is reversed. The largest digital ad campaigns, on the very largest websites, can be far more efficient than the quaint geographic targeting that newspapers offer.[3] There is nothing newspapers can do to change this: it is simply the way the math works. The fact that data mining gets more accurate with larger audiences is as indelible as $2 + 2 = 4$.

Nor, as we saw in the previous chapter, can we pretend that tiny online-only or hyperlocal sites will save local journalism. This book has documented the myriad ways in which size matters online, and newspapers are at a profound disadvantage compared to firms like Google or Facebook or Amazon. Still, *relative* size matters, too. And one silver lining for newspapers is that they are larger than other local news competitors.

Even the clearest online local news success stories employ only a few reporters—far fewer than the number of laid-off newspaper reporters in their respective cities. Worrisome, too, is the fact local news sites have gained traction mostly in the affluent, social capital–rich communities that need them least. Employing a few reporters in Minneapolis or West Seattle or Austin is great. But the same model has failed in many other places, even when the journalism produced was high quality.

Newspapers thus remain by far the most important source for local news. Not only do they have the largest local news audience, but they also set the news agenda for local communities, breaking far more stories than local TV.[4] While newspapers are at a size disadvantage when competing with Google, the logic is reversed at the local level: newspapers have a leg up on any nascent digital-only competitors. Like it or not, solutions to save local journalism are about saving newspapers, and easing their transition to the digital news era.

The Dynamics of Digital News Audience

Journalists and editors today are provided with an enormous amount of data on their digital audiences. What newsrooms do with that data, however, varies enormously. Many newspapers still reward reporters for making the front page of the print publication over topping the most emailed list, as Nikki Usher found at the *New York Times*.[5] Others, such as the *Des Moines Register*, have integrated analytics much more strongly into their daily workflow.[6]

Even those newsrooms that aggressively adopted digital audience metrics, though, have missed an important part of the picture. Newspapers need to focus not on total traffic, but on stickiness—on a site's growth rate over time. In short, newspapers need to think dynamically.

To understand why thinking dynamically makes a difference, consider a simple puzzle: Why are there guest bloggers?

From the earliest days of blogging, it was clear that the blogs that grew fastest were those with many posts throughout the day. The frequency of new posts was a key factor in stickiness, and the reverse chronological order format highlighted the newest posts. Bloggers soon discovered that taking a break, or even a short vacation, was disastrous. Users who had made the sites part of their daily reading soon stopped visiting. Bloggers therefore might return from vacation to find that they had lost most of their audience.

Once bloggers returned, their audience would start to grow again, but from the new, much lower baseline. It could take weeks or months to recover the previous level of traffic. The solution to this conundrum was to find someone to take over the blog while its main author was away. Guest bloggers typically do not stop the process of audience decline entirely, but they ensure that traffic shrinks at a smaller rate.

Political blogging is one of the simplest possible forms of content creation online. It thus shows more clearly how traffic dynamics play out over time—and even how the entire blogging ecosystem can be subject to selection pressure.

Consider, for example, the remarkable decline of the solo blogger. In the early days of blogging—say, 1998 to 2003—the overwhelming majority of blogs were solo authored. Yet by the mid-2000s, a shift had taken place. The large majority of "A-list" bloggers either banded together to join superblogs, or moved themselves onto the site of a news organization. Today unaffiliated, solo-authored blogs are the exception in the top ranks of the blogosphere. Moreover, those solo bloggers who held out the longest were those with exceptionally high posting rates.

This is evolution, of a sort. Call it user selection, or digital Darwinism (more on this in the final chapter). On a given day, users will pick sites with slight advantages at slightly higher rates. Favored sites thus grow just a bit more quickly. Many solo-authored blogs that remained independent didn't go away—they just didn't grow as fast, and ended up being dwarfed by their competitors.

This example shows how strong selection for a single characteristic—frequency of posting—has transformed the landscape of blogging over time. Yet there has been strong selection pressure for a host of other site characteristics, too. All else being equal, users select faster sites over slower ones. Sites that better exploit social media, such as Buzzfeed and the Huffington Post, saw their audience balloon—though many of these gains are now at risk, as we will discuss shortly. Sites with good content recommendation engines have grown at the expense of competing outlets.

The evolutionary character of online media stems from the fact that digital audiences are more dynamic than those in traditional media. Traditional media outlets could count on a more-or-less built-in audience. This is particularly true for print newspapers, whose audiences were remarkably stable over years or even decades.

Yet for websites this is not true. Online audience growth or decline comes at the margins. It comes from making users more likely to view that extra news story, more likely to come back soon. These tiny marginal effects accrue exponentially over time.

FALSE SOLUTIONS

Understanding the dynamic character of digital audiences in this way has important consequences. To begin with, it forces us to reconsider the numerous "solutions" offered to fix local journalism.

In recent years, plans to save local journalism have become a cottage industry. These schemes have run the gamut. Newspapers have alternatively been told to put up paywalls, and to shut down their presses and embrace the open web. News organizations have been told to think smaller, through a sharper focus on local and hyperlocal content. Still others have proposed that newspapers stop trying to make a profit at all, with journalism relying on philanthropy, government subsidies, nonprofit status, or even citizen-produced content. More recently, the growth of mobile phones and especially tablet devices has been hailed as a "digital do-over" for newspapers.

These proposals are so contradictory that they cannot all be wrong. Some of these are bad ideas; others are zero sum proposals that help some newspaper organizations—and usually the *largest* news organizations—at the expense of others. If we take seriously the notion that web traffic is dynamic, though, each of these proposals is built on a misdiagnosis of the problem. Positive sum solutions, those that grow the digital pie for all news organizations, have remained elusive.

We will take each of these proposals in turn.

The Problem with Paywalls

Perhaps no "solution" in recent years has been as celebrated as the erection of paywalls. Yet the benefits of paywalls are often exaggerated, and their true costs overlooked.

Many have claimed that newspapers' failure to erect paywalls in the early years of the web was their "original sin,"[7] the originating mistake of the newspaper crisis. In fact, paywalls were tried repeatedly, by a host of different news organizations, from the mid-1990s onward.

Financial publications, such as the *Wall Street Journal* and the *Financial Times*, quickly had success with paywalled content. But for most other newspapers, experience after experience showed that paywalls were a failure: they reduced web traffic and online advertising to a single-digit percentage of previous levels, while generating little new revenue.

These longtime negative assessments of paywalls changed dramatically in 2011, when the *New York Times* implemented a so-called metered paywall. Visitors to the *Times* would be given a set number of articles a month, and when that quota was reached, individuals would be asked to subscribe. The result was widely heralded as a success. By the end of 2013, approximately 30 percent of the *Times'* subscription revenue—and 10 percent of total revenue—came from digital subscriptions.[8] The perceived success of the *Times* led to a rush by other newspapers to implement similar systems. By 2014 more than 450 U.S. dailies had implemented a metered paywall.[9]

It's easy to understand why "soft" paywalls have outperformed previous versions. As the traffic numbers discussed earlier suggest, most newspaper site-users visit just a few times a month. More than 90 percent of site visitors never hit the paywall in the first place. Metered paywalls thus ask for subscription revenue only from heavier users. Paywalls allow newspapers to perform price discrimination—to figure out which users are most willing to pay, and then ask that group alone to pony up.

But while metered paywalls provide a better series of trade-offs than hard paywalls, they are not a free lunch. The biggest cost of paywalls lies in lower traffic. This lost traffic doesn't manifest as a one-time drop. More insidiously, it comes in the form of permanently lower traffic growth. This missing audience may look small at first, but the audience gap compounds over time. Even the *Times* itself—as its leaked innovation report noted—for years saw a steady, paywall-driven traffic decline.[10] The 2016 election season finally saw significant traffic growth, though as of this writing it is too early to tell whether this boost will be sustained. Its digital subscription growth, though, has been fast enough to keep up with falling print revenue.[11]

No local newspaper, however, has enjoyed anything like the *Times'* digital success. The *Times* owns the nation's best news brand, and it produces an enormous, varied, and uniformly high-quality bundle of content. The Bezos-era *Washington Post* has been able to pull off a similar feat, improving its digital product and winning big jumps in digital subscribers. But the success of these national brands is hardly representative. A more typical case is Gannett, the nation's largest print newspaper chain. In 2013, after adopting paywalls at all eighty of its community newspapers, Gannett reported that it had signed up only a paltry 46,000 subscribers.[12] Digital-only subscribers have finally started to increase, with Gannett reporting 341,000 digital subscribers added as part of the "Trump bump."[13] But because so many of these digital subscriptions are steeply discounted, and because of rapid erosion in its print business, Gannett still saw a nearly 9 percent year-over-year drop in revenue per newspaper. Few, if any, of its properties are viable as digital-only enterprises without laying off most of their already-depleted current staff.

Paywalls, then, are not in themselves a solution to what ails local newspapers. Thus far paywalls have acted as a tourniquet, slowing the bleeding of revenue away from the newspaper's core print business. That does not mean they are, on balance, a bad idea—after all, sometimes a tourniquet is a medical necessity. But the costs of paywalls are large, even if they are paid on the installment plan.

The Open Web

Paywalls may have problems, but so do most of the proposed alternatives. While many have argued that newspapers need to "stop giving it away for free," a smaller group has argued that newspapers need to go in the opposite direction. Newspapers, according to this logic, need to become digital-only publications—and in the process, save the 40–50 percent of their overhead devoted to printing presses, ink, paper, and delivery vans. Papers have been told to shut down the presses, "burn the boats," and commit irrevocably to the web.[14]

There are many problems with this view. For starters, it grossly overstates both the *amount* of traffic the newspaper sites receive, and *how valuable* that traffic is. The myth of monetization is the central driver behind these digital-only fantasies. Even the *New York Times* as of this writing gets less than 40 percent of its total revenue from digital sources.[15]

Online-only proposals for local news depend on misleading figures about the amount of money raised by digital advertising. Some of the confusion comes from newspapers' creative accounting of online ad revenue. In fact, a large fraction of digital advertising comes as a part of a joint print advertising buy.[16] "Full price" digital ads are often sold only because they come with corresponding discounts on print advertising. If newspapers really did end their print editions, much of this joint digital revenue would quickly disappear too.

Philanthropy, Nonprofit News, and Government Subsidies

Some have proposed that philanthropy, nonprofit journalism, or government subsidies could help solve the local crisis. But here again, the data show problems.

Talk about philanthropic or nonprofit journalism has been animated by a few prominent national examples, such as award-winning nontraditional news organizations ProPublica and the Center for Public Integrity. Alternatively, a handful of local efforts such as the New Haven Independent, or statewide efforts such as the Texas Tribune, have attracted significant attention. But these examples should not distract us from the big picture: philanthropic journalism is inadequate to the size of the local journalism crisis.

As of 2013, philanthropic efforts, personal wealth, and venture capital funding together accounted for just 1 percent of local journalism funding nationwide.[17] Even if newspaper-focused philanthropy could grow tenfold, local journalism would be forced to continue with a skeleton crew. There is simply not enough money to replicate the previously mentioned national examples in thousands of local communities.

High-profile shutdowns of supposedly successful local media startups, too, have highlighted the risks of relying on a few wealthy individuals to bankroll journalism. Billionaire Joe Ricketts started New York City local news site DNAinfo in 2009, and in March 2017 acquired the Gothamist network of online-only newspapers with outposts in Los Angeles, Chicago, Washington, D.C., and San Francisco. But in November 2017, just a week after the New York staff had voted to unionize, Ricketts shut down all the sites without warning and fired all 110 staffers.[18] As the Gothamist example shows, relying on the goodwill of a single deep-pocketed benefactor creates substantial risks of its own.

Given the size of the problem, other commentators have proposed direct, large-scale government funding for journalism.[19] Government funding has one big advantage: it is the one proposed solution that might be able to provide resources adequate to the scale of the problem. Because news is a public good, government subsidies can be justified by the same logic seen in dozens of other policy areas, from national defense to public education. And while concerns that government funding would compromise press independence are worth considering, there are examples of state-supported journalism with a long track record of political independence.

Still, large-scale government subsidies remain a political nonstarter. Hundreds of millions of dollars—and likely many billions of dollars—would be required annually to sustain local journalism at even a fraction of current levels. That level of resources requires national government action rather than a state or municipal-level program. The odds of the U.S. Congress passing new, large-scale government press subsidies is remote.

Alternatively, some have proposed allowing newspapers to become nonprofit organizations, a strategy that combines government tax subsidies and philanthropic efforts. Certainly offering tax benefits to news organizations and their donors is more politically tractable than direct appropriations. Yet the nonprofit strategy, too, is more challenging than many have let on.

In fact, nonprofit status *would not* lower newspapers' tax bills—for the simple reason that they now pay little or no tax, because their gross revenue is almost always offset by deductible expenses.[20] Moreover, newspapers likely could not legally qualify as nonprofits without cutting most of their non-hard news content—*the most popular part of the paper!*—and eliminating the majority of their commercial advertising. This is a lot to give up on the dubious theory that new tax incentives will inspire generosity among nascent donors. Even if current owners could somehow be inspired to step aside, the shift would dramatically worsen the financial plight of nearly all local newspapers. Nonprofit organizations are also not allowed to endorse candidates in partisan elections, meaning that newspapers would have to abdicate a small but important traditional role.

Both philanthropic journalism and government subsidies would lessen, somewhat, the pressure of local news organizations to find an audience. But this relief is only partial. The *point* of funding local journalism is that *people supposedly read it*. Both private benefactors and government funders want to see impact for their dollars. Whether the funding comes from a congressional committee or a Wall Street financier, stable future funding streams require similarly robust digital audiences.

Tablet and Mobile Devices

Another source of hope for some has been the rise of mobile and tablet news. One group of commentators has proposed that the shift to tablets offers newspapers a "digital do-over,"[21] an opportunity to learn from previous mistakes.

Certainly the growth in tablet and mobile ownership is impressive. The iPhone and iPad, both category-defining products, date to just 2007 and 2010 respectively. By 2017, 77 percent of U.S. adults owned a smartphone, and 51 percent owned a tablet device.[22] News is a popular activity for those who own both sets of devices; 45 percent of Americans say they often get news on a mobile device, while an additional 29 percent say that they sometimes do.[23] Unfortunately, though, the shift to mobile and tablet news makes the situation of local newspapers even more precarious.

Early audience data seemed to show that tablet users produced higher news engagement than readers on other platforms. Much of this effect, however, has turned out to be just selection bias. Affluent, tech-savvy, Apple-loving early adopters are heavy news consumers, a group especially likely to rely on news apps. As tablets and smartphones have diffused, and mostly cheaper Android devices have taken over most of the market, the portion of users relying on apps for all or part of their news actually shrunk.[24]

Instead of being a dramatic departure, then, news consumption on tablets and smartphones mirrors patterns of news on the web. Mobile apps, just like traditional web news, send the overwhelming majority of their audience to large, national news organizations. Like the web overall, the audience for mobile and tablet news is broad but exceedingly shallow. Roughly 5 percent of time on mobile devices goes toward hard or soft news—only a modest improvement over browsing patterns on the broader web.[25] While the portion of time spent on mobile news has remained consistent, though, independent news apps have *declined* as Facebook, Twitter, and Apple News have all increased in importance.

In the case of smaller news organizations, the shift toward tablets and mobile devices has been especially bad. For local sites, mobile traffic produces only a fraction of the ad revenue that desktop visitors do. Mobile advertising dollars continue to grow at an explosive pace, but this has been of little benefit to local newspapers: Google and Facebook together control two-thirds of tablet and mobile advertising.[26]

The move to smartphones and tablets also dramatically raises development costs. Newspapers have no choice but to redesign their sites in order to perform well on these new platforms. The (usually few) computer programmers and web designers working for newspapers overwhelmingly know web-focused languages and standards like HTML, CSS, and JavaScript. By contrast, apps are real software programs mostly written in Objective C (for iOS) or Java (for Android), programming languages few newspaper staffers are proficient in.[27] Building a newspaper app usually requires outsourcing development to a specialized software firm at great cost.

Monitoring user experience across a profusion of platforms is now a nightmare. Newspapers must support both iPhone and Android operation systems, different app versions and browser versions for both phones and tablets, and even both "landscape" and "portrait" format depending on how the user is holding the device. Large, national news outlets can more easily absorb these new development and testing costs than local newspapers can.

This multiplatform development effort is difficult to avoid. There are few mobile-only news readers, and even most who do read news on their phone prefer other platforms when available.[28] Much news is still consumed at work,[29] a setting where users are not going to be using their iPads. The result has been an often-terrible smartphone and tablet experience for local newspaper readers. Some smaller publications have given up entirely on building their own news apps, concluding that the development and maintenance costs are simply not worth it.[30]

For publishers inclined to give up on the shift to mobile and tablets, Facebook, Google, and Apple have all introduced initiatives to make the shift easier—for a price. Facebook's Instant Articles, Google's Accelerated Mobile Platform, and Apple's reworked News app differ in key details, but all are explicitly sold as solutions to news publishers' failures on mobile devices. By offering to host others' content directly on their own servers, digital giants ensure faster load times, a more responsive user experience, and high-quality content recommendation tailored to users' personal tastes (more later on why these features are key).

For news organizations, participating in these initiatives is a devil's bargain. On one hand, it offers a way to reach mobile users even without a decent mobile site or app. On the other, participating means giving up 30 percent of revenue on these platforms in perpetuity, and losing further control of their audiences. Research shows that many users do not remember the outlet where they saw news, meaning participation in Instant Articles or Apple News risks further eroding already-diminished brand equity.[31] Local news sites have so little leverage, though, that many will opt to take a bad deal over no deal at all.

A "Pivot to Video"

The latest "solution" to the journalism crisis is the so-called pivot to video. Starting in mid-2016, and accelerating over the following year, a number of digital publications laid off print journalists with the stated aim of replacing them with video production staff. These cuts were especially noticeable at national digital news organizations that had previously been seen as success stories, including Mic, the Huffington Post, Vice, Mashable, and BuzzFeed.[32]

There are many problems with the pivot to video as a solution to the journalism crisis, particularly at the local level. The pivot to video is the Myth of Monetization in another guise—problematic even for national outlets, but especially so for local news sites. Moreover, the pivot to video has been driven not by audience demand, but by unfavorable shifts in the advertising landscape. As banner ad dollars have continued to decline, advertisers have increasingly shifted to video ads, with video ad spending expected to climb from $10 billion in 2016 to $18 billion in 2020. Much of this push has come from Facebook, which has aggressively pushed news organizations to produce video content for Facebook to sell ads against.[33]

A genuine shift to video is not a strategy for cutting costs. Adding a handful of still photos to a news story is cheap, particularly if a reporter is already reporting from location (more on this later). By contrast, video content is far more expensive per user minute. Even worse, the auto-playing videos that most pivoting sites depend on are annoying for users. In a remarkable aside, journalist Zach Shoenfeld even began his story on the pivot to video by apologizing for the autoplaying video accompanying the article.[34]

The pivot to video, then, is not a pro-growth strategy. Many sites that have pivoted strongly to video have seen dramatic drops in audience.[35] Even worse, as we have already seen, these audience losses are not a one-time drop. If the pivot to video lowers stickiness, losses will snowball over time.

The pivot to video highlights the vulnerability of digital news audiences of all kinds to policy shifts at Google or (especially) Facebook. Video content from news outlets finds its largest audience on YouTube and Facebook, not the organizations that made these videos. And just as has happened in the past, investment in video could be wiped out overnight if one of the digital giants realizes it is no longer in its interest (more on that risk later). One potential complication as of this writing, for example, is that Apple's Safari and Google's Chrome have announced that they will block the autoplaying videos that shifting news organizations depend on.

Local news sites, and especially local newspapers, have been less affected by the so-called video pivot. But the tea leaves from large digital outlets are nonetheless ominous, and local sites should be suspicious of diving headlong into video by laying off print journalists. And if the video pivot does indeed presage a crash in digital advertising—as publishers like Josh Marshall have argued[36]—local news sites are unlikely to be spared.

The bottom line is that *any* successful strategy for digital local news *requires* sites to grow their audience. This is obviously true for sites relying on ad revenue, though local newspaper sites cannot expect the same level of ad revenue per person that larger websites earn. Audience growth is just as essential for plans that rely on selling subscriptions. The current core audience of local news sites is too small to provide digital sustainability. Visitors who spend just a few minutes a month on a site are not good subscriber prospects. Even nonprofit journalism efforts need to demonstrate that their work is reaching a broad audience to ensure continued funding.

Digital Audiences and Stickiness: What Works?

If the raft of solutions proposed earlier won't work, what will? Growing local news audiences online boils down to two questions. First, how can we make news stickier compared to all of the other content—from Facebook to email to pornography to shopping to YouTube—that competes for users' attention? Second, how can local news sites make themselves stickier compared to the large national news brands that soak up 85 percent of the news audience?

Newspapers, fortunately, do not have to start from scratch. As previous chapters have shown, there is two decades of research on building habits of digital readership. For newspapers, though, this research reads like an indictment. Local newspaper sites, and *especially* smaller newspapers, have long broken all the rules for building a sticky site. Newspapers need to adopt better models of web traffic—and with them, the tools, techniques, and strategies that web giants like Google have used to get so big in the first place.

Perhaps the single most consistent finding, across the entire web traffic literature, is that *faster load times* lead to higher traffic. Dozens of studies have replicated this result across different sites and diverse categories of content.[37] Delays as small as a tenth of a second have been shown to reduce traffic.

News sites today still load more slowly than any other type of content.[38] When Google CEO Eric Schmidt visited the Newspaper Association of America convention in 2009, his first complaint about digital newspapers was that "the sites are slow. They literally are not fast. They're actually slower than reading the paper."[39]

In recent years, though, some newspapers have gotten the message. Upon buying the *Washington Post*, Amazon.com CEO Jeff Bezos immediately insisted on reducing load times by 40 percent.[40] Since 2013 the *New York Times* has revamped its entire web architecture, everything from hardware to server configuration to its massive code base, to meet new speed targets.[41] The *Guardian* has dropped page loads from 12.1 seconds to 3.2 seconds.[42] The *Guardian* now aims to load core page elements—layout, headline, and article text—in no more than a second, even for mobile users. These are welcome changes, but they need to be replicated at hundreds of other organizations' sites. The fact that large newspapers got there first underscores the size disadvantages that small newspapers face.

Beyond speed, *site design and layout* have a large effect on site traffic and on purchase decisions. Some of this effect might stem from simple aesthetic considerations. But there are other factors, too, that make design especially important in building traffic.

Several lines of research show that site design and layout are used as a proxy for site quality and trustworthiness.[43] Design also has big impacts on users' abilities to navigate the site. Sites that are easier to navigate generate more return traffic and higher sales.

Site design seems to have effects on e-commerce revenue that are even stronger than its effects on raw traffic—something that should give newspapers pause. The paywall push means that newspapers are now e-commerce sites, as they scramble to sign up digital subscribers. Amateurish and dated web designs are disastrous for readers' perceptions of quality.

Another key finding in the literature is the crucial importance of *personalized content recommendation systems* (see chapter 3). Automated, algorithmic recommendations are a cornerstone of most large digital firms. Companies like Amazon and Netflix depend on content recommendation systems for a large part of their revenue, and an even bigger chunk of their profits.

Lists of "most popular" or "most emailed" articles are increasingly common on news and media websites, and they can raise traffic numbers if given a prominent spot on the page. But lots of research shows that recommendation systems can do much better. Google News' personalized news recommendation system, for example, increased traffic on its homepage dramatically.[44]

To be sure, recommendation systems are challenging to get right. Newspapers have limited staff expertise in these areas, and they often have trouble paying the high salaries this specialized knowledge commands. But recommendation systems deserve more investment: few technical changes can provide such a big boost to news traffic.

Technical issues like site speed and content recommendation are both important, and underappreciated. But building local news audiences depends not just on site features, but also on creating compelling digital content. Here, too, the results are clear: sites with *more content, more frequently updated*, are much better at building traffic. Large story volume is necessary, though not sufficient, for strong audience growth.

It is impossible to build audience with a mostly static site. By definition, static sites provide no reason to come back. As one senior executive at the *Atlantic* remarked to the author, "If users return to your site and find that nothing has changed, you have just taught them to come back less frequently." As the economic models in chapter 4 suggest, high-volume sites can beat low-volume sites even when those low-volume sites produce quality content well matched to the desires of readers.

The importance of fresh content is at the heart of recent discussions of so-called "hamster wheel journalism." The evolutionary pressure for more content more often has led to enormous focus on immediacy, and breakneck production of short news articles. In a widely discussed *Columbia Journalism Review* article, Dean Starkman decried these trends:

> The Hamster Wheel isn't speed; it's motion for motion's sake. The Hamster Wheel is volume without thought. It is news panic, a lack of discipline, an inability to say no. It is copy produced to meet arbitrary productivity metrics.[45]

Certainly Starkman is right that these tactics sometimes challenge traditional news values (more on that later). But these approaches are not just "mindless volume"; rather, they are the considered outcome of much research on what builds readership. The reason these techniques have taken over is that the news organizations that adopted them have grown faster than their competitors.

All else being equal, news organizations generate more traffic with lots of little stories, rather than fewer medium-sized ones. Data from Chartbeat shows less than 10 percent of users scroll down to the end of a typical news article—most users, in fact, scroll only to the halfway point.[46] This suggests that reporters often spend lots of time writing words that barely get read.

Increasingly, these findings are shaping newsroom policies. On May 6, 2014, both the Associate Press and Reuters (apparently coincidentally) issued separate memos asking reporters to keep most news stories under five hundred words. In addition to saving reporters' and editors' time, the AP's memo decried a "sea of bloated mid-level copy," declaring that "our digital customers know readers do not have the attention span for most long stories and are in fact turned off when they are too long."[47]

To be clear, research *does not* suggest that newspaper sites can maximize their traffic by eliminating all of their long articles. As we saw in chapter 3, research on recommender systems—among other lines of evidence—suggests that the best solution for most newspapers is *diversity* in article content and format. Longer feature articles dominate the "most read" lists at most digital newspapers. But local newspaper sites cannot build up a consistent daily audience just with lengthy features. A constant stream of short pieces is the first step to ensuring site stickiness.

Newspapers can also make significant gains even by just better utilizing the content they already produce. In particular, *headline testing and improved lede-writing* can result in substantial jumps of traffic.

One of the most striking differences between successful online media startups like Upworthy, Buzzfeed, or the Huffington Post is just how much time their editors spend writing headlines. Upworthy, a site that often promotes news and public affairs content, requires its staff to write twenty-five headlines for every story.[48] Interviews with Buzzfeed staff emphasize the same point: a majority of writers' time is spent writing the headline and the lede, even for stories with original reporting. Practices at the Huffington Post are similar.

Headline testing comes with perils for newspapers. Going too far down the clickbait path, with catchy headlines that misrepresent the article, can diminish the newspaper's brand and squander readers' trust. Still, the headline is by far the most-read part of the article, and the greatest opportunity to alter reader behavior. Again and again, online aggregators have taken other organizations' reporting and received a tsunami of traffic by adding an A/B tested headline and a quantifiably catchier lede.

Recent shifts in news organizations suggest that there has been greater investment in this area, and a growing acknowledgement of the importance of headlines. Among other investments of the Bezos era, the *Washington Post* has created a new team focused on rewriting headlines to boost traffic.[49] Headline writing is not an either/or choice between the tepid titles of many newspapers, and Upworthy-style "You Won't Believe What Happened Next" headlines. Newspapers can write more compelling headlines while still respecting their values and their brand identity.

In the same vein, optimizing news sites for social media can also boost readership. Many news sites find that Facebook is their single largest source of traffic, something especially true for sites like Buzzfeed and Huffington Post. Capturing even a trickle from the Facebook firehose can produce wild traffic spikes.

Optimizing for social media is about more than adding "like" and "tweet" buttons to the website, or requiring reporters to tweet, or even testing for Facebook-friendly headlines. Most mid-size and larger local papers now have at least one person focused on social media, which is a start. But the features of a good social media story need to be considered at *every* part of the news process, from story pitch to final publication. Successful digital news sites deploy dedicated social media teams to coordinate this process, and push a set of promising stories hard in the hope that they go viral. With the Huffington Post, for example, different sections and "verticals" are required to pitch stories to the social media team several times a day.

Facebook-referred traffic is actually even more biased toward large, national news outlets than web traffic as a whole. Newspapers need not (and should not) turn their sites wholly over to social content, but they do need a consistent stream of suitable articles. Even modest improvements would have an outsize impact on closing the gap between local papers and national outlets.

To be sure, there are limits to the gains social media can provide. Facebook visitors are mostly flybys, looking at a single page and spending less than a minute.[50] Facebook users are difficult to keep for that second or third page-view, let alone convert to paid subscribers. News organizations overly dependent on Facebook visitors are quietly ceding a lot of control.

Moreover, the benefits of even substantial investments in social media can evaporate without notice when Facebook or Twitter changes its rules. One prominent example is the *Washington Post*'s Social Reader. The app promised to "share what you read with your friends," and it added recently read articles to subscribers' news feeds. Social Reader's developers got substantial technical help and encouragement from Facebook's own staff in building the app, and at its height the app had more than seventeen million users. Yet in late spring 2012, without any warning, Facebook redesigned its site and altered its algorithms. Traffic plummeted almost overnight.[51] By December 2012, the *Post* had killed the app. The *Guardian*'s similar social reader app, also created with help from Facebook, suffered the same fate.

Many news sites now have similar stories. As this book goes to press, traffic from Facebook to news sites has declined dramatically from its peak in 2015.[52] New initiatives, designed in part to address backlash to social media's role in the 2016 election, may mean further shifts in the outlets Facebook favors and the total traffic Facebook sends to news sites. Recent algorithm shifts have claimed other victims, too. LittleThings, a site focusing on sharing feel-good news on social media, shut down after seeing its traffic fall by 75 percent after the early 2018 Facebook algorithm change.[53]

Lastly, *multimedia content* attracts more traffic than plain-vanilla text articles. This includes interactive elements and graphics, which have long been associated with high levels of reader engagement. But text stories that include videos or even simple slide shows typically outperform text alone. Some digital news sites already aggressively exploit this finding. Huffington Post and Buzzfeed, for example, have both invested heavily in slideshows (HuffPo) and scrollable image galleries (Buzzfeed). The Huffington Post is so committed to the strategy that, as of this writing, it requires that slideshows accompany most of its articles.

In this regard, local newspapers are missing an easy layup. Print newspapers are strongly limited in the number of photos they can publish, but there are no such limits online. Digital newspaper articles are often text-only, when they would earn more time and attention from users with a handful of photos or even a gallery.

For content that requires higher levels of investment, though, this finding is more equivocal. The *New York Times*' story "Snowfall," about a deadly Washington state avalanche, is an oft-cited example of how digital news organizations can tell stories in new and sometimes dazzling ways. But "Snowfall" required enormous investment of journalistic resources. It took John Branch six months to report the story, plus the work of a photographer, a researcher, three video people, and an eleven-person (!) graphics and design team. Because the *Times*' content management system could not support the story's rich content, the entire page format had to be built from scratch. Some of this functionality might eventually be built into the newspaper's standard digital platform, making future projects easier. Still, the bottom line remains: multimedia content might generate more traffic, but it also requires more resources to produce. For many editors considering pieces of rich content, the opportunity cost is simply too high.

The Infrastructure of Growth

The tactics we've discussed so far are not a comprehensive list of everything newspapers could do to grow their digital audience, but they are a start. The median local newspaper could be improved in every single one of these areas. If money were no object, the prescription would be simple: do everything, and do it now.

Of course, for newspapers, money is *exactly* the issue, and everything-at-once is not a viable strategy. Newspapers need to think marginally, to identify the changes that provide the most stickiness for the least additional cost.

Some strategies are so important that they should be implemented immediately. For any editors reading this, please take note: If your site is slow, you are bleeding traffic day after day after day. If your site does not work seamlessly on mobile or tablet devices, drop everything and fix it. If your home-page does not have at least some visible new content every hour, you are throwing away traffic. Fix these problems first.

Beyond these easy gains, though, the challenges of increasing stickiness get harder and the trade-offs trickier. For these more difficult questions testing is crucial. Newspapers have to perform live experiments on their websites in order to learn what they need to know. There is no substitute for data.

A/B testing is the single most important strategy that has allowed today's web giants to get big in the first place. As chapter 2 explained, big digital firms—and a growing legion of small ones—test nearly everything that could impact the user experience. The impact of this testing is enormous. Ron Kohavi, formerly of Amazon and now head of experiments at Microsoft, credits online experiments with adding hundreds of millions of dollars to Microsoft's bottom line.[54] Less appreciated but just as important, similar sums were saved by catching damaging features before they went live. Large firms such as Google, Microsoft, and Facebook may have more than a thousand experiments running at any given time.

Though A/B testing began to be employed at sites like Amazon.com and Yahoo in the 1990s, most newspapers still lack the infrastructure or expertise to perform online experiments. First, newspapers must reliably track individual users, both over time and across devices. This is not trivial. If users cannot be reliably separated into treatment and control groups no experiment can work. Newsroom subscriptions to services like Omniture and Chartbeat are one way to solve the problem of tracking users.

Second, newspapers need to be able to serve altered versions of their web pages. Most newspapers currently do not have this ability. Cloud computing platforms such as Amazon Web Services or Google App Engine/Compute Engine are cheap and relatively easy to use—though of course newspapers need to make sure that load times and responsiveness are equal across different servers. Several vendors now provide A/B testing as a service with just a few extra lines of code on the target webpage. New open source multivariate testing platforms, such as Facebook's PlanOut,[55] are even more sophisticated, and cost nothing other than developers' time.

Increasingly, then, newspapers have no excuse not to perform online experiments. Many news organizations are already doing substantial online testing. Large online-only news outlets, news divisions that are part of larger digital firms (e.g., Yahoo!), and a few prestige news brands have invested heavily in measurement.

Yet even among this group there remains too little understanding of what exactly news sites should be optimizing for. This uncertainty can also be seen in missives about the journalism crisis, which are filled with vague, contentless calls for "innovation." Newspapers have been told to "experiment, experiment, experiment" without specifying what hypotheses these experiments are supposed to test.

Often discussions of A/B testing in the newsroom have dealt with the total traffic gained or lost. But this reflects old-media thinking, the notion that audiences are mostly stable, and that any changes to the site bring a near-immediate boost or drop to that total. To be most effective, A/B testing has to begin from the understanding that web traffic is dynamic. Newspapers are looking not for changes in their total traffic, but rather changes in their *growth rate*. Positive changes that make people more likely to come back, or more likely to view that extra article, compound over months and years. Tests of smaller effects need to run for weeks or even months in order to accurately gauge their impact.

Moreover, A/B testing makes it all too easy to optimize for the wrong thing. Consider one early *Washington Post* effort to test headlines. To its surprise, the *Post* found that headlines chosen for maximum clicks actually *lowered* total news traffic.[56] Dramatic headlines attracted a larger fly-by social media audience, but turned off those readers most inclined to visit the second or third article. This example emphasizes, again, the need to focus on robust metrics that are less likely to lead analysts astray.

Costs

Testing may be crucial, but it tells us only half of what we need to know in order to help online local news. Just as important is measuring the costs of pro-stickiness tactics. The good news is that, with the growth of cloud computing, there is no need for newspapers to spend tens of thousands of dollars upfront on new hardware—though newspapers must spend money to hire new staff, especially technical staff. But the question of costs goes beyond new financial outlays and requires deeper thinking about the altered economics of newspapers. Staff time, even more than money, is the most crucial scarce resource for news organizations.

A large fraction of newspapers' budgets go to fixed costs, such as rent and capital equipment. As one editor-in-chief remarked to the author, "I don't know the [total] cost of anything." Yet investing in growth, fortunately, does not require accounting for total costs. Like stickiness itself, the price of growth strategies needs to be calculated on the margin: How much *extra* will it cost to hire a blogger, or a new web analytics specialist? What is the additional development cost to make the site faster, or the extra expense to put a Twitter crawl on the front page?

The biggest line item is the hiring of new technical staff, especially software engineers, web designers, and analysts with statistics training. In the author's conversations with newspaper executives, several complained about the difficulty in attracting and retaining programmers and other technical staff. When pressed, though, this difficulty turns out not to be mysterious.

The software engineers whom newspapers need—those experienced with web-scale technologies in a live production environment—can command six-figure salaries at tech firms, plus bonuses, stock options, and other forms of compensation. Not only can the best programmers earn more elsewhere, the working environment at newspapers is often unattractive to technical staff. Software engineers want to work at companies that employ a cadre of peers, and that view their work as core to the organization's mission—not at firms where their coworkers ask them to fix the printer.

All of these barriers could be overcome if news organizations committed to spend what it takes. Newspapers need to get over their sticker shock, pay market-rate salaries to programmers and analysts, and fix the workplace issues that make retention of digital staff difficult. Newspapers understand that other technical investments, such as printing presses, are mission critical. If the presses do not work, the paper does not reach its readers. But lack of digital staff has the same effect: without smart design and constant testing, the paper loses most of its digital audience. *Technical staffers are just as much a distribution cost as printing presses*, and just as mandatory.

Spending more in-house on technology staff can also help newspapers change their broken site development models. Many newspapers practice web development through punctuated equilibrium. Site templates will be static for years, until the site is embarrassing enough to demand a refresh, and an outside firm is hired to undertake a redesign. The resulting update might be pretty (or not), but the key design decisions are rarely informed by a deep understanding of how traffic flows through the site. Internal staffers are best positioned to understand traffic flow, and to make the key design decisions. Without in-house technical expertise, it is hard to get good results from outside contractors, because no one in the organization can adequately oversee the quality of the contracted work.

Moreover, even if an outside firm does a good job, they usually leave the work half-finished. The experience of Google, Yahoo!, and other digital firms shows that *optimizing* a web design often has a bigger impact than the initial shift to a new layout. The launch of a site design needs to be followed by many rounds of testing and tweaking, squeezing every ounce of additional stickiness out of the new site template. Design contracts often do not allow for this crucial final stage of the process, and many newspapers lack the expertise to carry out this work themselves.

Chain newspapers can suffer from similar problems, even when they do not hire outside firms. In theory, multi-newspaper firms should enjoy economies of scale in web design and analytics. Instead, though, newspaper companies often produce one-size-fits-none websites, in which all of the chain's newspapers are shoehorned into a single web template. Any design element needed by *one* of the firm's newspapers is imposed on *all* of them. The result is cluttered, ugly, and difficult to navigate—far from the clean, streamlined, even elegant designs that successful sites have gravitated toward.

On the content production side, as well as the technical side, most newspapers need to make hires and shift staff to new roles. Most local newspapers still do not have any high-volume bloggers, or a clear social media strategy. Many have hired a social media editor, but that alone does not a strategy make. Few local newspapers feature constantly updated content on their front page. Almost none have formal programs to identify and foster key digital skills among their existing reporters and editors. With the right metrics, for example, newsroom contests to pick the best-performing headlines can identify top performers and help newsroom staff as a whole improve their skills.

Even many newspapers that talk a good game about digital strategies for improving stickiness have their institutional incentives backward. Hundreds of newspapers fill their digital journalism jobs with their cheapest staffers, often even interns. But the data show that these jobs are among the most critical for building readership. This is the equivalent of an NFL team spending tens of millions on its receivers and offensive line, while using an undrafted free agent at quarterback. Salaries and nontangible rewards both have to shift, so that the best staffers—not just the newest or youngest or cheapest—are the ones filling high-impact roles.

It would be nice to think that newspapers could adopt growth-driven strategies just by picking up a few strategic hires. In reality, most local newspapers will need to make this shift through a combination of key hires, shifting existing staff, and—if revenue declines continue —layoffs. For the last category, understanding which staff to lay off is crucial.

Some digital journalists succeed by producing the hard news and showcase reporting that is core to the organization's mission—stories that have an outsize influence on the paper's brand regardless of their raw readership. Other digital journalists generate high readership among the paper's core audience, the heavy readers who visit habitually and are the best candidates for digital subscriptions. Still other journalists reach a broad but shallow audience, bringing in a few page views each from a wide cross-section of the community. A few digital journalists rank highly in two or even three of these categories. Most succeed at just one. And many digital journalists, unfortunately, rank poorly compared to their colleagues on all three metrics. These journalists produce little hard news, while attracting neither broad nor deep readership. They contribute neither home runs, nor a regular drumbeat of base hits.

These are the cases where a change must be made, and the problem diagnosed and fixed. Poor editorial supervision and story assignment is a common culprit. Better social media support, stronger headlines, and more photos can broaden a reporter's readership. But if the problem persists, the journalist or responsible editor needs to be reassigned—and if that does not work, he or she needs to be let go.

Hiring new staff can be expensive, and laying off current staff painful—but neither of these is the largest cost of retooling for digital growth. The biggest price by far comes from opportunity cost: reassigning staff to new roles, reporting some stories instead of others, trading off a dozen short articles for a single long feature, investing in some site features while neglecting other potential improvements. Growing a newspaper's digital audience requires the willingness to forgo much of what it is already doing. Some of these changes will inevitably be unpopular, both within the newsroom and among some in the current newspaper audience. But testing gives us the best assurance possible that these sacrifices will be worth it.

COOPERATION

A/B testing is indispensable, but it is expensive in terms of staffing and newsroom resources. One strategy to defray these costs is broader industrywide cooperation.

Online testing is particularly challenging for smaller organizations. Per reader, experiments are more costly with a smaller audience. The *New York Times* or the *Guardian* can spread the costs of testing infrastructure and hiring analytics staff across many hundreds of thousands of readers, while a mid-sized metro daily cannot. Even worse, the math of testing itself creates a challenge. Big firms like Google and Yahoo! have been able to test thousands upon thousands of potential improvements. Often these changes are small or seemingly trivial, such as a site's color scheme, or a margin's width in pixels. Yet the aggregate effect of this testing is profound. Nearly every element of these firms' web pages, every piece of their user experience, has been tested and optimized.

Newspapers, especially smaller-circulation ones, will never be able to detect such tiny effects. Web traffic is highly variable. Some of this variation in traffic is systematic, such as higher traffic on weekdays versus weekends, or a boost in traffic surrounding an election, or a particular story that goes viral. But most of these ups and downs are just random noise.

This noise means that two groups of randomly selected readers will never show exactly the same level of traffic growth over time. The treatment group will always be at least a little higher or lower than the control group. The challenge is to discern whether the gap between treatment and control is a genuine treatment effect or just the result of chance. Big sites like Google and Yahoo can be confident that even very small gaps between treatment and control represent real differences. If Google and Yahoo! have ten thousand times more traffic than a typical mid-sized newspaper, they can detect effects roughly one hundred times smaller.

Because of the statistical challenges of detecting small effects, and their limited analytic resources, newspapers need to join forces, sharing research and expertise with other news organizations. The advantages of cooperation are many. Newspapers can pursue a far broader research agenda and limit redundant effort. Analytics expertise is one of the scarcest resources in journalism, and sharing allows these skills to be leveraged highly. Joint work provides greater statistical power—especially important with smaller audiences and long testing windows—and it ensures that important results replicate.

Of course, much informal sharing already takes place. Ideas and research are shared on Twitter and blogs, at industry conferences, through email, and in one-on-one conversations. Newspapers such as the *New York Times* and the *Guardian* have been laudably forthcoming about their research findings and technical platforms (see previous discussion). The American Press Institute, the Knight Foundation, and the Pew Research Center, among several other industry groups and academic centers, have fostered sharing of research across news organizations.

Still, none of this is a substitute for more organized efforts. Newspapers need a forum through which they can outline a common research agenda, share results, receive peer feedback, and synthesize findings. Failed experiments need to be highlighted, too, in order to avoid the file drawer problem. Such a research group could be organized through a professional association, such as the American Association of News Editors or the Online News Association. Alternatively, foundations could provide the organizing role.

In many industries firms are understandably reluctant to share core business information, or to collaborate in building common infrastructure. But local newspapers are in an unusual situation. They rarely compete directly with one another. The *Seattle Times* is not a rival to the *Tampa Bay Times*, though both are now facing off against sites like CNN.com and Yahoo! and Buzzfeed. Moreover, as reporters and editors themselves loudly declare, journalism is not just another business. Journalism's commitment to openness is part of what makes it worth saving. Harnessing that public-spirited ethos, and being willing to share with their peers, is essential if newspapers are to adapt to the digital age.

The Last, Best Hope

The plight of newspapers is far worse than many journalists and editors realize. Local newspapers' digital audiences are simply too small to be sustainable as print ad revenue continues to shrink. No matter which strategy newspapers pursue—from paywalls to nonprofit journalism to doubling-down on mobile devices—digital audience growth is essential.

It is unclear how large the paying audience for digital local news can ever be. Ironically, though, the fact that newspaper websites *as websites* have long been terrible is one reason for optimism. Longstanding errors provide an opportunity for rapid improvements.

Doing better requires newspapers to think differently about web and mobile audiences. Newspapers need to invest heavily in measurement and online experiments. Just as important, they need to rethink what they are optimizing for: not raw traffic, but audience growth. Small gains in stickiness can compound enormously over time.

The strategy outlined in this book is unabashedly data-driven, which may be cause for suspicion. Some argue that a myopic focus on metrics has already damaged journalism, that page view–chasing has betrayed journalism's core values and alienated loyal readers. A renewed focus on metrics might be seen as an excuse to turn newspapers into a thousand local editions of Buzzfeed, complete with curiosity gap headlines and puppy slideshows and "Which local official are you?" quizzes.

These complaints about measurement, though, have the issue backward. Journalists portray themselves as indispensable public servants: as Bill Kovach and Tom Rosenstiel aptly put it, "The primary purpose of journalism is to provide citizens with the information they need to be free and self-governing."[57] But audience numbers are so shockingly low that newspapers are clearly failing in their civic role.

The silver lining is that journalists have a new toolkit with which to diagnose and mend the problem. Big scientific leaps have often followed improvements in measurement, as when Newton's laws followed the invention of the telescope. Journalism today is at such a juncture. Journalists no longer have to rely on the so-called "imagined audience" or faulty conventional wisdom. For the first time, individual journalists can directly measure the readership their stories receive. With practice, the hope is that journalists can distill broader lessons about how to attract readers to the stories that really matter.

Maximizing the wrong metrics can be disastrous, as examples discussed here show. But metrics can also be used to enlarge the audience for hard news, if newspapers are willing to put in the effort. Nearly every story characteristic can be tested: which headlines keep readers, which framing is most compelling, even which specific paragraphs chase away readers. As newspapers look beyond crude measures such as page views, and instead focus on deeper metrics such as reader attention and compounded audience growth, they can narrow the gap between expediency and their ideals.

That is not to say that tough trade-offs can always be avoided. But making smart compromises between commercial pressures and democratic values requires data, and most smaller newsrooms today are still flying blind. Do those slideshows of kittens expand the hard news audience, or do they crowd out coverage of the mayor's race? How much does a section's readership suffer when a reporter goes off to pursue a month-long investigation? If we want to maximize hard news readership, should reporters spend less time reporting and more time writing decent headlines? Every newsroom needs to be asking these questions. We cannot get the ethics of digital journalism right without first getting the facts about digital audience. Empowering editors and journalists begins by mapping out what exactly the costs and benefits of each tactic are.

Of course, all of these ethical debates are moot if newspapers do not survive in a recognizable form. The decline in the economic health of local newspapers is so severe that there are no guarantees. Traffic dynamics mean newspapers are racing the clock: readers lost today get ever harder to replace tomorrow.

Growing the digital newspaper audience is still possible—but we need to hurry.

The "Nature" of the Internet

The best products don't win. The ones everyone use[s] win. I know a lot
of people don't want to hear this.... But make no mistake, growth tactics
are how we got here.
    —Facebook Vice President Andrew Bosworth, internal memo titled
                                    "The Ugly," June 18, 2016

In February 1996 John Perry Barlow, best known as a lyricist for the
Grateful Dead, published a short manifesto titled "A Declaration of the
Independence of Cyberspace." In turgid prose that recalled Hegel more
than Jefferson, Barlow asserted that the internet was immune to regulation
and entirely divorced from the "Industrial World."[1] The internet was "the
new home of Mind," where "whatever the human mind may create can
be reproduced and distributed infinitely at no cost. The global conveyance
of thought no longer requires your factories to accomplish." Governments
could not hope to govern cyberspace, because the internet was not just a
technology but "an act of nature."

Barlow was hardly the first to invoke "natural" laws or biological
metaphors in talking about the internet. Southern California's tech culture
had been shaped by both *Whole Earth Catalog*-tinged counterculture[2] and
Joseph Schumpeter-inspired "evolutionary" capitalism. But Barlow's trea-
tise gave such views a wider audience. The essay was quickly mirrored on
forty thousand other sites, making it arguably the most impressive example
of viral content up to that point. Today the Declaration is often cited as
the zenith of 1990s techno-utopian silliness. Barlow himself, when asked

about the declaration in a 2004 interview, quipped that "we all get older and smarter."[3]

In crucial ways, though, we have *not* gotten smarter about the internet. Misconceptions about the "nature" of the internet are still the explicit rationale for our public policies. We hear them on the lips of the secretary of state and the chairman of the FCC and even the president of the United States. We read them in peer-reviewed publications and best-selling books. Half-trillion-dollar corporate Goliaths worry loudly about the threat they face from students in a garage—often falsifying their own underdog origins in the process.[4]

The problem in writing about "the" internet, then, is that there is not one internet but two. The first is the actual-existing internet most of us use daily, if not constantly. The second is what we will call the *imaginary internet*—the idealized, fictionalized, reified internet that "everyone knows" is democratizing communication and economic life. Again and again, our understanding of the real internet has been obscured by unfounded faith in the idealized one.

The gap between the imagined internet and the real one is not just a matter of emphasis or optimistic tone or rhetorical flourish. As this book has shown, confusing the two internets leads to basic factual errors.

On the imagined internet, many still suppose that audiences are spread thinly across tens of thousands of outlets. On the real internet, by contrast, a third of web visits go to the top ten firms. While the former FCC chairman Tom Wheeler imagines that the internet "spread[s] out ... economic activity,"[5] the real one lets two firms control more than half of online ad revenue. Trump administration FCC chair Ajit Pai similarly imagines that the internet provides "countless" online local news sources, while the FCC's real-world data shows most Americans have just a few real local online choices. On the imagined internet, personalization favors small sites. On the real one, scale economies and the mathematics of targeting mean that only the biggest sites can personalize ads and content efficiently. The imagined internet might be "post industrial," but on the real internet nearly all the profits go to those firms building giant factories. Scale economies dominate whether the heavy machinery is refining data or iron ore.

The imaginary internet also misleads us about the dynamics of digital audiences. On the imagined internet, audience churn is a leveling force.

In reality, unequal churn is what *creates* such intense digital concentration. The real web changes far faster at the bottom than at the top, while the largest sites enjoy relative security. On the imagined internet, switching costs are trivial and competition is "only a click away." On the real one, customers are *more* loyal to digital stores than brick-and-mortar retailers.

Our misunderstanding of the internet is especially consequential for news and civic content. On the imagined internet, the local newspaper audience is "larger than ever"; on the real one, attention to local news is just a rounding error. On the imagined internet, hyperlocal sites are supposed to capture small-but-valuable audiences; on the real internet, small-but-valuable audiences are an oxymoron. The economics of advertising, which used to pay higher per-reader rates to local versus national media, has been turned on its head.

Our fictionalized version of the internet does not even get the technical architecture right. The imagined internet is still a peer-to-peer network just as it was in 1995. Today on the real internet, though, most traffic never touches the public backbone. Small sites are not remotely equal in their computing hardware or their software stack or their fiber—unless of course they depend on digital giants like Amazon or Google to do the hosting for them, making the inequality even more profound. Content delivery networks and paid peering mean that big sites take a shortcut to users.

One goal of this book is to bridge the gap between the imaginary internet and the real one—between the internet so many celebrate and the more important, more complicated, and less equal internet now interwoven into our lives. Pointing out specific areas where reality fails to match up to our assumptions is the first step in that process.

But mythbusting means little if it cannot replace vapid folk theories of the internet with something better. Ironically, clearer thinking about the internet comes from taking all this talk about the"nature" of the internet seriously.

AN EVOLUTIONARY MODEL OF AUDIENCES

The use of biological metaphors has a long history in the rhetoric of technology, from Stewart Brand's focus on human "co-evolution" with technology to Schumpeter's discussion of technology change as "industrial mutation."[6] Recent communication scholarship on media "niches"[7] and "audience evolution,"[8] too, has relied on biological language to explain important shifts in the media landscape.

Yet if we want to understand online audiences, it is worth returning to Darwin's thought—and taking it rather more literally than previous scholarship has. Building upon what we've seen in earlier chapters, I propose an *evolutionary model of digital audiences*. Like Darwin's original argument, this model can be reduced to a series of premises that build on each other.[9]

Let's start with the first premise: *almost all sites online can support more audience than they currently have*. The technical architecture of the web allows near-instant audience growth. Audiences are not limited by printing capacity or broadcast range. Well-designed websites can stay up even when ten or even a hundred times the number of expected visitors arrive.

Second, *categories of content show stable audiences*. The collective audience share for news or weather or shopping has been remarkably consistent over time. The biggest audience shifts have been about opening up new content niches (e.g., YouTube and Netflix) or using the internet in previously difficult situations (e.g., smartphone and tablet devices). But the portion of audience going to news content, for example, has held steady at roughly 3 percent for twenty years.

Third, for both consumers and websites themselves, *resources are limited*. Work, family, and sleep compete for users' attention, as do myriad other types of media. Site revenue is limited. Staffing is limited, with true talent and expertise in even shorter supply.

Put these three premises together and the result (fourth premise) is *fierce competition for attention*. The notion that the web produces a no-holds-barred fight for audience is already something of a cliché, as we saw in chapter 1. But while severe competition for online audiences undeniably exists, the character and consequences of that competition have been grossly misunderstood.

Audience competition online has been assumed to result from a radical leveling of the playing field. Competition is so brutal, the argument goes, because it is so equal. Clay Shirky, for example, channels Thomas Hobbes in arguing that online competition is "the war of each against all."[10] It is a rare and revealing slip—not least because Hobbes himself notes that scientific endeavors and the "arts grounded upon words"[11] are a key exception to his claims about human equality. Most analysis of digital audiences has stopped at this point, with supposedly self-evident equality producing an intensely egalitarian melee.

But following the rest of Darwin's argument shows why equal competition cannot last. Consider the fifth premise: with limited resources, *websites differ in traits that allow them to build audiences.* As we have catalogued, some site characteristics matter enormously in the task of audience building. Site load time matters. Technical architecture matters. Layout, branding, and user learning matter. Countless other characteristics matter too—some across nearly all websites, others only within a given online niche.

Lastly, *sites with favorable traits grow their market share over time.* Favorable traits make a site stickier: they make users more likely to visit, more likely to stay longer when they do. For convenience we will term this model *audience selection*, after natural selection in biology. The label of audience selection may sound empowering, even meritocratic. But in fact, audiences rarely get to choose among many equally good options.

Darwin's account left out many key details, and indeed it was written a century before the discovery of DNA. But it still carried enormous power to connect macroscale biology—species and ecosystems—with the pressures on individual organisms. In Darwin's account, his eureka moment came while reading Thomas Malthus. Malthus argued that society is doomed to outstrip its food supply because human population grows geometrically. If every couple has four surviving children, for example, the population will double every generation. In a flash, Darwin realized that natural selection would not be cumulative, but *compounded*: the population of organisms with favorable traits multiplies with every succeeding generation. Natural selection is powered by exponential growth.

The central challenge of internet scholarship is similar. Scholars have publicly struggled to connect the macro structure of digital audiences with micro-level behavior—individual choices about what to click on, read, watch, and listen to.[12] This book shows that the intuitive leap is the same for digital media as for biology: to understand that even tiny daily differentials in audience growth compound exponentially. Hundreds of features on a site influence how long users stay, and how likely they are to return—everything from the speed at which the page loads to the general layout to the freshness of the content. Tiny effects multiply with every user visit, and publishers with above-average stickiness grow their market share over time. This process is responsible for the macro-level structure of the web.

Audience selection thus means that growth is a function of how large a site's audience *already is*. Only current visitors get to appreciate a bounty of fresh content or speedy load times. Moments of competitive equality are thus fleeting. A small early edge can snowball into an insurmountable advantage. Half a percent more in daily growth can turn into a fivefold size advantage in less than a year.

The news gets worse for small organizations. As we have seen, stickiness is expensive. Large sites not only have a bigger user base across which to spread those costs, but they also earn more per visitor. The same user is worth much more to Facebook or Google than she is to a local newspaper. Treating audience churn as an organic and evolutionary process, then, does not lead to radical leveling. The internet's destructive energies—"creative" or not—are not applied equally.

Digital Distribution Is Never Free

This evolutionary model of traffic has profound consequences for every aspect of digital media. First and foremost is this: when competition for attention is a ceaseless Darwinian struggle, *digital distribution is never free*.

Economist Milton Friedman (among others) was fond of the phrase "There's no such thing as a free lunch." Friedman's point was that someone somewhere is always paying the cost of a "free" meal. When American pubs before prohibition invented the practice of "free" lunches, those lunches were paid for by raising the cost of drinks—and by making the free food extremely salty, so that patrons would need high-priced drinks to quench their thirst.

The same principle holds for digital audiences. Someone always has to pay the costs of digital distribution—which is to say, *the costs of audience building*. The billions of dollars spent on server farms and software platforms are distribution costs. Site design and mobile app design are distribution costs, since clunky interfaces stunt audience growth. Fresh content is a distribution cost, since few readers want to read the same piece twice.

Distribution costs also include search costs, which are spread across digital giants, smaller publishers, and users alike. Google and Facebook pay by filtering through billions of items to find those most likely to satisfy users. Publishers pay search costs, too, by optimizing their content for visibility in search engines and social sites, or simply by buying advertising. Buzzfeed and the Huffington Post pay millions of dollars to ensure that Facebook features their stories—money that goes to everything from site design to content management platforms, testing infrastructure to writers' salaries. These are distribution costs just as surely as if Facebook was paid directly to publish Buzzfeed's content. Not least of all, individual consumers pay part of these costs by spending the effort to find content that suits their interests.

These distribution costs upend our understanding of the internet as a neutral platform. The Internet Protocol won out over early competing network standards in large part because of its minimal, bare bones approach. A reliance on "rough consensus and running code" meant that the internet was already running on millions of machines while corporate or government-backed alternatives were still on the drawing board.[13]

But the internet's minimalism is now a critical weakness. With key functionality for audience-building missing, digital publishers are forced to rely on proprietary platforms: Google, Facebook, the iOS and Android operating systems, even Amazon's AWS and Microsoft's cloud hosting services. Every recent rapidly growing publishing upstart—from Buzzfeed to the Huffington Post, Gawker to Upworthy to Vice to Vox.com—has been utterly dependent on these private platforms.

The most important question is this: *do small publishers have a reasonable chance to build an audience*? Today the answer is no, not without help from big digital firms.

Political Voice

These expensive but unconventional distribution costs challenge our notions of internet openness, and force us to reconsider an enormous volume of internet scholarship.

Hundreds of pieces of scholarship have claimed that the internet expands political voice, and makes it cheaper for citizens and groups to reach audiences. In the words of Jennifer Earl and Katrina Kimport, the internet is supposed to provide "cost affordances" to groups, individuals, and small-scale publishers.[14] Yet Darwinian competition for attention has destroyed most of these cost affordances over time. To be sure, there has been enormous *shifting* of distribution costs. Google and Facebook invest billions in their platforms, which can be leveraged by myriad groups and publications for audience building. Some groups and organizations can even pay for audience building in nontraditional currencies. But it is a profound mistake to see digital distribution as cheap or even "free."

Expensive distribution helps explain continuing inequalities in digital participation. Many studies continue to find that the political internet remains a "weapon of the strong."[15] Blogs hosted on independent sites have been pushed to the brink of extinction (see chapter 7), with evolutionary dynamics funneling political discussion to a few popular sites. While this is a partial check on a fragmented public sphere, it limits the shelf space for political debates and curtails much of the internet's promised openness.

The same difficulties are visible in the organizational layer of politics. Interest groups especially are supposed to benefit from the cost affordances of the internet. Work by Trevor Thrall, Dominik Stecula, and Diana Sweet, though, has found that cost affordances are minimal, and that interest groups actually find it *more* difficult to attract public attention in the digital media environment.[16] David Karpf's book *Analytic Activism* has similarly shown that new data-driven political organizing benefits from massive scale.[17] Fearsome attention competition means that it is still difficult for small-scale activists to achieve public notice.

Peer Production of Content

If attention competition handicaps political groups, it is especially discouraging for peer production of civic content.

Several of the most widely cited works of internet scholarship have claimed that the internet would make distributed content production commonplace. Loose collections of citizens would be able to function as media outlets, publishing civic information, political opinions, and even original reporting. Wikipedia and political blogs have both been invoked repeatedly as successful examples of distributed content creation.

Yet as work by Yochai Benkler, Aaron Shaw, and Benjamin Mako Hill has noted, the question is not whether peer production is possible, but instead under what conditions is peer production *likely to succeed*?[18] Again and again, real-world peer production of content has been unable to compete with traditional corporate models.

Evolutionary audience models explain this failure by highlighting the intractable problem of stickiness. Fast load times, good web designs, A/B testing platforms, streamlined mobile apps, constantly updated content—among dozens of other features—are far easier to achieve with a hierarchical organizational structure. Even sites that depend heavily on users to make and filter content, such as Facebook, Twitter, and Reddit, are for-profit corporations that rely on command and control for important decisions—not to mention billions of dollars of private capital.

Scholarship on peer production of content is much like the study of island ecologies to understand evolution.[19] Wikipedia has from its inception enjoyed rare protection from corporate competitors. Encyclopedia Brittanica and even Microsoft Encarta could not match Wikipedia on price, speed, or coverage of popular culture. But Wikipedia's highly unusual niche undermines the claim that peer production can be a model for other types of content. Wikipedia is the digital equivalent of the dodo bird: a fantastic evolutionary solution that works only when isolated from competition.

INTERNET GOVERNANCE, NET NEUTRALITY, AND ANTITRUST

Better models of digital audiences are crucial, too, in reframing scholarship on internet governance.

Over the past two decades, scholarship has highlighted the way in which states, private firms, and other institutions exert power over the internet. One worry has been corporate actors' ability to shape the information ecosystem with little public debate.[20] As Robert G. Picard argues, big digital firms "are increasingly shifting the mechanism of control and influence over media from public to private spheres, reducing the ability of the public to influence it through democratically determined policy, and making public oversight of media and communication systems and operations more difficult."[21] This influence stems partly from the fact that seemingly neutral technical decisions often reinforce power relationships:

in Laura DeNardis's words, "Arrangements of technical architecture are arrangements of power."[22]

This book adds to the internet governance literature in several ways. First, evolutionary models of traffic strengthen the link between big firms' *architectural* power and their *economic* power. From firms' perspective, their ability to control stickiness—to ensure their own growth—is key to their influence. This book provides a better explanation of how audience concentration emerges, and how firms' investments and technical choices serve to entrench their own position.

Some media scholars have worried that because "content is king,"[23] the internet will reproduce concentration among content producers. This belief in the market power of content producers has long been the centerpiece of academic critiques about media concentration. For example, Benjamin Bagdikian's 2004 book *The New Media Monopoly* noted with particular concern that five large content firms controlled 80 percent of media revenue.[24] Scholarship by Eli Noam, among others, has challenged this view, arguing that distribution not content production is the crucial bottleneck, and that this gap will only grow in the future.[25]

This book is similarly worried about monopolies in distribution—but it argues that *distribution must be considered more broadly still.* Distribution is not just ISPs and physical pipes, but rather *all* the components of stickiness that go into audience building. Big firms like Google and Facebook need to be seen as *attention utilities.* They provide crucial distribution architecture for which there are no adequate substitutes. Being demoted in the news feed or the results page has dire consequences for content producers.

Net Neutrality and Beyond

A broader understanding of infrastructure is crucial, too, in understanding renewed debates about net neutrality. The evolutionary, constantly-compounding audience models in this book offer a new and better explanation of why net neutrality is both *indispensable* and *insufficient* for an open internet.

The founding myth of the internet, and later the World Wide Web, was that the technology treated every computer online and every packet of data equally.[26] Yet internet service providers have repeatedly tried to create a "fast lane" for certain favored companies who pay for better access to customers.

In February 2015 the Federal Communication Commission issued a major decision in support of network neutrality. The FCC order prohibited internet providers from blocking lawful content, throttling sites or types of usage, and charging for traffic prioritization. And unlike previous FCC efforts, the 2015 decision reclassified internet traffic under Title II, the core part of its mandate under the Communications Act of 1934. The 2015 net neutrality order, though, provided only a fleeting victory. With the election of Donald Trump, and the elevation of Ajait Pai from commissioner to chairman, the FCC repealed net neutrality protections in December 2017.

Evolutionary models of digital audiences help explain why the end of net neutrality enforcement is such a dire threat to content producers, and especially *smaller* content producers. If service providers like Comcast and Time Warner and Verizon can require publishers to pay for fast-loading sites and apps, content producers will be forced to pay up or face a growing audience gap. Comcast and Time Warner are thus in a position for a mafia-style shakedown: "Nice site you've got here, it would be a shame if load times increased and you had snowballing traffic losses." To be sure, ISPs have repeatedly argued that any impact would be small, a claim belied by the millions of dollars they have spent opposing the regulation. If this book has taught us anything, it is this: small effects compounded hundreds of times over are *not* small effects.

The Trump FCC's repeal of net neutrality is discouraging. Yet one of the core lessons of this book is that *net neutrality alone is not enough*. Even if we could return the internet to its original end-to-end architecture, that would not be enough to eliminate the concentration of audience and power in a few big sites. Ensuring an open internet is thus not just a job for the FCC or international telecom regulators. It requires help from a broader set of regulators, too.

Strengthening Antitrust Enforcement

Net neutrality, then, is not enough on its own. In order to maintain meaningful internet openness, regulators in the United States and the European Union need to aggressively enforce existing antitrust law.

Understanding the compounded, evolutionary nature of digital audiences is crucial for that effort. The ability of firms to control their own growth is a key element of monopoly power.

The United States and European Union account for roughly 80 percent of Google and Facebook's revenue, making these two markets key for shaping the firms' behavior. Though basic antitrust laws are similar on both sides of the Atlantic, since 2013 there has been a growing split about how to apply the law—a disagreement with enormous consequences.

U.S. law defines a firm as a monopoly if it has "significant and durable market power—that is, the long term ability to raise price or exclude competitors."[27] In the first part of this test—the ability to alter prices—the market power of these firms is obvious. Google, Facebook, Microsoft, Amazon, and Apple all have market share far beyond the established thresholds for market power in their core business. All except Amazon have produced 30+ percent profit margins year after year after year, an impossibility in competitive markets with unrestricted entry.[28]

Yet U.S. regulators have been gun shy even when firms have been caught red-handed. In 2012, for example, Google was caught promoting its own products and services over those of competitors, even when its own data showed that users preferred outside content.[29] This is textbook anticompetitive behavior, and Federal Trade Commission staff concluded that there had been "real harm to consumers and to innovation." Yet in 2013 the full Commission voted against taking the case to trial, instead settling for a weaker settlement that left Google free to demand exclusive contracts with partner sites.

Some raised the specter of political influence: the *Wall Street Journal* documented extensive contact between Google and Obama administration officials in the weeks before the FTC's decision. But when a key confidential FTC report was accidentally leaked, it became clear that Google's mythmaking operation played a key role too. Even in a report expected to be kept confidential, the FTC's lawyers blithely repeated the claim that "competition is only a click away."[30] They concluded that Google users "are not locked in," using a misunderstanding of lock-in refuted by Google chief economist Hal Varian himself.[31] And the report concluded that the "durability of Google's monopoly power is questionable."[32]

The FTC's 2013 decision not to pursue Google ended its previously-close partnership with EU antitrust regulators. In June 2017, EU officials concluded their investigation by slapping Google with a €2.42 billion fine for promoting its own comparison shopping product over those of competitors. [33] Margrethe Vestager, the European Commissioner for Competition, suggested that there may be more cases against Google to come. Some U.S. commentators and Google itself have archly suggested that the EU's decision was motivated by protectionism. Yet the EU's decision is sound, according to both U.S. and EU rules.

Google's durable market power is crystal clear if we judge internet firms by the same rules as *every other industry*. Other firms' factories are seen as barriers to entry, but Google's data factories are somehow left out of the analysis. Microsoft's multimillion-line code base and army of locked–in customers are viewed as durable advantages; Google's somehow are not. The biggest digital firms are all marketmakers that take roughly a third of all revenue that moves through their ecosystem. Marketmakers are infamously difficult to displace once established.

Google and other digital giants certainly have a few novel advantages. Targeting economies provide pricing power, ensuring that firms with a larger user base are able to extract more dollars per user. A/B testing can dramatically reduce the risk of missteps by big firms, and limit entry opportunities for new competitors (chapter 2). But those advantages are *in addition to* plenty of old-school advantages that matter just as much as they do in bricks-and-mortar industries.

Historically, communication technologies have tipped quickly from open to locked down—a pattern that the telegraph, telephone, and broadcasting (among others) all followed.[34] The internet has now passed this tipping point in nearly all of its established niches. Over the past decade, even the best-funded competitors have failed to break into established digital niches—as examples like the Google Plus social network and Windows Phone operating system show. Even the nominal success of Bing, which has managed to become the number-two search engine, is only a pyrrhic victory. Microsoft spent more than a decade, investing tens of billions of dollars and absorbing an astonishing $12.4 billion in cumulative losses,[35] to establish Bing as a credible competitor. It is cheaper and easier to build a manned space program than it is to build a modern search engine.

One key feature of U.S. antitrust law, dating back to the 1890 Sherman Act itself, is its concern about harm to small businesses even—or rather especially—if these small businesses were not direct competitors to the big trusts.[36] The goal of antitrust regulation, as even conservative jurists like Frank Easterbrook emphasize, is to promote social wealth.[37] Society as a whole is poorer if Standard Oil doubles the price of gasoline, or if farmers have to pay extortionary railroad fees to get their crops to market. Antitrust laws are supposed to prevent monopolists from pursuing private gains at the expense of big costs imposed on others. Today that risk is enormous and pervasive throughout the digital economy, which forms an ever-larger portion of the economy as a whole.

Ironically, the history of firms like Google, Facebook, and Amazon show why antitrust is so crucial. In the latter half of the 1990s, Microsoft managed to beat Netscape in the so-called browser wars. Microsoft's strategy was to deliberately break the open standards that the web had been built on, and make the internet into a walled garden that could be accessed only with Microsoft's products. The Justice Department's lengthy investigation of Microsoft produced a modest settlement. But far more important, the ongoing investigation curtailed anticompetitive conduct that would have crushed then-nascent firms like Google, Amazon, or eBay.

If antitrust enforcement is critical, the tools these firms have used obsessively to grow their audience can also make the work of regulators easier. A/B testing, in particular, is a powerful way to measure digital firms' power in ways that go beyond longtime yardsticks like HHI. Regulators can see, with real-world experimental data, just how much big firms' choices matter for sites downstream, and just how locked in current users really are. Even more helpful to regulators is that much of the data they need to make better decisions already exists, in the thousands of online experiments running around the clock. Asking for this data, and regularly incorporating it into rule-making and enforcement, is key to twenty-first-century antitrust law.

DEMOCRACY AND NATIONAL SECURITY

Yet, as important as fights over net neutrality and antitrust law are, recent events have shown that the rise of digital giants isn't just a threat to innovation or to the pocketbooks of consumers. It also strengthens the hands of state actors—including state actors working to undermine democracy. Two decades after Barlow's Declaration, cyberspace is less independent from state power than ever before.

Part of state influence comes from online surveillance. The 2013 Snowden disclosures sparked a heated public debate about the capabilities of the NSA, Britain's GCHQ, and other allied intelligence services. Pervasive digital surveillance remains a critical issue, and one that this book has been able to address only in passing.

State surveillance, though, is closely intertwined with the power of big digital firms. The NSA's capabilities have piggybacked upon the networks, tools, and techniques of companies like Google, Facebook, and Verizon. The NSA's infrastructure copies digital giants' data warehouses, it depends critically on software architectures that Google and Facebook developed, and it even hires former Facebook staff. And, of course, the biggest digital firms increasingly serve as a one-stop-shop for all kinds of personal data: email, browsing history, location data, and increasingly even credit-card purchase data. The temptation for governments to use this data through legal or covert means is strong.

Any effective response to "surveillance capitalism"[38] must begin with the evolutionary audience dynamics that led us here. User surveillance at firms like Google came first and foremost out of the imperative to grow faster than others. A/B testing and audience data collection were used to improve and personalize recommendations even before they were applied to targeted advertising—indeed, before Google had a clear business model at all.

Any attempt to curtail surveillance, then, has to deal with the growth imperative. Surveillance undergirds techniques that produce faster growth. It is essential for autocomplete search results, for location-based services, for voice-activated assistants, for personalized news recommendations and social media timelines, and countless other highly sticky features.

This means, like it or not, that individual firms *cannot* simply decide not to track their users. *Slower growth on an evolutionary web is just slow-motion suicide.* Privacy advocates whose only proposal is "don't track us" miss the key role of stickiness and compounded audience. Actions by firms like Apple, which has integrated machine learning to block third-party trackers in its Safari brower, are one possible step—one giant taking unilateral action to hurt rivals like Google and Facebook. By contrast, solutions that depend on voluntary action by a few small firms are untenable on their face. For firms that do want to limit their collection of private data, there is currently no solution to this prisoner's dilemma. Strong regulation is the only way out of this catch-22.

Public Discourse and Disinformation

Evolutionary audiences create other vulnerablities, too: they provide novel and often insidious ways for states to influence public discourse. Recent work by Samantha Bradshaw and Phil Howard has catalogued the rapid emergence of "cyber troops"—organized government, military, or political party teams trying to shape public opinion on social media—in more than two dozen countries.[39]

Some states have developed and used these capabilities to constrain domestic media. For example, China's internet is set off from the rest of the world by a "great firewall" that filters political content, and the Chinese government monitors online behavior and intervenes to limit collective action. At critical moments the Chinese government mobilizes hundreds of thousands of citizens to shape online discussion, though usually by distraction rather than directly confronting disfavored speech.[40]

Even more disturbing is the example of Russia, whose efforts go far beyond just domestic censorship and surveillance. As we have seen, the web provides business models for fake news and other types of questionable content. But Russia seems to have used coordinated campaigns at unprecedented scale to amplify these dynamics and shape the news agenda.

While the full extent of Russian influence on the 2016 U.S. election is still unclear as of this writing, what we do know is disturbing. Russia employs thousands of professional internet trolls, each typically controlling numerous fake accounts. Eight of the ten most popular Facebook stories in the months before the election were wholly fabricated.[41] In key battle-ground states, such as Michigan, false news stories were shared on Twitter more often than real ones in the weeks before the 2016 election.[42]

These digital methods are particularly effective because they are supplemented by traditional spycraft. Rule-breaking or illegal "black hat" methods of improving placement in search engines and social media have long been an annoyance, but state intelligence services have gone far beyond what ordinary criminals or talented hackers can accomplish. For example, *Time* magazine reports that a Russian programmer who worked in the United States "returned to Moscow and brought with him a trove of algorithms that could be used in influence operations," promptly being hired by the Russian intelligence services.[43] Pervasive industrial espionage was also a key factor in Google's decision to pull out of mainland China.

In the aftermath of the 2016 campaign, Google, Facebook, and Twitter all announced efforts to fight fake accounts and this kind of influence operation. But these kinds of state actor threats are incredibly difficult for even the largest private firms to defend against. Consider just one point of vulnerability: the thousands of tech industry workers who live or have family in foreign countries. The core algorithms behind Facebook and Google are secret from the public, but they are frighteningly accessible to hostile governments. Vladimir Putin has a larger, smarter, better financed, and far more ruthless social media strategy than any news organization. Large digital firms have become a single point of failure not just for communications networks, but potentially for democracy itself.

Newspapers: He Who Pays the Piper

Hostile nations' ability to hack digital media is a new and worrying threat. But in the long term, the changing economics of media is just as ominous. It is no longer true that local media is more targeted then national media. National media usually gets more money than local media for the same readers, and the democratic consequences of this grand advertising inversion are profound.

The modern American newspaper emerged in the mid to late 1800s, when the rotary press and cheap pulp newsprint allowed successful papers to get far bigger—and in the process put hundreds of smaller papers out of business. The shift in the economics of news also meant the birth of press independence, as papers in more valuable advertising markets increasingly became independent of political parties.[44] As Joseph Pulitzer himself explained, "Circulation means advertising, and advertising means money, and money means independence."[45]

The past decade has demonstrated that Pulitzer's equation also runs in reverse. Newspapers' print circulation has been more than halved, and their digital audience remains just a fraction of a percent of time online. Ad revenue has cratered as audiences have declined. Despite constant talk about a "shift" to digital, online audiences at most newspapers continue to shrink.[46]

All of these changes threaten newspapers' influence and independence. Critically, though, this threat comes because distribution costs have been *shifted* instead of *lowered*. As we have seen repeatedly, everything that goes into audience building is a distribution cost. The fact that these audience acquisition and maintenance costs are mostly paid by other firms is a curse instead of a blessing, because newspapers no longer control their own audience.

Much industry discussion and scholarly debate has obscured this key problem. Claims that the internet reduces distribution costs are ubiquitous—even this author has made them in previous work. It is false that newspaper audiences are larger than ever, or that newspapers have a revenue problem without an audience problem. And even discussions of "postindustrial journalism," while insightful in some ways, get key parts of the problem wrong. A print newspaper is not less "industrial" because it rents its presses instead of owning them outright. By the same token, digital newspapers are not "postindustrial" if they depend critically on the industrial plants of Google, Facebook, or Apple in order attract an audience. Smokestack economies remain a key reason, though hardly the only one, why digital audiences are so concentrated.

Google, Facebook, and Apple have now all made bids to move news organizations' content onto their own platforms. Facebook's Instant Articles, Google's Accelerated Mobile Pages (AMP), and Apple News were all pitched as a way to improve many news sites' ugly, broken, and dismally slow mobile performance. Facebook and Apple's solutions are particularly damaging to the autonomy of news outlets, as they work only within Facebook and Apple's own apps and platforms. Open-source AMP is better, but it still breaks web standards and increases publisher dependence on Google—with news articles often hosted directly from Google's own caching servers. AMP may be better than the alternatives, but it magnifies the loss of control news organizations have already experienced.

Newspapers are not wholly helpless, as we have seen. With a better understanding of stickiness, newspapers and civic content producers can make smarter investments and maximize their chance to build an audience. In the midst of the panic over fake news, many citizens who hate "mainstream media" still have strong affection for their local newspaper. This goodwill remains an enormous asset, and mid-size newspapers have little to fear from small hyperlocal startups. But there is no hiding the fact that many newspapers—and increasingly other news organizations—now depend on the actions of policymakers and digital giants for their very survival.

The theory of evolution is also the story of extinction, not just growth. Species and ecosystems can be stable for millions of years until, suddenly, they are not. When the food is gone, the niche is too, and tipping points are not always obvious in advance. Boilerplate language about "ecosystems" and "diversity" is little comfort given how real ecosystems work. And in any case, what we have built online is not an ecosystem at all, but a pair of commercial monocultures. Nearly the entire internet energy pyramid now rests on the Facebook and Google duopoly. As events like the Irish potato famine show, every monoculture is only a single pathogen away from destruction.

At some point, inevitably, we reach the limits of biological metaphors. The evolutionary model can help us understand the dynamics of digital audiences, but the internet remains a wholly artificial realm. The internet has no "nature." If the internet destroys local news, or subverts democracy, or ushers in a new gilded age, this is not the inevitable result of natural laws, but the consequence of human choices. The hope of this book is that, by understanding how our choices add and multiply together, our decisions will be wiser. But it is also a warning about complacency, about misunderstanding the character of the internet we all depend on. If we want the internet to remain open we must first understand it—and then we must fight for it.

APPENDIX ON DATA, METHODOLOGY, AND MODELS

APPENDIX TO CHAPTER 4: A FORMAL MODEL OF WEB TRAFFIC AND ONLINE AD REVENUE

Chapter 4 offers a simple formal model of online revenue for websites. In this Appendix, we will walk through the mathematics behind the model. Those familiar with increasing returns models from many other areas of economics will find the approach here broadly similar.

Suppose there are M sites, each producing 1 type of content, but each site produces its own variety p_j, $0 \leq p_j \leq 1$. There are N consumers, each with a daily consumption budget C, and a preference for the variety p^i. For purposes of notation, i will index consumers as a super-script; j will index sites as a subscript, and we will suppress the indexes if the context is clear.

Each site produces content at rate λ_j with quality ω_j. Let c_j^i be the consumption of site j by individual i. Consumption is determined by the quality of content, the refresh rate (λ_j), and an individual's preference for variety. Doing the simplest thing:

$$c_j^i = \gamma_j^i \left(1 - |p^i - p_j|\right) \lambda_j \omega_j,$$

where γ_j^i is a constant of proportionality.

Each individual's consumption is subject to the budget constraint C, which is the amount of time the viewer has to enjoy the web. To take the easiest case first, we initially assume C is constant for all consumers. If searching on the web were free, we could say $C = \sum_{j=1}^{M} c_j^i$, for each $i = 1, \ldots, N$. However, we assume there is a fixed cost to the viewer's attention each time he navigates to a new site. Let s_i be the number of sites in i's viewing porfolio, and let t_0 be the search cost. Then

$$C = s_i t_0 + \sum_{j=1}^{M} c_j^i.$$

In general, many of the c_j^i, may be zero.

With complete information, then, the consumer knows each site's content quality, quantity, and variety. By analogy, one can imagine a consumer deciding which markets to shop at. He knows the location of the markets and their wares, and he must choose to travel to many markets to purchase exactly the variety and quality of goods he wants. In this case, he must assume high transportation costs. Or the consumer may lower travel costs by going to a single supermarket while perhaps conceding some preference for quality, quantity, or variety.

We will write π_j for the profit of site j. Profit is just revenue minus the cost. Set the revenue of site j to be a function of the total consumption, $R\left(\sum_{i=1}^{N} c_j^i\right)$. Initially the precise mechanism for turning consumers' attention into dollars is taken to be exogenous to the model. For now, we assume conservatively that R is increasing. There are two components of the cost to site j: a fixed cost α and a cost of production. Traditionally, production costs are the number of workers in the labor force times the wage rate. Supposing content quantity is proportional to the labor force and content quality is proportional to the wage rate, we write the profit function as

$$\pi_j = R\left(\sum_{i=1}^{N} c_j^i\right) - \alpha - (\beta\lambda_j)(\delta\omega_j)$$

where β and δ are constants of proportionality.

Utility for consumers is derived from consumption of site content. Every possible triple of site quantity, quality, and variety determines the amount of content an individual is willing to consume. That is, consumption measures utility indirectly. Each individual has a preference ordering

$$c_{j_k}^i \geq c_{j_{k+1}}^i \geq 0$$

for $k = 1, \ldots, M$. It is rational for an individual to consume sites in preferential order $c_{j_1}^i, c_{j_2}^i, \ldots$, paying the search cost at each transition until his consumption budget is exhausted.

Example: 2 Sites and 1 Consumer

With two sites, $j = 1, 2$, we can assume the first site is closer to our lonely viewer's preferences, $|p - p_1| \leq |p - p_2|$. If the quality/quantity factor of site 2 is sufficiently high, the consumer will consume more of site 2. Precisely, if

$$\frac{\gamma_1 \left(1 - |p - p_1|\right)}{\gamma_2 \left(1 - |p - p_2|\right)} \leq \frac{\lambda_2 \omega_2}{\lambda_1 \omega_1},$$

we can cross-multiply to get

$$c_1 = \gamma_1 \left(1 - |p - p_1|\right) \lambda_1 \omega_1 \leq \gamma_1 \left(1 - |p - p_2|\right) \lambda_2 \omega_2 = c_2.$$

This means that sites can make a sufficient investment in quantity and quality to draw consumers past sites closer to the consumers' preferences.

Example: 2 Sites and Many Individuals

Suppose the consumers are distributed uniformly in the variety preference space, and the proportionality constant is fixed, $\gamma_j^i = \gamma$ for all i and j. If revenue grows faster than production cost as a function of the quantity/quality factor, profit will grow with investment in production. Formally, calling the production cost W, if $R' > W'$, then $\pi' = R' - W' > 0$. Thus, even mild economies of scale in production or revenue will produce profit growth from production investment.

The maximum available revenue for a site occurs when all the viewers spend their entire consumption budgets on that one site, so the maximum possible revenue is $R(NC)$. If this level of production is profitable, then there is a monopolistic equilibrium. That is, all individuals will spend all their budgets on one site. That one site is profitable, and no other site is consumed. This is optimal for consumers, because they all deem the quantity/quality to be sufficiently high that they don't have to waste precious consumption time changing sites.

Strong Preferences for Variety and Other Extensions

The mathematical core of the model is highly extensible, as the rest of the chapter shows. One extension is to give users limited preference windows, as follows:

$$\gamma_j^i = \begin{cases} \gamma & : |p^i - p_j| < \epsilon \\ 0 & : |p^i - p_j| \geq \epsilon \end{cases}$$

Now it is impossible to capture everyone's complete attention, so long as at least some consumers' preference windows exclude the midpoint of the variety space.

Alternatively, we might allow sites to produce multiple categories of content, offering an analog to aggregators or portal sites. Here additional assumptions are required: for example, dichotomizing the utility that consumers receive from a given category of content ("all or nothing"), assuming that users' preferences across categories are independent, and positing that there is at least some diminishing marginal utility for additional content in a given category. The higher the number of categories, the more the central limit theorem takes over, providing an increasing advantage to portal sites or aggregators.

The main chapter goes into additional examples, all of which reframe the core results (or offer different utility payoffs) instead of offering genuinely new math. All of the model extensions reinforce the main point, though: once the core assumptions about increasing returns are accepted, it becomes difficult to find any auxiliary assumptions that will prevent strong market concentration.

Appendix to Chapter 5: The Dynamics of Digital Audiences

The discussion in chapter 5, on change in digital audiences over time, delves into a series a highly technical subjects. This section will briefly discuss power laws and the mathematics of dynamical systems that underlie our simulations.

The first order of business is to address a sometimes unhelpful debate on what counts as a power law in empirical data. In formal terms, a power law distribution is characterized by a density function that is proportional to $1/x^{\alpha}$, where the (negative) power α corresponds to the slope of the line when plotted on a log-log scale. A profusion of papers on power laws from the late 1990s onward, and a subsequent popular press discussion of power laws and "long tails," has sparked a corrective backlash among some researchers (e.g., Clauset et al., 2009). Some of these papers have chastised researchers for using the term when other distributions may fit better—sometimes a lot better, but usually only slightly.

For the data sources used here, there is little substantive difference whether the distribution of audience is a power law, an extreme log-normal, a power law with exponential cutoff, etc. Most real-world datasets show deviations from a pure power law in the "head" with the largest observations. This volume often uses the term "log-linear distribution" to denote this broad family of related distributions.

In general, though, there are good reasons to prefer the power law label, even when other distributions may fit the data slightly better. *Of course* other related distributions often fit better: they have two or more parameters, while pure power laws have only one. Parsimony is a cardinal virtue in model building, and each additional parameter provides latitude for mischief. As John von Neumann reportedly said, "With four parameters I can fit an elephant, and with five I can make him wiggle his trunk."[1]

In any case, our data show a good fit to a pure power law, the discussion in the previous paragraphs notwithstanding. A simple way to check the regularity of the traffic distribution is to estimate the exponent of the power law for each day in our data. While an OLS regression line for the log-log web traffic distribution produces a near-perfect R^2, this technique overweights the smallest observations, as there are an order of magnitude more of them. We use the maximum likelihood techniques described in Newman (2005), which give us an estimated daily exponent (α) that varies between 1.98 and 2.13 for the 1,096 days in our sample.

Day-to-day changes in stochastic dynamical systems, such as stock markets, are often modeled with log-normal distributions. In our modeling we thus consider changes in the *logarithms* of the web-traffic market shares. We are particularly interested in the day-to-day relative growth rate

$$g_t = \frac{x_{t+1} - x_t}{x_t}.$$

Note that "growth," in this definition, can be negative as well as positive. Additionally, we cannot observe the growth rates for sites falling out of the top three hundred with our data. This skews the distribution of the observed growth rates for the smallest sites, but does not change any of the findings that follow.

The notation $x_j(t)$ will represent the market share of the site occupying rank j at time t. We can thus write the market share on the next day as

$$x_{(j)}(t+1) = x_j(t) + g_j x_j(t). \tag{A.1}$$

On the left-hand side, the j is in parentheses because the website that occupied rank j at time t may occupy a different rank on the next day. The term g_j is a random variable describing the daily growth rate of the sites at rank j. At each time t, a new g_j is sampled. If g_j is negative, the market share decreases such that $x_{(j)}(t+1) < x_j(t)$. If g_j is zero, there is no change in market share.

Importantly, g_t for each rank in our data is approximately log-normally distributed, though with heavier tails than a pure log-normal distribution would produce.

Appendix to Chapter 7: Local Digital News Outlets

A critical component of the analysis in chapter 7 involves identifying local news sites.

For our purposes, local websites are operationalized as sites that have experienced higher levels of usage within a given media market than they do in the rest of the nationwide sample. How much higher? The simplest rule is to look at any usage difference big enough that is unlikely to have been produced by chance. The study uses a standard difference of means test, comparing sites' mean audience reach within a market to its reach in the rest of the national panel.

Sites where the observed local vs. national gap in usage is at least three times larger than the estimated standard error are examined as possible local sites. Formally, this is equivalent to a t-score > 3. The samples are large enough that z-scores or t-scores are equivalent. Qualitative assessments (detailed later) suggest that this decision rule for discerning local from national content works extremely well for the types of sites we hope to examine. A lower decision threshold—such as 2.5—produces few additional genuinely local sites, with the vast majority of additional sites false positives. As we would expect, much lower decision thresholds, such as $t > 1.5$, swamp the analysis with false positives. Given that the data are roughly normally distributed, sampling error alone should produce a t-statistic > 2.0 about 2.5 percent of the time. In a dataset of more than a million observations, such a low threshold produces an unmanageably high false positive rate.

If a difference-of-means test provides a powerful heuristic to distinguish local from national content, the other important task is to distinguish between sites that provide news and sites that do not. The initial research design called for this study to use comScore's proprietary "web dictionary," which places tracked sites into one of many of categories and subcategories, including a category for "News/Information."

However, comScore's coding scheme was discovered to have significant limitations. Substantively identical news sites are often placed in different categories and subcategories. Even within the same market, it is common to find television station sites or newspaper sites spread across several different categories and groupings.

This initially puzzling result likely stems from comScore's subscriber model. Media organizations that subscribe to comScore *get to choose* the category or subcategory in which their site is placed. This can result in a "Lake Wobegon effect," in which subscribing media organizations each choose the category or subcategory that looks most favorable. Most subscribing news organization thus get to say that they are at the top of their chosen category.

Since it is essential that we know the affiliation (if any) between online news sources and traditional media outlets, the comScore data need to be supplemented. Because of these limits with the comScore categorization, the author himself coded sites for news content, locality, and traditional media affiliation.

While the comScore data categories are imprecise and inconsistently applied, they do provide some guidance. A newspaper site might end up in "Regional/Local" or "News/Information: Newspapers" or "News/Information: General News," but it is unlikely to end up in "Retail." First, ten broadcast markets were chosen using random numbers generated by random.org. For February, March, and April, all sites with a t-score > 3 in these 10 markets were examined. The comScore category was recorded for all sites that provided local news. News sites were found in the three comScore "News/Information" subcategories, in the "Regional/Local" category, and in the "Entertainment" category (particularly the "Entertainment: TV" and "Entertainment: Radio" subcategories). There was no discernible difference between local TV stations that ended up in the "Entertainment" category and those that ended up in "News/Information" or "Regional/Local." Even with radio, a number of hard news stations were placed in the "Entertainment" category.

The study also requires setting a consistent, cross-market audience share standard for inclusion in the analysis. Without such a standard, far more local news sites will be found in bigger markets than in smaller ones, since sites that receive five or fewer visitors are not included in the comScore data. For example, a site that got five panelist visits in Burlington, Vermont, would be omitted from the analysis, while a site that got eight visits in New York City would be included, even though the market reach of the Burlington site is eighteen times higher.

Since the study aims to provide the broadest possible survey of online local news, this base threshold is set as low as the data allow. First, minimum standards for inclusion in the analysis are based on monthly audience reach rather than other traffic metrics. Less-trafficked sites usually score far better on audience reach than they do on page views or time spent on the site. Second, these audience reach metrics should be as small as consistent cross-market comparison permits. To repeat, sites must have at least six local market visitors in order to have shown up in the comScore data at all. The smallest markets (such as Burlington or Madison, WI) have between six hundred and seven hundred panelists.

Since six visitors equal 1 percent of six hundred panelists, 1 percent audience reach is the smallest threshold we can use and still include cities like Burlington and Madison in the analysis, at least without worrying about data censoring. Even slightly lower thresholds would affect many or most of our one hundred markets. Requiring sites to receive 0.5 percent audience reach requires a panel size of at least 1,200 respondents to avoid censoring, excluding thirty-three of our markets. Requiring 0.3 percent audience reach requires 1,800 panelists and would impact fifty-four of the one hundred broadcast markets. Moreover, any additional sites found by lowering the threshold would add up to only a tiny fraction of all news consumed in the local market. (Local news sites just above the 1 percent audience-reach cutoff average less than 1/100th of 1 percent of all local page views.)

While the 1 percent threshold here is chosen because of the limits of the data, at least one prominent scholar has proposed a similar threshold on normative as well as pragmatic grounds. Eli Noam (2004, 2009) argues that outlets should have 1 percent market share to count as media voices in his proposed Noam Index of media diversity.[2] As Noam (2004) explains, "To keep the index practical there should be a cut-off of a minimal size for a voice. One per cent seems a reasonable floor: small but not trivial."[3]

Putting these requirements together means that local news site candidates are all sites in the sample with the following characteristics:

- Sites in the "News/Information" category, "Local/Regional" category, or the "Entertainment" category.
- Sites where the difference in audience reach within a market vs. nationally produces a t-statistic > 3.
- Sites that achieve 1 percent audience reach in at least one of the three months examined.

More than 1,800 sites in the data possess all three of the above characteristics. The coding guidelines specify an inclusive definition for news sites. Websites were counted as news and information outlets if they provided regularly updated, independent information about local news, community affairs, local officials, or issues of regional concern. This definition is not format-dependent, and in principle it would include sites such as local blogs. Static content by itself *was not* enough to count as a news source; sites needed to have had front-page content updated within the preceding two weeks. This coding was labor-intensive, but did provide for an extremely detailed, firsthand look at what local news sites consist of.

The data presented almost no margin cases or difficult coding decisions. The overwhelming majority of sites identified by the aforementioned three-pronged test were traditional media outlets. Ultimately, 1,074 of the candidate sites were classified as local news sites.

Because of the mandate to examine internet-only local news sources in particular, special care was taken to accurately record a site's affiliation with broadcast or print sources. Every television station was confirmed to have broadcast or cable distribution, and every print outlet was confirmed to have a paper version.

In ninety-five out of the 1,074 news sites, higher usage levels ($t > 3$) were recorded in more than one media market. These cases overwhelmingly involved a large newspaper or (less often) a regional television station with a statewide or regional audience. Since the focus here is on local news, rather than state or regional news, these secondary regional markets are excluded from the definition of local content. The *Seattle Times* may have above-average readership in Spokane, WA, but it does not consistently cover Spokane's local politics.

There are two exceptions to this rule, however: AL.com and Michigan Live. Both are statewide sites that feature content from newspapers in several different broadcast markets. Participating newspapers forgo their own home pages to host content on these statewide platforms. These outlets are thus counted as local in every market with a participating news organization.

Variables for Regression Analysis

Previous work has examined both the demographics of national digital news consumption and structural factors that shape local news consumption in traditional media.[4] Of particular interest, previous studies have found that larger markets produce more broadcast news.[5] *TV Market Population* is each media market's population, according to the Census Bureau's American Community Survey.

Some research has shown that broadband users use the web far differently than dial-up users, and that they consume more and richer types of web-based content.[6] To investigate the potential impact of high-speed access, *Broadband Pct.* is FCC data on the percentage of the market that subscribes to 768 bps or faster broadband.

Since local newspapers and TV stations provide most online local news, it is particularly important to examine the structure of offline local media. Regarding newspapers, the models test several variables. *Newspaper Circ/Capita* reports the total newspaper circulation per person in a given market. *Daily Newspapers* gives the number of daily newspapers that reach at least 5 percent of the market population. *Newspaper Parent Companies* is the number of parent daily newspaper firms in the television market. These variables hopefully provide some leverage over which (if any) matters most: the number of newspaper firms, the size of the newspaper audience, or just the number of outlets that reach a minimum threshold of readership.

Television broadcasters are approached similarly. Since we find few local news outlets associated with noncommercial broadcasters, we focus on the number and type of commercial TV stations. *Commercial TV Stations* records the number of full-power commercial television broadcasters. Additionally, we are interested in whether ownership patterns predict the number of online outlets found and the amount of local news consumed. *Locally Owned TV Stations* measures the number of commercial stations with owners in the market. *Minority-Owned Stations* captures the number of local television stations under minority ownership according to FCC records. *Newspaper-TV Cross-Ownership* reports the number of parent companies in the market that own *both* a daily newspaper and a commercial television station.

While newspaper-TV cross-ownership is of particular concern, the local radio market is also potentially important. *News-Format Radio Stations* records the number of broadcast radio stations with a news-based format. *Radio-TV Cross-Ownership* measures the number of parent entities that own both a broadcast TV station and a radio station.

We also investigate possible ties between the racial and ethnic makeup of a market and its online news production. *Black Pct.* and *Hispanic Pct.* capture the portion of residents who are African American and Hispanic, respectively. One might hypothesize that markets with large immigrant Hispanic populations may consume less English-language local news. Models thus include interaction effects between racial and ethnic makeup and market size: *Hispanic Pct. × Market Pop.* and *Black Pct. × Market Pop.* These terms test whether racial and ethnic diversity has different effects in larger vs. smaller markets, as some of the cases discussed earlier might suggest.

The analysis also controls for effects of income and age. *Income* uses per-capita earnings data provided by BIA. *Age 65+* is the fraction of the population in the market that is sixty-five years or older.

Lastly, because there may be month-specific factors that impact the amount of news consumed, two dummy variables for the months of February and March are included. April is the omitted category. These coefficients should be interpreted as the difference between consumption in April and the listed month.

NOTES

Chapter 1. Rethinking the Attention Economy

1. For a full discussion of Google's early experiments, see Mayer, 2007. Mayer has used slightly different figures in describing the experiments' impact in other speeches.

2. Subsequent experiments have shown that it can take weeks or months for slowed-down users to return to their previous level of usage; see Hölzle, 2012.

3. Berners-Lee, 2000, p. 23.

4. Ingram, 2017.

5. Simon, 1971.

6. Goldhaber, 1997.

7. Ibid.

8. J. Webster, 2014, p. 1.

9. See discussion in Krugman, 1997, pp. 52–55.

10. Ibid., p. 54.

11. von Thunen [1826], 1966.

12. Blumler and Kavanagh, 1999.

13. Negroponte, 1995, p. 58.

14. Reynolds, 2006.

15. Mele, 2013.

16. Sifry, 2009.

17. Bai, 2009.

18. Morton, 2011.

19. Benkler, 2006, pp. 3–4.

20. Shirky, 2009, pp. 59–60.

21. Rosen, 2011.

22. Hindman, 2009, pp. 86–87.

Chapter 2. A Tilted Playing Field

1. Schwartz, 1998.

2. See discussion in chapter 1, especially Benkler, 2006.

3. AT&T, 1908, p. 21.

4. See, for example, O'Reilly, 2005; Wu, 2011.

5. The major exception, the Chinese site Weibo, illustrates the same logic: the fact that social networks in China and the United States barely overlap has allowed

a different firm to seize this niche in China. Other internet services, from instant messaging to Skype, show the same pattern.

6. E.g. Pariser, 2011, p. 41.

7. Hundt, 1996.

8. See, for example, Briscoe, Odlyzko, and Tilly, 2006.

9. Cialdini and Goldstein, 2004; Asch, 1955.

10. Kirkpatrick, 2011, p. 101.

11. Ksiazek, Peer, and Lessard, 2014.

12. Sonderman, 2012.

13. Toth, 2014.

14. Sonderman, 2011.

15. Bain, 1954, 1956; Haldi and Whitcomb, 1967.

16. A. D. Chandler, 1977.

17. Pearn, 2012; see also Munroe, 2013.

18. Ghemawat, Gobioff, and Leung, 2003.

19. Burrows, 2006; Lo et al., 2015.

20. J. Dean and Ghemawat, 2008; Chang et al., 2008.

21. Bhatotia et al., 2011.

22. Shute et al., 2012; Corbett et al., 2012.

23. Verma et al., 2015, p. 1.

24. On Google's acquisition of UK-based machine learning startup DeepMind, see "What DeepMind brings to Alphabet," 2016. Access to Google's computing power was reportedly a key factor in why DeepMind agreed to be acquired by Google. On TensorFlow, see Abadi et al., 2016.

25. Jouppi et al., 2017.

26. S. Levy, 2012; McMillan, 2012.

27. TeleGeography, 2012.

28. Labovitz et al., 2009.

29. Google, 2013.

30. DeepMind, 2016.

31. McKusick and Quinlan, 2009.

32. Mayer, 2007.

33. Hölzle, 2012.

34. Schurman and Brutlag, 2009.

35. Artz, 2009.

36. Hölzle, 2012.

37. Singhal and Cutts, 2010.

38. Bowman, 2009.

39. On the relation between site design, traffic, and revenue, see Flavián et al., 2006; Cyr, 2008.

40. Kohavi et al., 2013.

41. Tang et al., 2010.

42. Kohavi et al., 2013.

43. McKusick and Quinlan, 2009.

44. Pike et al., 2005; Chattopadhyay et al., 2011; Melink et al., 2010.

45. Palmer, 2002.

46. Bohn and Hamburger, 2013; see also Buchanan, 2013.

47. Brian, 2014.

48. Kohavi et al., 2013.

49. Ibid., p. 4.

50. Davis, 1921, p. 169.

51. Nelson, 1970; Shapiro, 1983.

52. Hoch and Deighton, 1989.

53. Shaprio and Varian, 1998, pp. 113–14, emphasis added.

54. Wells, Valacich, and Hess, 2011; McKnight, Choudhury, and Kacmar, 2002.

55. H. E. Krugman, 1972; Tellis, 2003, 1988.

56. Lambrecht and Tucker, 2013.

57. Semel, 2006.

58. Yarow, 2013.

59. Hargittai et al., 2010.

60. Jansen, Zhang, and Mattila, 2012, p. 445.

61. Jansen, Zhang, and Schultz, 2009.

62. Pan et al., 2007. Another interpretation of these results might be that users have entrenched habits and site-specific skills, as we will discuss later.

63. Microsoft has removed the initial study from the web. Note that even if Microsoft consistently performed *worse* on this challenge, it might benefit from this sort of direct comparison. If Microsoft wins 40 percent of the time (for example), but has only 30 percent market share, more Google users will be told they chose Bing than the other way around. Note that this assumes that an individual's choice is not related to his or her current browser usage, which is likely false in real life, as browsers increasingly learn from users' past behavior.

64. Ataullah and Lank, 2010, p. 337.

65. Ayres et al., 2013.

66. Zara, 2012.

67. Ataullah and Lank, 2010, p. 337.

68. Iyengar and Hahn, 2009.

69. Stroud, 2011.

70. Hargittai and Shaw, 2015.

71. Hargittai, 2010.

72. Hargittai et al., 2010.

73. Stigler and Becker, 1977; Wernerfelt, 1985, 1991.

74. On this point see, for example, Wernerfelt, 1991, p. 232.

75. Shapiro and Varian, 1998.

76. Ajax is an acronym for Asynchronous JavaScript and XML.

77. J. J. Garrett, 2005.

78. E. Johnson, Bellman, and Lohse, 2003; see also Murrary and Häubl, 2007, p. 62.

79. See discussion in Brynjolfsson and Smith, 2000.

80. Shankar, Smith, and Rangaswamy, 2003; Ha and Perks, 2005; Aksoy et al., 2013.

81. Murray and Häubl, 2007.

82. Quoted in Beam, 2010.

83. Ibid.

84. Schmidt, 2014.

85. Wheeler, 2013.

86. Arthur, 1989; David, 1985.

Chapter 3. The Political Economy of Personalization

1. Negroponte, 1995, p. 153.

2. See, for example, Kennard Gates, 2000; Kennard, 1999.

3. Sunstein, 2001, 2009.

4. Schafer, Konstan, and Riedl, 2001.

5. Zuckerberg quote from Pariser, 2011.

6. Zelizer, 2009.

7. Bucy, 2004; Deuze, 2003; but see Stromer-Galley, 2004.

8. Thurman and Schifferes, 2012; Thurman, 2011.

9. See, for example, Haim, Graefe, and Brosius, 2017, and Möller, Trilling, Helberger, and van Es, 2018.

10. Hindman, 2018.

11. Stigler, 1961, p. 216.

12. Ibid., p. 220.

13. Mayer-Schoenberger and Cukier, 2013.

14. Netflix, 2007.

15. This chapter's overview of AT&T's participation in the contest draws heavily from from the team's official history (AT&T 2009, 2010), and from Yehuda Koren's (2009) recounting of the contest.

16. Funk, 2006.

17. Ibid.

18. Ibid.; see also Gorrell, 2006.

19. AT&T, 2009.

20. AT&T, 2010.

21. AT&T, 2009, emphasis in original.

22. AT&T, 2009.

23. Hunt, 2010.

24. AT&T, 2009.
25. Netflix, 2007.
26. Amatriain and Basilico, 2012.
27. Ibid.
28. Koren, 2009.
29. Banko and Brill, 2001, p. 28.
30. Funk, 2006.
31. Koren, 2009.
32. Pariser, 2011.
33. Amatriain and Basilico, 2012.
34. Ibid.
35. Das et al., 2007.
36. Ibid., p. 271.
37. Ibid., p. 279.
38. Liu, Dolan, and Pedersen, 2010.
39. Ibid., p. 32.
40. Kirshenbaum, Forman, and Dugan, 2012, p. 11.
41. Boyd, 2011.
42. Pandey et al., 2011.
43. Ibid.
44. Ibid., p. 3.
45. Hindman, 2018.
46. Cadwalladr and Graham-Harrison, 2018.
47. Kosinski, Stillwell, and Graepel, 2013.
48. Frier, 2018.
49. Negroponte, 1995, pp. 57–58.
50. See discussion in Neuman, 1991.

Chapter 4. The Economic Geography of Cyberspace

1. Ohlin, 1935.
2. Krugman, 1979, 1980.
3. E.g., Dixit and Stiglitz, 1977.
4. Pai, 2017; see also Faulhaber, Singer, and Urschel, 2017.
5. Pooley and Winseck, 2017; see also chapter 6.
6. Box, 1979.
7. For example, see Steiner, 1952; Negroponte, 1995; see also the discussion later in this chapter.
8. For an overview of research on bundling see Adams and Yellen, 1976; Shapiro and Varian, 1998; Bakos and Brynjolfsson, 1999.
9. Adams and Yellen, 1976

10. This example loosely adapted from Shapiro and Varian, 1998; see also a similar example of bundling in Hamilton, 2004.

11. Hamilton, 2004.

12. Carroll, 2008.

13. Bakos and Brynjolfsson, 1999.

14. On how bundling digital products is different, see Bakos and Brynjolfsson, 2000.

15. Nalebuff, 2004.

16. Chandler, 1964; Flink, 1990, but see Raff, 1991.

17. Peles, 1971, p. 32.

18. Ingram, 2017.

19. Meyer, 2004, p. 45.

20. Lewis and Rao, 2015; Johnson et al., 2016.

21. Brodersen et al., 2015.

22. Pandey et al., 2011; see discussion in chapter 3.

23. Mutter, 2012.

24. Last, 2002.

25. See, for example, Bagdikian, 1985.

26. C. Anderson, 2004.

27. Steiner, 1952; Beebe, 1977—though see J. G. Webster and Wakshlag, 1983 for an influential critique. For an older but still excellent overview of economic models of program choice, see Owen and Wildman, 1992.

28. Ehrenberg, 1968; Kirsch and Banks, 1962.

29. Goodhardt and Ehrenberg, 1969.

30. J. Webster, 2014, p. 30.

31. Koren, 2009.

32. Prior, 2006.

33. Boczkowski and Mitchelstein, 2013.

34. Stroud, 2011; Iyengar and Hahn, 2009; R. K. Garrett, 2009.

35. Levendusky, 2013; see also Gentzkow and Shapiro, 2011.

36. J. Webster, 2014; Ariely and Norton, 2008.

37. Monsell, 2003; Kahneman, 2011.

38. Krug, 2013.

39. Somaiya, 2014.

40. Hotelling, 1929; see also Downs, 1957.

41. Unequal browsing time also limits portal sites' production. Additional content no longer automatically increases profitability, because at high levels of production fewer and fewer users have the time budget needed to consume additional content.

Alternatively, we might reintroduce narrow preference windows, making it so that some users get no utility from the middle-of-the-road content produced by portal sites. However—as we have already seen in this chapter—this change arguably makes the model *less* rather than more realistic.

42. Tankersley, 2015. Note also Steve Wildman's (1994) work on "one-way flows" in news production.

43. Benton, 2016.

44. Cairncross, 2001.

45. Hindman, 2009.

46. Athey, Mobius, and Pál, 2017.

47. P. Krugman, 2009.

48. D. Dean et al., 2012.

Chapter 5. The Dynamics of Web Traffic

1. Glaeser, 2005.

2. On this point, see Hindman, 2009.

3. Dahlgren, 2005; Benkler, 2006; Hindman, 2009; Meraz, 2009; Caldas et al., 2008.

4. Barabási and Albert, 1999.

5. Newman, 2005; Clauset, Shalizi, and Newman, 2009.

6. For early examples of this, see Goel and Richter-Dyn, 1974.

7. Rioul and Vetterli, 2002.

8. Anderson and Mattingly, 2007.

9. Caldentey and Stacchetti, 2010.

10. Volz and Meyers, 2009.

11. Redner, 1998.

12. Small and Singer, 1982.

13. Levy and Solomon, 1997.

14. Gabaix, 1999.

15. Fernholz (2002) notes that the stock market deviates slightly from a power law at both the extreme head and at the tail of the distribution. The very largest firms are slightly smaller than mathematical models predict, which Fernholz attributes to antitrust laws and real-world limits. Concentration at the very top of the market has been increasing, though—perhaps because of weakened antitrust enforcement (more on that in chapter 8). At the other end of the market, many small firms stay privately owned instead of becoming public companies, shortening what would otherwise be a longer tail.

16. Fernholz, 2002, p. 95.

17. PriceWaterhouseCoopers, 2008.

18. Interactive Advertising Bureau [IAB], 2010.

19. Companies such as Chartbeat can provide reasonable time measures across different sites that use their instrumentation, but can measure only behavior on

their partners' sites. This makes their data useful for analysis within the network of affiliates, but still limited in key ways (more on the time-measurement approach and comScore's data in the next chapter).

20. See Meiss et al., 2008; E. Johnson, Lewis, and Reiley, 2003.

21. The key difference between power law and lognormal distributions, interestingly enough, has to do with what happens to observations that go to zero. If observations that go to zero (or the lower bound) are replaced, then the distribution becomes a power law; if they are *not* replaced the distribution becomes lognormal. See Mitzenmacher, 2004; Gabaix, 1999.

22. Clauset et al., 2009.

23. Fernholz, 2002.

Chapter 6. Less of the Same: Online Local News

1. This account of the founding of Patch.com is taken from Carlson, 2013.

2. Carr, 2013.

3. Romenesko, 2013.

4. Jack Marshall, 2016.

5. Carr, 2013.

6. Jarvis, 2013.

7. Mitchell, Gottfried, Barthel, and Shearer, 2016.

8. See, for example, Noam, 2009.

9. *Prometheus v. FCC*, 2004, is one prominent example.

10. Kirchoff, 2010.

11. Olmstead, Mitchell, and Rosenstiel, 2011.

12. Graves, 2010.

13. Cook and Pettit, 2009.

14. Boczkowski, 2010.

15. Olmstead, Mitchell, and Rosenstiel, 2011.

16. See, for example, Hindman, 2009.

17. Department of Justice and Federal Trade Commission, 2010.

18. Because HHI attempts to assess firms' market power, I combine the market shares of multiple outlets in the same market owned by the same firm. For example, page views on the *Atlanta Journal-Constitution* site, the WSB-TV site, and the WSB-radio site are all summed together.

19. Kopytoff, 2011.

20. Schaffer, 2010.

21. Pew, 2010.

22. On this point, see Gelman, 2010.

23. Negative binomial models are closely related to poisson regression models. Whereas poisson models have only a single parameter λ, which governs both

the mean and the variance of the distribution, negative binomial models add the parameter α to capture overdispersion. While overdispersed count data are often the norm in the social sciences, in this case both models produce estimates of α very close to zero. When $\alpha = 0$, as it does here, poisson and negative binomial models are identical.

24. Greenslade, 2012.

25. Morton, 2011.

26. Waldfogel, 2002.

27. Chyi and Tenenboim, 2017.

28. FCC 2017, p. 87.

Chapter 7. Making News Stickier

1. Pew Internet and American Life Project, 2017b.

2. Graves, Kelly, and Gluck, 2010.

3. Kanagal et al., 2013; Pandey et al., 2011.

4. Pew, 2010.

5. Usher, 2014a.

6. Usher, 2014b.

7. Mutter, 2009.

8. New York Times Company, 2013. Note, though, that by the end of 2016 digital subscriptions had crept up to 15 percent of total revenue—though this shift reflects decline in print as much as digital growth. For more on this topic, see the discussion in New York Times Company, 2016.

9. Ellis, 2014.

10. New York Times, 2014; see also Usher, 2014c.

11. Lee and Molla, 2018.

12. Chittum, 2014.

13. Gannett Co., 2018.

14. The "burn the boats" quote is from entrepreneur and investor Marc Andreessen, referenced in Schonfeld, 2010.

15. Lee and Molla, 2018.

16. See, for example, McClatchy Company, 2013.

17. Holcomb and Mitchell, 2014.

18. A. Newman and Leland, 2017.

19. McChesney and Nichols, 2011.

20. Usher and Layser, 2010.

21. Mutter, 2014.

22. Pew Internet and American Life Project, 2017a.

23. Barthel and Mitchell, 2017.

24. Mitchell, Rosenstiel, Santhanam, and Christian, 2012.

25. Knight Foundation, 2016; Nielsen, 2014.

26. eMarketer, 2014.

27. E.g., Pontin, 2012.

28. Mitchell et al., 2012.

29. Boczkowski, 2010.

30. Pontin, 2012.

31. Kalogeropoulos and Newman, 2017.

32. As of this writing, the pivot to video has now received an outpouring of commentary; noteworthy essays on the downturn include Moore, 2017, Josh Marshall, 2017, and Thompson, 2017.

33. Cohen, 2017.

34. Shoenfeld, 2017.

35. Benes, 2017.

36. Josh Marshall, 2017; see also Thompson, 2017.

37. E.g., Schurman and Brutlag, 2009.

38. Castillo, 2014.

39. Moos, 2009.

40. Author conversations with multiple *Post* staffers.

41. Konigsburg, 2014.

42. Hamann, 2014.

43. Bart et al., 2005; Wells, Valacich, and Hess, 2011.

44. Das et al., 2007; Liu, Dalan, and Pedersen, 2010.

45. Starkman, 2010.

46. Manjoo, 2013.

47. Wemple, 2014b, 2014a.

48. Upworthy, 2013.

49. Somaiya, 2014.

50. Mitchell, Jurgowitz, and Olmstead, 2014.

51. Ellis, 2012.

52. Bell, 2018.

53. Moses, 2018.

54. Kohavi et al., 2013; see discussion in chapter 2.

55. Bakshy, Eckles, and Bernstein, 2014

56. Author conversation with senior executives at the *Washington Post*.

57. Kovach and Rosenstiel, 2007.

CHAPTER 8. THE "NATURE" OF THE INTERNET

1. Barlow, 1996. Capitalization in original text.

2. Turner, 2006; see also Helmreich, 1998.

3. Doherty, 2004.

4. On the manufactured underdog origins of many tech firms, see Heath and Heath, 2011.

5. Wheeler, 2013.

6. Turner, 2006; Schumpeter, 1942.

7. Dimmick, 2002.

8. Napoli, 2011; see also Stober, 2004.

9. This account of Darwin is drawn especially from Ernst Mayr's (1982) digest of Darwin in his classic book *The Growth of Biological Thought*. See also Bowler, 1989; Gould, 2002.

10. Shirky, 2010.

11. Hobbes, 1996.

12. O'Hara et al., 2013; for a more general discussion of the micro-macro problem, see Watts, 2011, pp. 61–64.

13. Abbatte, 1998.

14. Earl and Kimport, 2011.

15. Schlozman, Verba, and Brady, 2010; see also Schradie, 2012.

16. Thrall, Stecula, and Sweet, 2014.

17. Karpf, 2016.

18. Benkler, Shaw, and Hill, 2015.

19. MacArthur and Wilson, 1976.

20. One this point see Vaidhyanathan, 2012; Mueller, 2010.

21. Picard, 2014.

22. DeNardis, 2014.

23. The phrase "content is king" seems to have been coined by Bill Gates in a 1996 essay published on the Microsoft website that has long since been taken offline.

24. Bagdikian, 2004.

25. E. M. Noam, 2015; see also Odlyzko, 2001.

26. Wu, 2003.

27. FTC, n.d.

28. Amazon is something of a special case, with its core business long optimized for explosive growth rather than for profit. Their AWS cloud computing business, though, is exceptionally profitable and responsible for a large chunk of the firms' market valuation.

29. Mullins, Winkler, and Kendall, 2015.

30. Federal Trade Commission, 2012, p. 112.

31. Shapiro and Varian, 1998; see chapter 2.

32. Federal Trade Commission, 2012, p. 112.

33. Scott, 2017.

34. Wu, 2011; though for a critique, see Starr, 2011.

35. Yarow, 2013.

36. For a good discussion of this point, see Orbach, 2013.
37. Easterbrook, 2008.
38. Zuboff, 2015.
39. Bradshaw and Howard, 2017.
40. King, Pan, and Roberts, 2013, 2017.
41. Silverman, 2017.
42. Howard et al. 2017.
43. Calabresi, 2017.
44. Petrova, 2011.
45. Quoted in Starr, 2004, p. 257.
46. Chyi and Tenenboim, 2017.

Appendix on Data, Methodology, and Models

1. Quoted in Dyson, 2004.
2. Noam, 2004 and 2009.
3. Noam, 2004.
4. Hindman, 2009; Hamilton, 2004; Napoli, 2012.
5. Shiman, 2007; Crawford, 2007.
6. Smith, 2010.

BIBLIOGRAPHY

Abadi, M., Barham, P., Chen, J., Chen, Z., Davis, A., Dean, J., ..., Isard, M., et al. (2016). Tensorflow: a system for large-scale machine learning. In OSDI (16, 265–83).

Abbatte, J. (1998). *Inventing the Internet.* Cambridge, MA: MIT Press.

Adams, W. J., and Yellen, J. L. (1976). Commodity bundling and the burden of monopoly. *Quarterly Journal of Economics, 90:* 475–98.

Aksoy, L., van Riel, A., Kandampully, J., Wirtz, J., den Ambtman, A., Bloemer, J., ..., Gurhan Canli, Z., et al. (2013). Managing brands and customer engagement in online brand communities. *Journal of Service Management, 24*(3), 223–44.

Amatriain, X., and Basilico, J. (2012, April). *Netflix recommendations: beyond the 5 stars.* Blog post. Retrieved from http://techblog.netflix.com/2012/04/netflix-recommendations-beyond-5-stars.html.

Anderson, C. (2004, December). The long tail. *Wired.* Retrieved from http://www.wired.com/wired/archive/12.10/tail.html.

Anderson, D., and Mattingly, J. C. (2007). Propagation of fluctuations in biochemical systems, II: nonlinear chains. *IET Systems Biology, 1*(6), 313–25.

Ariely, D., and Norton, M. I. (2008). How actions create—not just reveal—preferences. *Trends in Cognitive Sciences, 12*(1), 13–16.

Arthur, W. (1989). Competing technologies, increasing returns, and lock-in by historical events. *The Economic Journal, 99*(394), 116–31.

Artz, D. (2009). *The secret weapons of the AOL optimization team.* Presentation, O'Reilly Velocity Conference, June 22–24. Retrieved from http://assets.en.oreilly.com/1/event/29/The_Secret_Weapons_of_the_AOL_Optimization_Team_Presentation.pdf.

Asch, S. E. (1955). Opinions and social pressure. *Scientific American 193*(5), 31–35.

Ataullah, A. A., and Lank, E. (2010). Googling Bing: reassessing the impact of brand on the perceived quality of two contemporary search engines. In *Proceedings of the 24th BCS Interaction Specialist Group Conference*, Dundee, September 6–10 (pp. 337–45). British Computer Society.

Athey, S., Mobius, M. M., and Pál, J. (2017). The impact of aggregators on internet news consumption. Stanford University Graduate School of Business Research Paper 17–8. Retrieved from https://ssrh.com/abstract-2897960.

AT&T. (1908). Annual report. Retrieved from http://www.beatriceco.com/bti/porticus/bell/pdf/1908ATTar_Complete.pdf.

———. (2009). *Statistics can find you a movie.* Retrieved from http://www.research.att.com/articles/featured_stories/2010_01/2010_02_netflix_article.html.

———. (2010). *From the lab: winning the Netflix Prize.* Retrieved from http://www.youtube.com/watch?v=ImpV70uLxyw.

Ayres, I., Atiq, E., Li, S., and Lu, M. (2013). Randomized experiment assessing the accuracy of Microsoft's Bing It On challenge. *Loyola Consumer Law Review, 26,* 1.

Bagdikian, B. H. (1985). The U.S. media: supermarket or assembly line? *Journal of Communication, 35*(3), 97–109.

Bagdikian, B. H. (2004). *The new media monopoly.* Boston, MA: Beacon Press.

Bai, M. (2009). Bloggers at the gate. *Democracy, 12,* 108–14.

Bain, J. S. (1954). Economies of scale, concentration, and the condition of entry in twenty manufacturing industries. *American Economic Review, 44*(1): 15–39.

———. (1956). *Barriers to new competition: their character and consequences in manufacturing industries.* Cambridge, MA: Harvard University Press.

Bakos, Y., and Brynjolfsson, E. (1999). Bundling information goods: pricing, profits, and efficiency. *Management Science, 45*(12), 1613–30.

———. (2000). Bundling and competition on the internet. *Marketing Science, 19*(1), 63–82.

Bakshy, E., Eckles, D., and Bernstein, M. S. (2014). Designing and deploying online field experiments. In *Proceedings of the 23rd International Conference on the World Wide Web* (pp. 283–92). ACM.

Banko, M., and Brill, E. (2001). Scaling to very very large corpora for natural language disambiguation. In *Proceedings of the 39th Annual Meeting of the Association for Computational Linguistics*, Toulouse, FR (pp. 26–33). Association for Computational Linguistics.

Barabási, A., and Albert, R. (1999). Emergence of scaling in random networks. *Science, 286*(5439), 509.

Barlow, J. P. (1996). *A declaration of the independence of cyberspace.*

Bart, Y., Shankar, V., Sultan, F., and Urban, G. L. (2005). Are the drivers and role of online trust the same for all websites and consumers? A large-scale exploratory empirical study. *Journal of Marketing, 69*(4), 133–52.

Barthel, M., and Mitchell, A. (2017). Americans' attitudes about the news media deeply divided along partisan lines. Pew Internet and American Life Project. Retrieved from http://www.journalism.org/2017/05/10/americans-attitudes-about-the-news-media-deeply-divided-along-partisan-lines/.

Beam, C. (2010, September). The other social network. *Slate.* Retrieved from http://www.slate.com/articles/technology/technology/2010/09/the_other_social_network.html.

Beebe, J. H. (1977). Institutional structure and program choices in television markets. *Quarterly Journal of Economics, 91*(1), 15–37.

Bell, E. (2018, January). Why Facebook's news feed changes are bad news for democracy. *The Guardian.* Retrieved from https://www.theguardian.com/media/media-blog/2018/jan/21/why-facebook-news-feed-changes-bad-news-democracy.

Benes, R. (2017). Side effect of the pivot to video: audience shrinkage. *Digiday.* Retrieved from https://digiday.com/media/side-effect-pivot-video-audience-shrinkage/.

Benkler, Y. (2006). *The wealth of networks: how social production transforms markets and freedom.* New Haven, CT: Yale University Press.

Benkler, Y., Shaw, A., and Hill, B. M. (2015). Peer production: a form of collective intelligence. In T. Malone and M. Bernstein (eds.), *Handbook of collective intelligence* (pp. 175–203). Cambridge, MA: MIT Press.

Benton, J. (2016, March). The game of concentration: the internet is pushing the American news business to New York and the coasts. *NiemanLab*. Retrieved from http://www.niemanlab.org/2016/03/the-game-of-concentration-the-internet-is -pushing-the-american-news-business-to-new-york-and-the-coasts/.

Berners-Lee, T. (2000). *Weaving the Web*. New York: HarperBusiness.

Bhatotia, P., Wieder, A., Akkuş, İ. E., Rodrigues, R., and Acar, U. A. (2011). Large-scale incremental data processing with change propagation. In *Proceedings of the 3rd USENIX Conference on Hot Topics in Cloud Computing*, Portland, OR. Retrieved from https://dl.acm.org/citation.cfm?id=2170462.

Blumler, J., and Kavanagh, D. (1999). The third age of political communication: influences and features. *Political Communication, 16*(3), 209–30.

Boczkowski, P. J. (2010). *News at work: imitation in an age of information abundance*. Chicago, IL: University of Chicago Press.

Boczkowski, P. J., and Mitchelstein, E. (2013). *The news gap: when the information preferences of the media and the public diverge*. Cambridge, MA: MIT Press.

Bohn, D., and Hamburger, E. (2013, January). Redesigning Google: how Larry Page engineered a beautiful revolution. *The Verge*. Retrieved from http://www.theverge .com/2013/1/24/3904134/google-redesign-how-larry-page-engineered-beautiful -revolution.

Bowler, P. J. (1989). *Evolution: the history of an idea*. Berkeley: University of California Press.

Bowman, D. (2009). *Goodbye, Google*. Blog post, March 20. Retrieved from http://stopdesign.com/archive/2009/03/20/goodbye-google.html.

Box, G. E. (1979). Robustness in the strategy of scientific model building. *Robustness in statistics, 1*, 201–36.

Boyd, E. B. (2011, August). Brains and bots deep inside Yahoo's CORE grab a billion clicks. *Fast Company*. Retrieved from http://www.fastcompany.com/1770673/brains -and-bots-deep-inside-yahoos-core-grab-billion-clicks.

Bradshaw, S., and Howard, P. N. (2017). *Troops, trolls and troublemakers: a global inventory of organized social media manipulation*. Retrieved from http://comprop.oii.ox.ac.uk /wp-content/uploads/sites/89/2017/07/Troops-Trolls-and-Troublemakers.pdf.

Brian, M. (2014, June). Google's new "material design" UI coming to Android, Chrome OS and the web. *Engadget*. Retrieved from https://www.engadget.com/2014 /06/25/googles-new-design-language-is-called-material-design/.

Briscoe, B., Odlyzko, A., and Tilly, B. (2006). Metcalfe's Law is wrong: communications networks increase in value as they add members, but by how much? *IEEE Spectrum, 43*(7), 34–39.

Brodersen, K. H., Gallusser, F., Koehler, J., Remy, N., Scott, S. L., et al. (2015). Inferring causal impact using Bayesian structural time-series models. *The Annals of Applied Statistics, 9*(1), 247–74.

Brynjolfsson, E., and Smith, M. D. (2000). Frictionless commerce: a comparison of internet and conventional retailers. *Management science, 46*(4), 563–85.

Buchanan, M. (2013, May). The design that conquered Google. *New Yorker*. Retrieved from http://www.newyorker.com/online/blogs/elements/2013/05/the -evolution-of-google-design.html.

Bucy, E. (2004). Second generation net news: interactivity and information accessibility in the online environment. *International Journal on Media Management, 6*(1–2), 102–13.

Burrows, M. (2006). The Chubby lock service for loosely-coupled distributed systems. In *Proceedings of the 7th Symposium on Operating Systems Design and Implementation*, Seattle, WA (pp. 335–50). USENIX Association.

Cadwalladr, C., and Graham-Harrison, E. (2018, March). Revealed: 50 million Facebook profiles harvested for Cambridge Analytica in major data breach. *The Guardian.* Retrieved from https://www.theguardian.com/news/2018/mar/17/cambridge -analytica-facebook-influence-us-election.

Cairncross, F. (2001). *The death of distance: how the communications revolution is changing our lives.* Cambridge, MA: Harvard Business School Press.

Calabresi, M. (2017, May). Inside Russia's social media war on America. *Time.* Retrieved from http://time.com/4783932/inside-russia-social-media-war-america/.

Caldas, A., Schroeder, R., Mesch, G., and Dutton, W. (2008). Patterns of information search and access on the World Wide Web: democratizing expertise or creating new hierarchies? *Journal of Computer-Mediated Communication, 13*(4), 769–93.

Caldentey, R., and Stacchetti, E. (2010). Insider trading with a random deadline. *Econometrica, 78*(1), 245–83.

Carlson, N. (2013, November). The cost of winning: Tim Armstrong, Patch, and the struggle to save AOL. *Business Insider.* Retrieved from http://www.businessinsider .com.au/tim-armstrong-patch-aol-2013-10.

Carr, D. (2013, December). AOL chief's white whale finally slips his grasp. *New York Times.* Retrieved from http://www.nytimes.com/2013/12/16/business/media/aol -chiefs-white-whale-finally-slips-his-grasp.html.

Carroll, J. (2008, April). This is really a newspaper. *San Francisco Chronicle.* Retrieved from http://www.sfgate.com/entertainment/article/This-is-really-a-newspaper -3287998.php.

Castillo, M. (2014, November). News sites top list of slowest-loading websites. *Adweek.* Retrieved from http://www.adweek.com/news/technology/news-sites-top-list -slowest-loading-web-pages-161619.

Chandler, A. D. (1964). *Giant enterprise: Ford, General Motors, and the automobile industry.* New York: Harcourt Brace.

———. (1977). *The visible hand: The managerial revolution in American business.* Cambridge, MA: Bellknap.

Chang, F., Dean, J., Ghemawat, S., Hsieh, W. C., Wallach, D. A., Burrows, M., . . . Gruber, R. E. (2008). Bigtable: a distributed storage system for structured data. *ACM Transactions on Computer Systems (TOCS), 26*(2), 4.

Chattopadhyay, B., Lin, L., Liu, W., Mittal, S., Aragonda, P., Lychagina, V., . . . Wong, M. (2011). Tenzing: a SQL implementation on the MapReduce framework. In *Proceedings of the VLDB Endowment*, Seattle, WA (pp. 1318–1327).

Chittum, R. (2014). Gannett's print-focused paywalls flounder: the quality imperative and charging for news online. *Columbia Journalism Review.* Retrieved from https://archives.cjr.org/the_audit/gannetts_paywall_plan-flounder.

Chyi, H. I., and Tenenboim, O. (2017). Reality check: multiplatform newspaper readership in the United States, 2007–2015. *Journalism Practice, 11*(7), 798–819.

Cialdini, R. B., and Goldstein, N. J. (2004). Social influence: compliance and conformity. *Annual Review of Psychology, 55,* 591–621.

Clauset, A., Shalizi, C. R., and Newman, M. E. (2009). Power-law distributions in empirical data. *SIAM Review, 51*(4), 661–703.

Cohen, D. (2017, April). Facebook's new video content deals with publishers that emphasize produced videos. *Ad Age.* Retrieved from http://www.adweek.com/digital /facebook-video-content-deals-publishers-produced-video-content/.

Cook, W. A., and Pettit, R. C. (2009). *comScore Media Metrix U.S. methodology.* Advertising Research Foundation.

Corbett, J. C., Dean, J., Epstein, M., Fikes, A., Frost, C., Furman, J., ..., Hochschild, P., et al. (2012). Spanner: Google's globally-distributed database. In *Proceedings of OSDI 2012: Tenth Symposium on Operating System Design and Implementation*, Hollywood, CA (pp. 251–264).

Crawford, G. (2007). Television station ownership structure and the quantity and quality of TV programming. Federal Communications Commission Media Ownership Study, Washington, D.C.

Cyr, D. (2008). Modeling web site design across cultures: relationships to trust, satisfaction, and e-loyalty. *Journal of Management Information Systems, 24*(4), 47–72.

Dahlgren, P. (2005). The Internet, public spheres, and political communication: dispersion and deliberation. *Political Communication, 22*(2), 147–62.

Das, A., Datar, M., Garg, A., and Rajaram, S. (2007). Google News personalization: scalable online collaborative filtering. In *Proceedings of the 16th International Conference on World Wide Web* (pp. 271–280). ACM.

David, P. A. (1985). Clio and the economics of QWERTY. *American Economic Review, 75*(2), 332–37.

Davis, E. (1921). *The history of the New York Times 1851–1921.* New York: New York Times.

Dean, D., DiGrande, S., Field, D., Lundmark, A., O'Day, J., Pineda, J., and Zwillenberg, P. (2012). The Internet economy in the G-20. *BCG Perspectives.* Retrieved from https://www.bcgperspectives.com/content/articles/media_entertainment_strategic _planning_4_2_trillion_opportunity_internet_economy_g20/.

Dean, J., and Ghemawat, S. (2008). MapReduce: simplified data processing on large clusters. *Communications of the ACM, 51*(1), 107–13.

DeepMind. (2016). *DeepMind AI reduces Google data centre cooling bill by 40%.* Press release. Retrieved from https://deepmind.com/blog/deepmind-ai-reduces-google -data-centre-cooling-bill-40/.

DeNardis, L. (2014). *The global war for Internet governance.* New Haven, CT: Yale University Press.

Department of Justice & Federal Trade Commission. (2010, August). *Horizontal merger guidelines.* Revised August 19. Retrieved from https://www.justice.gov/sites/default/files/atr/legacy/2010/08/19/hmg-2010.pdf.

Deuze, M. (2003). The web and its journalisms: considering the consequences of different types of newsmedia online. *New Media & Society, 5*(2), 203–30.

Dimmick, J. W. (2002). *Media competition and coexistence: the theory of the niche.* New York: Routledge.

Dixit, A. K., and Stiglitz, J. E. (1977). Monopolistic competition and optimum product diversity. *American Economic Review, 67*(3), 297–308.

Doherty, B. (2004, August). John Perry Barlow 2.0. *Reason.* Retrieved from https://reason.com/archives/2004/08/01/john-perry-barlow-20.

Downs, A. (1957). *An economic theory of democracy.* New York: Harper.

Dyson, F. (2004). A meeting with Enrico Fermi. *Nature, 427,* 297.

Earl, J., and Kimport, K. (2011). *Digitally enabled social change: activism in the Internet age.* Cambridge, MA: MIT Press.

Easterbrook, F. H. (2008). The Chicago School and exclusionary conduct. *Harvard Journal of Law and Public Policy, 31,* 439.

Ehrenberg, A.S.C. (1968). The factor analytic search for program types. *Journal of Advertising Research, 8*(1), 55–63.

Ellis, J. (2012, May). The Guardian: yep, it was "major changes" by Facebook that caused drop in social reader traffic. *NeimanLab.* Retrieved from http://www.niemanlab.org/2012/05/the-guardian-yep-it-was-major-changes-by-facebook-that-caused-drop-in-social-reader-traffic/.

———. (2014, May). If my newspaper puts up a metered paywall, how many people will pay? here's some data. *NeimanLab.* Retrieved from http://www.niemanlab.org/2014/05/if-my-newspaper-puts-up-a-metered-paywall-how-many-people-will-pay-heres-some-data/.

eMarketer. (2014, March). *Driven by Facebook and Google, mobile ad market soars 105% in 2013.* Retrieved from http://www.emarketer.com/Article/Driven-by-Facebook-Google-Mobile-Ad-Market-Soars-10537-2013/1010690.

Faulhaber, G. R., Singer, H. J., and Urschel, A. H. (2017). The curious absence of economic analysis at the Federal Communications Commission: an agency in search of a mission. *International Journal of Communication, 11,* 1214–33.

Federal Communication Commission [FCC]. (2017, November). Order on reconsideration and proposed rulemaking FCC-17-156. Retrieved from https://apps.fcc.gov/edocs_public/attachmatch/FCC-17-156A1.pdf.

Federal Trade Commission. (2012). *Google inc.* Memorandum. File 111-0163. Project DXI. Retrieved from https://graphics.wsj.com/google-ftc-report/img/ftc-ocr-watermark.pdf.

———. (n.d.). *Monopolization defined.* Retrieved from https://www.ftc.gov/tips-advice/competition-guidance/guide-antitrust-laws/single-firm-conduct/monopolization-defined.

Fernholz, E. R. (2002). *Stochastic portfolio theory.* New York: Springer.

Flavián, C., Guinalíu, M., and Gurrea, R. (2006). The role played by perceived usability, satisfaction and consumer trust on website loyalty. *Information & Management, 43*(1), 1–14.

Flink, J. J. (1990). *The automobile age.* Cambridge, MA: MIT Press.

Frier, S. (2018, March). Trump's campaign said it was better at Facebook. Facebook agrees. *Bloomberg.* Retrieved from https://www.bloomberg.com/news/articles/2018-04-03/trump-s-campaign-said-it-was-better-at-facebook-facebook-agrees.

Funk, S. (2006, December). *Try this at home.* Blog post. Retrieved from http://sifter .org/~simon/journal/20061211.html.

Gabaix, X. (1999). Zipf's law for cities: an explanation. *Quarterly Journal of Economics, 114*(3), 739–67.

Gannett Co. (2018, February). Gannett Reports Fourth Quarter and Full-Year 2017 Results. Press release. Retrieved from https://www.gannett.com/news/press-releases/2018/2/20/gannett-reports-fourth-quarter-and-full-year-2017-results/

Garrett, J. J. (2005). Ajax: a new approach to web applications. Retrieved from http://www.adaptivepath.com/ideas/ajax-new-approach-web-applications.

Garrett, R. K. (2009). Politically motivated reinforcement seeking: reframing the selective exposure debate. *Journal of Communication, 59*(4), 676–99.

Gates, B. (2000). *Business at the speed of thought: succeed in the digital economy.* New York: Warner Business Books.

Gelman, A. (2010). When small numbers lead to big errors. *Scientific American, 303*(4), 31.

Gentzkow, M., and Shapiro, J. M. (2011). Ideological segregation online and offline. *Quarterly Journal of Economics, 126*(4), 1799–839.

Ghemawat, S., Gobioff, H., and Leung, S.-T. (2003). The Google file system. In *ACM SIGOPS Operating Systems Review, 37*(5), pp. 29–43. ACM.

Glaeser, E. L. (2005). Urban colossus: why is New York America's largest city? *Federal Reserve Bank of New York Economic Policy Review, 11*(2), 7.

Goel, N. S., and Richter-Dyn, N. (1974). *Stochastic models in biology.* Caldwell, NJ: Blackburn Press.

Goldhaber, M. H. (1997). The attention economy and the net. *First Monday, 2*(4).

Goodhardt, G., and Ehrenberg, A. (1969). Duplication of television viewing between and within channels. *Journal of Marketing Research, 6*(2).

Google. (2013). *Efficiency: how we do it.* Retrieved from http://www.google.com/about /datacenters/efficiency/internal/.

Gorrell, G. (2006). Generalized Hebbian algorithm for incremental singular value decomposition in natural language processing. In *Proceedings of EACL*, Trento, Italy (pp. 97–104).

Gould, S. J. (2002). *The structure of evolutionary theory.* Cambridge, MA: Harvard University Press.

Graves, L. (2010). Traffic jam: we'll never agree about online audience size. *Columbia Journalism Review.* Retrieved from https://archives.cjr.org/reports/traffic_jam.php.

Graves, L., Kelly, J., and Gluck, M. (2010). Confusion online: faulty metrics and the future of digital journalism. Tow Center for Digital Journalism, Columbia University, New York. Retrieved from http://towcenter.org/research/confusion -online-faults-metrics-and-the-future-of-journalism/

Greenslade, R. (2012, June). Local news crisis: what crisis? audiences are bigger than ever. *The Guardian.* Retrieved from http://www.theguardian.com/media/greenslade /2012/jun/29/local-newspapers-newspapers.

Ha, H.-Y., and Perks, H. (2005). Effects of consumer perceptions of brand experience on the web: brand familiarity, satisfaction and brand trust. *Journal of Consumer Behaviour, 4*(6), 438–52.

Haim, M., Graefe, A., and Brosius, H. B. (2017). Burst of the filter bubble? Effects of personalization on the diversity of Google News. *Digital Journalism, 6*(3), 330–343.

Haldi, J., and Whitcomb, D. (1967). Economies of scale in industrial plants. *Journal of Political Economy, 75*(4), 373–85.

Hamann, P. (2014). Breaking news at 1000ms. TECH.insight conference. Retrieved from https://speakerdeck.com/patrickhamann/breaking-news-at-1000ms-tech-dot -insight-2014.

Hamilton, J. (2004). *All the news that's fit to sell: how the market transforms information into news.* Princeton, NJ: Princeton University Press.

Hargittai, E. (2010). Digital na(t)ives? variation in internet skills and uses among members of the "net generation." *Sociological Inquiry, 80*(1), 92–113.

Hargittai, E., Fullerton, L., Menchen-Trevino, E., and Thomas, K. Y. (2010). Trust online: young adults' evaluation of web content. *International Journal of Communication, 4*(1), 468–94.

Hargittai, E., and Shaw, A. (2015). Mind the skills gap: the role of internet know-how and gender in differentiated contributions to Wikipedia. *Information, Communication & Society, 18*(4), 424–42.

Heath, C., and Heath, D. (2011). *The myth of the garage.* New York: Crown Business.

Helmreich, S. (1998). *Silicon second nature: culturing artificial life in a digital world.* Berkeley: University of California Press.

Hindman, M. (2009). *The myth of digital democracy.* Princeton, NJ: Princeton University Press.

———. (2018, March). How Cambridge Analytica's Facebook targeting model really worked—according to the person who built it. *The Conversation.* Retrieved from https://theconversation.com/how-cambridge-analyticas-facebook-targeting -model-really-worked-according-to-the-person-who-built-it-94078.

Hobbes, T. (1651 [1996]). *Leviathan* (R. Tuck, ed.). Cambridge, England: Cambridge University Press.

Hoch, S. J., and Deighton, J. (1989). Managing what consumers learn from experience. *Journal of Marketing, 53*(2): 1–20.

Holcomb, J., and Mitchell, A. (2014). The revenue picture for American journalism and how it is changing. State of the News Media, 2014. Washington, D.C.: Pew Research Center.

Hölzle, U. (2012, January). The Google gospel of speed. *Think Quarterly.* Retrieved from http://www.google.com/think/articles/the-google-gospel-of-speed-urs -hoelzle.html.

Hotelling, H. (1929). Stability in competition. *Economic Journal, 39*(153), 41–57.

Howard, P. N., Bolsover, G., Kollanyi, B., Bradshaw, S., and Neudert, L.-M. (2017). *Junk news and bots during the U.S. election: what were Michigan voters sharing over Twitter?* Data Memo. Oxford, England: Project on Computational Propaganda. Retrieved from http://comprop.oii.ox.ac.uk/2017/03/26/junk-news-and-bots-during-the -uselection-what-were-michigan-voters-sharing-over-twitter.

Hundt, R. (1996). Speech delivered at the Wall Street Journal Business and Technology Conference. Washington, D.C., September 18. Retrieved from http://transition .fcc.gov/Speeches/Hundt/spreh636.txt.

Hunt, N. (2010). Netflix Prize update. Blog Post, March 23. Retrieved from http://blog
.netflix.com/2010/03/this-is-neil-hunt-chief-product-officer.html.

Ingram, M. (2017, January). How Google and Facebook have taken over the digital ad
industry. *Fortune.* Retrieved from http://fortune.com/2017/01/04/google
-facebook-ad-industry/.

Interactive Advertising Bureau [IAB]. (2010). *Measurement guidelines.* Retrieved
from http://www.iab.net/iab_products_and_industry_services/508676
/guidelines.

Iyengar, S., and Hahn, K. S. (2009). Red media, blue media: evidence of ideological
selectivity in media use. *Journal of Communication, 59*(1), 19–39.

Jansen, B. J., Zhang, L., and Mattila, A. S. (2012). User reactions to search engines logos:
investigating brand knowledge of web search engines. *Electronic Commerce Research,
12*(4), 429–54.

Jansen, B. J., Zhang, M., and Schultz, C. D. (2009). Brand and its effect on user
perception of search engine performance. *Journal of the American Society for
Information Science and Technology, 60*(8), 1572–95.

Jarvis, J. (2013, December). The almost-post mortem for Patch. *BuzzMachine.* Retrieved
from http://buzzmachine.com/2013/12/16/patch-almost-post-mortem/.

Johnson, E., Bellman, S., and Lohse, G. (2003). Cognitive lock-in and the power law of
practice. *Journal of Marketing, 67*(2), 62–75.

Johnson, G. A., Lewis, R. A., and Reiley, D. H. (2016). When less is more: data and
power in advertising experiments. *Marketing Science, 36*(1), 43–53.

Jouppi, N. P., Young, C., Patil, N., Patterson, D., Agrawal, G., Bajwa, R., ..., Borchers,
A., et al. (2017). In-datacenter performance analysis of a tensor processing unit. In
Proceedings of the 44th Annual International Symposium on Computer Architecture,
Toronto, Canada (pp. 1–12). ACM.

Kahneman, D. (2011). *Thinking, fast and slow.* New York: Farrar, Straus and
Giroux.

Kalogeropoulos, A., and Newman, N. (2017). "I saw the news on Facebook": brand
attribution when accessing news from distributed environments. Reuters Institute
for the Study of Journalism. Retrieved from https://papers.ssrn.com/sol3
/papers.cfm?abstract_id=3005412.

Kanagal, B., Ahmed, A., Pandey, S., Josifovski, V., Garcia-Pueyo, L., and Yuan, J. (2013).
Focused matrix factorization for audience selection in display advertising. In
Proceedings of the 29th International Conference on Data Engineering (ICDE)
(pp. 386–97). IEEE.

Karpf, D. (2016). *Analytic activism: digital listening and the new political strategy.* New
York: Oxford University Press.

Kennard, W. E. (1999, April). From the vast wasteland to the vast broadband. Speech to
the National Association of Broadcasters. Retrieved from http://transition.fcc
.gov/Speeches/Kennard/spwek914.html.

King, G., Pan, J., and Roberts, M. E. (2013). How censorship in China allows
government criticism but silences collective expression. *American Political Science
Review, 107*(2), 326–43.

———. (2017). How the Chinese government fabricates social media posts for strategic distraction, not engaged argument. *American Political Science Review, 111*(3), 484–501.

Kirchoff, S. M. (2010, September). The U.S. newspaper industry in transition. Congressional Research Service. Retrieved from http://fas.org/sgp/crs/misc/R40700.pdf

Kirkpatrick, D. (2011). *The Facebook effect: the inside story of the company that is connecting the world.* New York: Simon and Schuster.

Kirsch, A. D., and Banks, S. (1962). Program types defined by factor analysis. *Journal of Advertising Research, 2*(3), 29–31.

Kirshenbaum, E., Forman, G., and Dugan, M. (2012). A live comparison of methods for personalized article recommendation at Forbes.com. *Joint European Conference on Machine Learning and Knowledge Discovery in Databases*, Bristol, England (pp. 51–66).

Knight Foundation. (2016, May). Mobile first news: how people use smartphones to access information. Retrieved from https://www.knightfoundation.org/media/uploads/publication_pdfs/KF_Mobile-Report_Final_050916.pdf.

Kohavi, R., Deng, A., Frasca, B., Walker, T., Xu, Y., and Pohlmann, N. (2013). Online controlled experiments at large scale. In *Proceedings of the 19th ACM SIGKDD international conference on Knowledge Discovery and Data Mining*, Chicago, IL (pp. 1168–76). ACM.

Konigsburg, E. (2014). *The surprising path to a faster NYTimes.com.* Velocity New York conference, September 16. Retrieved from https://speakerdeck.com/nytdevs/the-surprising-path-to-a-faster-nytimes-dot-com.

Kopytoff, V. G. (2011, January). AOL bets on hyperlocal news, finding progress where many have failed. *New York Times.* Retrieved from http://www.nytimes.com/2011/01/17/business/media/17local.html.

Koren, Y. (2009). The Netflix Prize: quest for $1,000,000. Lecture, Rutgers University. Retrieved from http://www.youtube.com/watch?v=YWMzgCsFIFY.

Kosinski, M., Stillwell, D., and Graepel, T. (2013). Private traits and attributes are predictable from digital records of human behavior. *Proceedings of the National Academy of Sciences, 110*(15), 5802–5.

Kovach, B., and Rosenstiel, T. (2007). *The elements of journalism: what newspeople should know and the public should expect.* New York: Three Rivers Press.

Krug, S. (2014). *Don't make me think, revisited: a common sense approach to web usability.* Berkeley, CA: New Riders.

Krugman, H. E. (1972). Why three exposures may be enough. *Journal of Advertising Research, 12*(6), 11–14.

Krugman, P. (1979). Increasing returns, monopolistic competition, and international trade. *Journal of International Economics, 9*(4), 469–79.

———. (1980). Scale economies, product differentiation, and the pattern of trade. *American Economic Review, 70*(5), 950–59.

———. (1997). *Development, geography, and economic theory.* Cambridge, MA: MIT Press.

———. (2009). The increasing returns revolution in trade and geography. *American Economic Review, 99*(3), 561–71.

Ksiazek, T. B., Peer, L., and Lessard, K. (2014). User engagement with online news: conceptualizing interactivity and exploring the relationship between online news videos and user comments. *New Media & Society, 65*(10), 1988–2005.

Labovitz, C., Iekel-Johnson, S., McPherson, D., Oberheide, J., Jahanian, F., and Karir, M. (2009). ATLAS Internet Observatory 2009 annual report. Retrieved from https://www.nanog.or/meetings/nanog47/presentations/monday/Labovitz_Observe Report_N47_Mon.pdf

Lambrecht, A., and Tucker, C. (2013). When does retargeting work? information specificity in online advertising. *Journal of Marketing Research, 50*(5), 561–76.

Last, J. (2002, March). Reading, writing, and blogging. *Weekly Standard.* Retrieved from http://www.weeklystandard.com/Content/Public/Articles/000/000/001/009flofq.asp.

Lee, E., and Molla, R. (2018, February). The New York Times digital paywall business is growing as fast as Facebook and faster than Google. *Recode.* Retrieved from https://www.recode.net/2018/2/8/16991090/new-york-times-digital-paywall -business-growing-fast-facebook-google-newspaper-subscription.

Levendusky, M. (2013). *How partisan media polarize America.* Chicago, IL: University of Chicago Press.

Levy, M., and Solomon, S. (1997). New evidence for the power-law distribution of wealth. *Physica A: Statistical and Theoretical Physics, 242*(1–2), 90–94.

Levy, S. (2012, April). Going with the flow: Google's secret switch to the next wave of networking. *Wired.* Retrieved from http://www.wired.com/2012/04/going -with-the-flow-google/.

Lewis, R. A., and Rao, J. M. (2015). The unfavorable economics of measuring the returns to advertising. *Quarterly Journal of Economics, 130*(4), 1941–73.

Liu, J., Dolan, P., and Pedersen, E. (2010). Personalized news recommendation based on click behavior. In *Proceedings of the 15th International Conference on Intelligent User Interfaces*, Hong Kong (pp. 31–40). ACM.

Lo, D., Cheng, L., Govindaraju, R., Ranganathan, P., and Kozyrakis, C. (2015). Heracles: improving resource efficiency at scale. In *Proceedings of the 42th Annual International Symposium on Computer Architecture*, Portland, OR.

MacArthur, R. H., and Wilson, E. O. (1976). *The theory of island biogeography.* Princeton, NJ: Princeton University Press.

Manjoo, F. (2013, June). You won't finish this article. *Slate.* Retrieved from http://www .slate.com/articles/technology/technology/2013/06/how_people_read_online_why _you_won_t_finish_this_article.html.

Marshall, J. [Jack]. (2016, February). Patch rebounds after spilt from AOL. *Wall Street Journal.* Retrieved from https://www.wsj.com/articles/patch-rebounds-after-split -from-aol-1454445340.

Marshall, J. [Josh]. (2017, November). There's a digital media crash. But no one will say it. *Talking Points Memo.* Retrieved from http://talkingpointsmemo.com/edblog/theres -a-digital-media-crash-but-no-one-will-say-it.

Mayer, M. (2007, June). *Scaling Google for every user.* Keynote presentation, Google Seattle Conference on Scalability. Retrieved from http://www.youtube.com/watch?v =Syc3axgRsBw.

Mayer-Schoenberger, V., and Cukier, K. (2013). *Big data.* New York: Houghton Mifflin Harcourt.

Mayr, E. (1982). *The growth of biological thought: Diversity, evolution, and inheritance.* Cambridge, MA: Harvard University Press.

McChesney, R., and Nichols, J. (2011). *The death and life of American journalism: the media revolution that will begin the world again.* New York: Nation Books.

McClatchy Company. (2013). Annual report. Retrieved from http://media.mcclatchy .com/smedia/2014/03/24/17/45/SYS83.So.32.pdf.

McKnight, D. H., Choudhury, V., and Kacmar, C. (2002). The impact of initial consumer trust on intentions to transact with a website: a trust building model. *Journal of Strategic Information Systems, 11*(3), 297–323.

McKusick, M. K., and Quinlan, S. (2009, August). GFS: evolution on fast-forward. *ACM Queue.* Retrieved from http://queue.acm. org/detail.cfm?id=1594206.

McMillan, R. (2012, July). Facebook mimics Google with underwater cable to Asia. Retrieved from http://www.wired.com/2012/07/facebook-submarine/.

Meiss, M., Menczer, F., Fortunato, S., Flammini, A., and Vespignani, A. (2008). Ranking web sites with real user traffic. In *Proceedings of the International Conference on Web Search and Web Data Mining*, Palo Alto, CA (pp. 65–76). ACM.

Mele, N. (2013). *The end of big: how the Internet makes David the new Goliath.* New York: Macmillan.

Melnik, S., Gubarev, A., Long, J. J., Romer, G., Shivakumar, S., Tolton, M., and Vassilakis, T. (2010). Dremel: interactive analysis of web-scale datasets. *Proceedings of the VLDB Endowment, 3*(1-2), 330–39.

Meraz, S. (2009). Is there an elite hold? traditional media to social media agenda setting influence in blog networks. *Journal of Computer-Mediated Communication, 14*(3), 682–707.

Meyer, P. (2004). *The vanishing newspaper: saving journalism in the information age.* Columbia: University of Missouri Press.

Mitchell, A., Gottfried, J., Barthel, M., and Shearer, E. (2016). *The modern news consumer.* Pew Research Center. Retrieved from http://www.journalism.org/2016/07/07/the -modern-news-consumer/.

Mitchell, A., Jurgowitz, M., and Olmstead, K. (2014, March). Search, social and direct: pathways to digital news. Pew Research Center. Retrieved from http://www .journalism.org/2014/03/13/social-search-direct/.

Mitchell, A., Rosenstiel, T., Santhanam, L. H., and Christian, L. (2012, October). The future of mobile news. Pew Research Center. Retrieved from http://www.journalism .org/2012/10/01/future-mobile-news/.

Mitzenmacher, M. (2004). A brief history of generative models for power law and lognormal distributions. *Internet Mathematics, 1*(2), 226–51.

Möller, J., Trilling, D., Helberger, N., and van Es, B. (2018). Do not blame it on the algorithm: an empirical assessment of multiple recommender systems and their impact on content diversity. *Information, Communication & Society, 21*(7), 959–77.

Monsell, S. (2003). Task switching. *Trends in Cognitive Sciences, 7*(3), 134–40.

Moore, H. N. (2017, September). The secret cost of pivoting to video. *Columbia Journalism Review.* Retrieved from https://www.cjr.org/business_of_news /pivot-to-video.php.

Moos, J. (2009, April). Transcript of Google CEO Eric Schmidt's Q&A at NAA [Newspaper Association of America]. Retrieved from http://www.poynter.org/latest -news/top-stories/95079/transcript-of-google-ceo-eric-schmidts-qa-at-naa/.

Morton, J. (2011). Costly mistakes. *American Journalism Review.* Retrieved from http://ajrarchive.org/article.asp?id=4994.

Moses, L. (2018, February). Little Things shuts down, a casualty of Facebook news feed change. *Digiday.* Retrieved from https://digiday.com/media/littlethings-shuts -casualty-facebook-news-feed-change/.

Mueller, M. L. (2010). *Networks and states: the global politics of internet governance.* Cambridge, MA: MIT Press.

Mullins, B., Winkler, R., and Kendall, B. (2015, March). Inside the U.S. antitrust probe of Google. *Wall Street Journal.* Retrieved from http://www.wsj.com/articles/inside -the-u-s-antitrust-probe-of-google-1426793274.

Munroe, R. (2013). Google's data centers on punch cards. *XKCD.* Retrieved from https://what-if.xkcd.com/63/.

Murray, K. B., and Häubl, G. (2007). Explaining cognitive lock-in: the role of skill-based habits of use in consumer choice. *Journal of Consumer Research, 34*(1), 77–88.

Mutter, A. (2009, February). Mission possible? Charging for web content. *Newsosaur.* Retrieved from http://newsosaur.blogspot.com/2009/02/mission-possible-charging -for-content.html.

———. (2012, December). Digital ad share dives sharply at newspapers. *Newsosaur.* Retrieved from https://newsosaur.blogspot.com/2012/12/digital-ad-share-dives -sharply-at.html.

———. (2014, January). Mobile offers local media a digital do-over. *Newsosaur.* Retrieved from http://newsosaur.blogspot.com/2014/01/mobile-offers-local-media-digital -do.html.

Nalebuff, B. (2004). Bundling as an entry barrier. *Quarterly Journal of Economics, 119*(1), 159–87.

Napoli, P. M. (2011). *Audience evolution: new technologies and the transformation of media audiences.* New York: Columbia University Press.

———. (2012). *Audience economics: media institutions and the audience marketplace.* New York: Columbia University Press.

Negroponte, N. (1995). *Being digital.* New York: Knopf.

Nelson, P. (1970). Information and consumer behavior. *Journal of Political Economy, 78*(2): 311–29.

Netflix. (2007). *Frequently asked questions.* Retrieved from http://www.netflixprize .com/faq.

Neuman, W. (1991). *The future of the mass audience.* Cambridge, UK: Cambridge University Press.

New York Times. (2014, March). Innovation. Internal report. Retrieved from http://mashable.com/2014/05/16/full-new-york-times-innovation-report/.

New York Times Company. (2013). Annual report. Retrieved from http://investors .nytco.com/files/doc_financials/annual/2013/2013_Annual_Report.pdf.

———. (2016). Annual report. Retrieved from http://s1.q4cdn.com/156149269 /files/doc_financials/annual/2016/Final-Web-Ready-Bookmarked-Annual -Report-(1).pdf.

Newman, A. and Leland, J. (2017, November). DNAinfo and Gothamist are shut down after vote to unionize. *New York Times.* Retrieved from https://www.nytimes.com /2017/11/02/nyregion/dnainfo-gothamist-shutting-down.html.

Newman, M. (2005). Power laws, Pareto distributions and Zipf's Law. *Contemporary Physics, 46*(5), 323–51.

Nielsen. (2014, July). So many apps, so much time. Retrieved from http://www.nielsen .com/us/en/insights/news/2014/smartphones-so-many-apps–so-much-time.html.

Noam, E. M. (2004). How to measure media concentration. *Financial Times.* September 7.

———. (2009). *Media ownership and concentration in America.* New York: Oxford University Press.

Noam, E. M. (2015). Is content king? Columbia Business School Research Paper 15-42. Retrieved from https://ssrn.com/abstract=2588295.

Odlyzko, A. (2001). Content is not king. *First Monday, 6*(2). Retrieved from http://firstmonday.org/article/view/833/742.

O'Hara, K., Contractor, N. S., Hall, W., Hendler, J. A., and Shadbolt, N. (2013). Web science: understanding the emergence of macro-level features on the World Wide Web. *Foundations and Trends in Web Science, 4*(2–3), 103–267.

Ohlin, B. (1935). *Interregional and international trade.* Cambridge, MA: Harvard University Press.

Olmstead, K., Mitchell, A., and Rosenstiel, T. (2011). *The top 25: navigating news online.* Pew Journalism Project. Retrieved from http://www.journalism.org/2011/05 /09/top-25/.

Orbach, B. (2013). How antitrust lost its goal. *Fordham Law Review, 81*(5), 2253–77.

O'Reilly, T. (2005). Web 2.0: Compact definition. *O'Reilly Radar.* Retrieved from http://radar.oreilly.com/2005/10/web-20-compact-definition.html.

Owen, B. M., and Wildman, S. S. (1992). *Video economics.* Cambridge, MA: Harvard University Press.

Pai, A. (2017, April). *The importance of economic analysis at the FCC.* Remarks of the FCC Chairman at the Hudson Institute. Retrieved from https://apps.fcc.gov/edocs _public/attachmatch/DOC-344248A1.pdf.

Palmer, J. W. (2002). Website usability, design, and performance metrics. *Information Systems Research, 13*(2), 151–67.

Pan, B., Hembrooke, H., Joachims, T., Lorigo, L., Gay, G., and Granka, L. (2007). *Journal of Computer-Mediated Communication, 12*(3), 801–23.

Pandey, S., Aly, M., Bagherjeiran, A., Hatch, A., Ciccolo, P., Ratnaparkhi, A., and Zinkevich, M. (2011). Learning to target: what works for behavioral targeting. In *Proceedings of the 20th ACM International Conference on Information and Knowledge Management*, Glasgow, Scotland (pp. 1805–14). ACM.

Pariser, E. (2011). *The filter bubble: what the internet is hiding from you.* New York: Penguin.

Pearn, J. (2012, January). *How many servers does Google have?* Blog post. Retrieved from https://plus.google.com/114250946512808775436/posts/VaQu9sNxJuY.

Peles, Y. (1971). Economies of scale in advertising beer and cigarettes. *Journal of Business, 44*(1): 32–37.

Petrova, M. (2011). Newspapers and parties: how advertising revenues created an independent press. *American Political Science Review, 105*(04), 790–808.

Pew. (2010). How news happens: a study of the news ecosystem of one American ciy. The Pew Research Center Project for Excellence in Journalism. Retrieved from http://www.journalism.org/analysis_report/how_news_happens/.

Pew Internet and American Life Project. (2017a). *Mobile technology fact sheet.* Accessed June 2017. Retrieved from http://www.pewinternet.org/fact-sheets/mobile -technology-fact-sheet/.

———. (2017b). *Newpsapers fact sheet.* Accessed June 2017. Retrieved from http://www.journalism.org/fact-sheet/newspapers/.

Picard, R. G. (2014). The future of the political economy of press freedom. *Communication Law and Policy, 19*(1), 97–107.

Pike, R., Dorward, S., Griesemer, R., and Quinlan, S. (2005). Interpreting the data: parallel analysis with Sawzall. *Scientific Programming, 13*(4), 277–98.

Pontin, J. (2012, May). Why publishers don't like apps. *MIT Technology Review.* Retrieved from http://www.technologyreview.com/news/427785/why-publishers-dont -like-apps/.

Pooley, J., and Winseck, D. (2017). A curious tale of economics and common carriage (net neutrality) at the FCC: a reply to Faulhaber, Singer, and Urschel. *International Journal of Communication, 11*, 2702–33.

PriceWaterhouseCoopers. (2008, December). Independent audit report to Hitwise. Retrieved from http://www.hitwise.com/us/privacy-policy/audit-report.

Prior, M. (2006). *Post-broadcast democracy.* New York: Cambridge University Press.

Raff, D. M. (1991). Making cars and making money in the interwar automobile industry: economies of scale and scope and the manufacturing behind the marketing. *Business History Review, 65*(04), 721–53.

Redner, S. (1998). How popular is your paper? An empirical study of the citation distribution. *European Physical Journal B, 4*(2), 131–34.

Reynolds, G. (2006). *An army of Davids: how markets and technology empower ordinary people to beat big media, big government, and other Goliaths.* Washington, D.C.: Nelson Current.

Rioul, O., and Vetterli, M. (2002). Wavelets and signal processing. *Signal Processing Magazine, 8*(4), 14–38.

Romenesko, J. (2013, August). Listen to AOL CEO Tim Armstrong fire Patch's creative director during a conference call. *JimRomenesko.com.* Retrieved from http://jimrom

enesko.com/2013/08/10/listen-to-aol-ceo-tim-armstrong-fire-his-creative-director
-during-a-conference-call/.

Rosen, J. (2011, July). This house believes: *The Economist* debates. *The Economist.*
Retrieved from http://www.economist.com/debate/overview/208/The
_news_industry.

Schafer, J., Konstan, J., and Riedl, J. (2001). E-commerce recommendation applications.
Data Mining and Knowledge Discovery, 5(1), 115–53.

Schaffer, J. (2010). Exploring a networked journalism collaborative in Philadelphia: an
analysis of the city's media ecosystem with final recommendations. J-Lab: The
Institute for Interactive Journalism. Retrieved from http://www.issuelab.org/resource
/exploring_a_networked_journalism_collaborative_in_philadelphia.

Schlozman, K. L., Verba, S., and Brady, H. E. (2010). Weapon of the strong?
Participatory inequality and the Internet. *Perspectives on Politics, 8*(2), 487–509.

Schmidt, E. (2014, October). Speech at the headquarters of Native Instruments, Berlin,
Germany. Retrieved from http://googlepolicyeurope.blogspot.com/2014/10/the
-new-grundergeist.html.

Schonfeld, E. (2010, March). Andreessen's advice to old media: "burn the boats."
TechCrunch. Retrieved from http://techcrunch.com/2010/03/06/andreessen
-media-burn-boats/.

Schradie, J. (2012). The trend of class, race, and ethnicity in social media inequality: who
still cannot afford to blog? *Information, Communication & Society, 15*(4), 555–71.

Schumpeter, J. A. (1942). *Socialism, capitalism and democracy.* New York: Harper and
Brothers.

Schurman, E., and Brutlag, J. (2009). Performance related changes and their user impact.
O'Reilly Velocity conference presentation, San Jose, CA. Retrieved from http://blip
.tv/oreilly-velocity-conference/velocity-09-eric-schurman-and-jake-brutlag
-performance-related-changes-and-their-user-impact-2292767.

Schwartz, S. (1998). *Atomic audit: the costs and consequences of U.S. nuclear weapons since
1940.* Washington, D.C.: Brookings Institution Press.

Scott, M. (2017, June). Google fined record $2.7 billion in EU antitrust ruling. *New York
Times.* Retrieved from https://www.nytimes.com/2017/06/27/technology/eu-google
-fine.html.

Semel, T. (2006, May). Navigating Yahoo! Interview with Ken Auletta. Retrieved from
http://www.newyorker.com/videos/060511onvi_video_semel.

Shankar, V., Smith, A. K., and Rangaswamy, A. (2003). Customer satisfaction and loyalty
in online and offline environments. *International Journal of Research in Marketing,
20*(2), 153–75.

Shapiro, C. (1983). Optimal pricing of experience goods. *Bell Journal of Economics, 14*(2),
497–507.

Shapiro, C., and Varian, H. R. (1998). *Information rules: a strategic guide to the network
economy.* Cambridge, MA: Harvard Business Press.

Shiman, D. (2007). The impact of ownership structure on television stations' news and
public affairs programming. Federal Communications Commission Media
Ownership Study. Retrieved from https://apps.fcc.gov/edocs_public/attachmatch
/DA-07-3470A5.pdf.

Shirky, C. (2009). *Here comes everybody: the power of organizing without organizations.* New York: Penguin.

———. (2010, November). *The Times' paywall and newsletter economics.* Blog post. Retrieved from http://www.shirky.com/weblog/2010/11/the_times_paywall _and_newsletter_economics/.

Shoenfeld, Z. (2017, June). MTV News—and other sites—are frantically pivoting to video. It won't work. *Newsweek.* Retrieved from http://www.newsweek.com/mtv -news-video-vocativ-media-ads-pivot-630223.

Shute, J., Oancea, M., Ellner, S., Handy, B., Rollins, E., Samwel, B.,…, Jegerlehner, B., et al. (2012). F1: the fault-tolerant distributed RDBMS supporting Google's ad business. In *Proceedings of the 2012 International Conference on Management of Data,* Scottsdale, AZ (pp. 777–78). ACM.

Sifry, M. (2009, November). Critiquing Matthew Hindman's "The Myth of Digital Democracy". *TechPresident.* Retrieved from http://techpresident.com/blog-entry /critiquing-matthew-hindmans-myth-digital-democracy.

Silverman, C. (2017, November). This analysis shows how viral fake election news stories outperformed real news on Facebook. Retrieved from https://www.buzzfeed.com /craigsilverman/viral-fake-election-news-outperformed-real-news-on-facebook.

Simon, H. A. (1971). Designing organizations for an information-rich world. In Greenberger, M., ed., *Computers, communications, and the public interest.* Baltimore, MD: Johns Hopkins University Press.

Singhal, A., and Cutts, M. (2010, April). Using site speed in web search ranking. Blog post, Google. Retrieved from http://googlewebmastercentral.blogspot.com/2010 /04/using-site-speed-in-web-search-ranking.html.

Small, M., and Singer, J. (1982). *Resort to arms: international and civil wars, 1816–1980.* Thousand Oaks, CA: Sage Publications.

Smith, A. (2010). *Home broadband 2010.* Retrieved from http://www.pewinternet.org /2010/08/11/home-broadband-2010/.

Somaiya, R. (2014, November). *Washington Post* releases free app for Kindle, in first collaboration with Amazon. *New York Times.* Retrieved from http://www.nytimes .com/2014/11/20/business/media/jeff-bezos-makes-his-mark-on-washington-post -with-new-kindle-app.html.

Sonderman, J. (2011, August). News sites using Facebook comments see higher quality discussion, more referrals. *Poynter.* Blog post. Retrieved from http://www.poynter .org/latest-news/media-lab/social-media/143192/news-sites-using-facebook-com ments-see-higher-quality-discussion-more-referrals/.

———. (2012, October). How the Huffington Post handles 70+ million comments a year. *Poynter.* Blog post. Retrieved from http://www.poynter.org/latest-news/top -stories/190492/how-the-huffington-post-handles-70-million-comments-a-year/.

Starkman, D. (2010). The hamster wheel. *Columbia Journalism Review, 49,* 24–28.

Starr, P. (2004). *The creation of the media: the political origins of modern communications.* New York: Basic Books.

———. (2011, June). The Manichean world of Tim Wu. *American Prospect.* Retrieved from http://prospect.org/article/manichean-world-tim-wu.

Steiner, P. O. (1952). Program patterns and preferences, and the workability of competition in radio broadcasting. *Quarterly Journal of Economics, 66*(2): 194–223.

Stigler, G. (1961). The economics of information. *Journal of Political Economy, 69*(3), 213–25.

Stigler, G. J., and Becker, G. S. (1977). De gustibus non est disputandum. *American Economic Review*, 76–90.

Stober, R. (2004). What media evolution is: a theoretical approach to the history of new media. *European Journal of Communication, 19*(4), 483–505.

Stromer-Galley, J. (2004). Interactivity-as-product and interactivity-as-process. *Information Society, 20*(5), 391–94.

Stroud, N. (2011). *Niche news: the politics of news choice.* New York: Oxford University Press.

Sunstein, C. (2001). *Republic.com.* Princeton, NJ: Princeton University Press.

———. (2009). *Republic.com 2.0.* Princeton, NJ: Princeton University Press.

Tang, D., Agarwal, A., O'Brien, D., and Meyer, M. (2010). Overlapping experiment infrastructure: more, better, faster experimentation. In *Proceedings of the 16th ACM SIGKDD International Conference on Knowledge Discovery and Data Mining,* Washington, D.C. (pp. 17–26). ACM.

Tankersley, J. (2015, April). Why the PR industry is sucking up Pulitzer winners. *Washington Post.* Retrieved from http://www.washingtonpost.com/news/wonk/wp/2015/04/23/why-the-pr-industry-is-sucking-up-pulitzer-winners/.

TeleGeography. (2012). *Global internet map 2012.* Retrieved from http://global-internet-map-2012.telegeography.com/.

Tellis, G. J. (1988). Advertising exposure, loyalty, and brand purchase: a two-stage model of choice. *Journal of Marketing Research, 25*(2): 134–44.

———. (2003). *Effective advertising: understanding when, how, and why advertising works.* Thousand Oaks, CA: Sage Publications.

Thompson, D. (2017, November). How to survive the media apocalypse. *The Atlantic.* Retrieved from https://www.theatlantic.com/business/archive/2017/11/media-apocalypse/546935/.

Thrall, A. T., Stecula, D., and Sweet, D. (2014). May we have your attention please? Human-rights NGOs and the problem of global communication. *International Journal of Press/Politics*, 135–59.

Thurman, N. (2011). Making "The Daily Me": Technology, economics and habit in the mainstream assimilation of personalized news. *Journalism: Theory, Practice & Criticism, 12*(4), 395–415.

Thurman, N., and Schifferes, S. (2012). The future of personalization at news websites: lessons from a longitudinal study. *Journalism Studies 13*(5–6): 775–90.

Toth, O. (2014, May). Moving the conversation to where you want to have it. *Huffington Post.* Retrieved from http://www.huffingtonpost.com/otto-toth/were-moving-the-conversation_b_5423675.html.

Turner, F. (2006). *From counterculture to cyberculture: Stewart Brand, the Whole Earth Network, and the rise of digital utopianism.* Chicago, IL: University of Chicago Press.

Turow, J. (2012). *The Daily You: how the new advertising industry is defining your identity and your worth.* New Haven, CT: Yale University Press.

Upworthy. (2013, December). *What actually makes things go viral will blow your mind. (Hint: it's not headlines like this.)* Blog post. Retrieved from http://blog.upworthy.com/post/69093440334/what-actually-makes-things-go-viral-will-blow-your-mind.

Usher, N. (2014a). *Making news at the New York Times.* Ann Arbor: University of Michigan Press.

———. (2014b). Moving the newsroom: post-industrial news spaces and places. Tow Center for Digital Journalism, Columbia University, New York.

———. (2014c, May). The New York Times' digital limbo. *Columbia Journalism Review.* Retrieved from http://archives.cjr.org/the_audit/the_new_york_times_digital_li.php.

Usher, N., and Layser, M. D. (2010). The quest to save journalism: a legal analysis of new models for newspapers from nonprofit tax-exempt organizations to L3Cs. *Utah Law Review, 2010*(4), 1315–71.

Vaidhyanathan, S. (2012). *The Googlization of everything: and why we should worry.* Berkeley, CA: University of California Press.

Verma, A., Pedrosa, L., Korupolu, M. R., Oppenheimer, D., Tune, E., and Wilkes, J. (2015). Large-scale cluster management at Google with Borg. In *Proceedings of the European Conference on Computer Systems (EuroSys).* Bordeaux, France.

Volz, E., and Meyers, L. (2009). Epidemic thresholds in dynamic contact networks. *Journal of the Royal Society Interface, 6*(32), 233.

von Thunen, J. H. ([1826] 1966). *Isolated state: an English edition of der isolierte staat.* Oxford, England: Pergamon Press.

Waldfogel, J. (2002). *Consumer substitution among media.* FCC Media Ownership Working Group Paper. Retrieved from https://transition.fcc.gov/ownership/materials/already-released/consumer090002.pdf.

Watts, D. J. (2011). *Everything is obvious: *once you know the answer.* New York: Crown Business.

Webster, J. (2014). *The marketplace of attention.* Cambridge, MA: MIT Press.

Webster, J. G., and Wakshlag, J. J. (1983). A theory of television program choice. *Communication Research, 10*(4), 430–46.

Wells, J. D., Valacich, J. S., and Hess, T. J. (2011). What signals are you sending? How website quality influences perceptions of product quality and purchase intentions. *MIS Quarterly, 35*(2), 373–96.

Wemple, E. (2014a, May). Associated Press polices story length. *Washington Post.* Retrieved from http://www.washingtonpost.com/blogs/erik-wemple/wp/2014/05/12/associated-press-polices-story-length/.

———. (2014b, May). Reuters polices story length too. *Washington Post.* Retrieved from http://www.washingtonpost.com/blogs/erik-wemple/wp/2014/05/12/reuters-polices-story-length-too/.

Wernerfelt, B. (1985). Brand loyalty and user skills. *Journal of Economic Behavior & Organization, 6*(4), 381–85.

———. (1991). Brand loyalty and market equilibrium. *Marketing Science, 10*(3), 229–45.

"What DeepMind brings to Alphabet." (2016, December). *The Economist.* Retrieved from https://www.economist.com/news/business/21711946-ai-firms-main-value-alphabet-new-kind-algorithm-factory-what-deepmind-brings.

Wheeler, T. (2013). *Net effects: the past, present, and future impact of our networks.* Washington, D.C.: Federal Communications Commission. Retrieved from http://www.amazon.com/NET-EFFECTS-Present-Future-Networks-ebook/dp/B00H1ZS4TQ.

Wildman, S. S. (1994). One-way flows and the economics of audience-making. In J. S. Ettema and D. C. Whitney (eds.), *Audiencemaking: how the media create the audience* (pp. 115–41). Thousand Oaks, CA: Sage Publications.

Wu, T. (2003). Network neutrality, broadband discrimination. *Journal of Telecommunications and High Technology Law, 2,* 141–76.

———. (2011). *The master switch: the rise and fall of information empires.* New York: Random House.

Yarow, J. (2013, October). One last look at the giant money pit that is Microsoft's online operations. *Business Insider.* Retrieved from http://www.businessinsider.com/microsofts-online-operations-losses-2013-10.

Zara, C. (2012, September). Bing vs Google: Microsoft's Pepsi Challenge backfires. *International Business Times.* Retrieved from http://www.ibtimes.com/bing-vs-google-microsoft%C5%9B-pepsi-challenge-backfires-780715.

Zelizer, B. (2009). Journalism and the academy. In K. Wahl-Jorgensen and T. Hanitzsch (eds.), *The handbook of journalism studies* (pp. 29–41). New York: Routledge.

Zuboff, S. (2015). Big other: surveillance capitalism and the prospects of an information civilization. *Journal of Information Technology, 30*(1), 75–89.

INDEX

Italic pages refer to figures and tables